SCOTTISH LAW COMMISSION
(Scot Law Com No 162)

Report on the Law of the Tenement

Laid before Parliament by the Lord Advocate under section 3(2) of the Law Commissions Act 1965

Ordered by the House of Commons *to be printed*
25 March, 1998

583

EDINBURGH: The Stationery Office
£18.50

0 10 259698 0

The Scottish Law Commission was set up by section 2 of the Law Commissions Act 1965 for the purpose of promoting the reform of the law of Scotland. The Commissioners are:

The Honourable Lord Gill, *Chairman*
Dr E M Clive
P S Hodge Q C
Professor K G C Reid
Mr N R Whitty

The Secretary of the Commission is Mr J G S Maclean. Its offices are at 140 Causewayside, Edinburgh EH9 1PR.

SCOTTISH LAW COMMISSION

Item 5 of our Fifth Programme of Law Reform

The Law of the Tenement

To: The Rt Hon the Lord Hardie, QC
Her Majesty's Advocate

We have the honour to submit our Report on the Law of the Tenement.

(*Signed*) BRIAN GILL, *Chairman*

E M CLIVE

P S HODGE

KENNETH G C REID

N R WHITTY

J G S MACLEAN, *Secretary*
30 December 1997

Contents

Part 5 - Management Scheme A

Part 6 - Management Scheme B

Part 1 Introduction

Background to the report

1.1 This is the first in a series of reports on property law, a subject which is included in our *Fifth Programme of Law Reform*.[1] It follows on publication of a discussion paper on the law of the tenement,[2] and on extensive consultation thereafter. Our provisional proposals were put to a seminar, held in association with the University of Glasgow, on 25 September 1996, and were well received. The seminar was attended by members of the legal profession, by property managers, and by a number of other interested persons.[3] A seminar had also been held in the previous year, in association with the University of Edinburgh.[4] In the light of the comments made on those occasions and of further work and reflection, we have been able to formulate the final recommendations which now appear in this report. Appendix 1 to the report contains a draft bill which is intended to give effect to our recommendations.

Summary of report

1.2 A list of recommendations is given in Part 11 of the report. They are intended to apply to all tenements, whether currently existing or built in the future, and whether used for residential or for commercial purposes. They are to apply both to custom-built tenements and to buildings originally designed for single occupancy but which have come later to be subdivided. We have two key recommendations. In the first place, we suggest that the existing common law rules which demarcate ownership within a tenement be clarified and re-stated in modern statutory language. In the second place, we seek to fill a widely acknowledged gap in the existing law by providing a proper system of management. The draft bill contains two separate management schemes, Scheme A and Scheme B.[5] Scheme A, which may be varied and which is subject to the provisions of existing titles, will in principle apply to all tenements. But Scheme A may be disapplied by deed of conditions and replaced by some other management scheme. The more elaborate Scheme B is offered as a possible alternative to Scheme A but developers and owners are free to devise a scheme of their own. The overall effect of our proposals is that every tenement will have a management scheme, and hence a mechanism for ensuring that repairs are carried out and that decisions are reached on other matters of mutual interest and concern.

1.3 Our recommendations touch also on a large number of other subjects including compulsory insurance, emergency repairs, access for repairs, obligations of support and shelter, the liability of incoming owners for repairs and other costs, and demolition of a tenement. Taken together these recommendations amount to a code of tenement law which would replace the existing common law of the tenement.

1.4 If enacted, our recommendations will affect a very large number of people in the day-to-day running of their property. We suggest that there ought to be a gap, perhaps of a year,[6] between enactment of the legislation and its coming into force, so that the legislation can be publicised as widely as possible and leaflets prepared for owners and those considering purchasing a flat.

---

1 Scot Law Com No 159, (1997) Item 6, paras 2.32-2.42.

2 Discussion Paper No 91- *Law of the Tenement*, published December 1990 (referred to in subsequent footnotes as "Discussion Paper No 91". A list of those who submitted written comments on the discussion paper is given in Appendix 2.

3 A list of those who attended the seminar and who submitted written comments on our proposals is given in Appendix 4.

4 A list of those who attended the seminar and who submitted written comments on our proposals is given in Appendix 3. The seminar was held in Edinburgh on 7 September 1995.

5 Contained, respectively, in Schedules 1 and 2 to the draft Bill, and discussed in Parts 5 and 6 of this report.

6 Clause 32(2) of the draft Bill provides that the Act should come into force 12 months after it is passed.

Acknowledgements

1.5 We have been fortunate in the responses which we have received from consultees, and we gratefully acknowledge their help. Only a small number can be mentioned here by name, but a complete list of consultees will be found in the appendices to this report. Representatives of the Property Managers Association Scotland Limited gave generously of their time on a whole range of issues. The Royal Institution of Chartered Surveyors in Scotland and the Royal Incorporation of Architects in Scotland both provided valuable assistance on technical matters. Expert advice was given by Professor J W G Blackie of the University of Strathclyde and by Mr Alan Barr of the University of Edinburgh on, respectively, delictual liability for damage to tenement property and taxation.

Professor Robert Rennie of the University of Glasgow gave a paper at one of our seminars and helped us in a number of other ways. Finally, Professor C G van der Merwe of the University of Stellenbosch, who is the author of the standard work on the comparative law of apartment ownership,[7] placed his knowledge and expertise at our disposal, travelling to Scotland for both of our seminars and giving a paper at one.

7 C G van der Merwe, *Apartment Ownership* (1994) (referred to in this report as "van der Merwe") (being vol VI, chapter 5 of the International Encyclopaedia of Comparative Law).

Part 2 The Existing Law

Historical and comparative survey

2.1 Tenements have a long history in Scotland. The tenement or "land" was known in medieval times, especially in Edinburgh. As usual, the law came later. The "law of the tenement" - in the sense of a special and self-contained set of rules governing the ownership and maintenance of tenement buildings - dates only from the seventeenth century. The first work to offer a systematic exposition of the law was Stair's *Institutions*, which was published in 1681.[1] Stair's brief account, while presumably based on the custom of burghs, may have been influenced by the law in other European countries, particularly by the Germanic institution of *Stockwerkseigentum*, to which it bears a strong resemblance. In more modern times there has been case law, although never in profusion. The explosion of tenement construction in the nineteenth century was accompanied by only a modest increase in useful litigation, although to some extent custom eked out case law.[2] At the close of the century Rankine's *Landownership* summarised the effect of the cases and offered suggested solutions for the many gaps which still remained in the law. Since then modern scholars have built on Rankine's work although they have not always agreed with one another.[3] By the end of the twentieth century tenements comprised more than a quarter of the occupied housing stock in Scotland,[4] but the law remained based on a handful of reported cases and on the disputed extrapolations of professors.

2.2 The contrast with other countries is instructive.[5] In Europe the codification movement led to the rules of flatted property being re-stated in a codified form, beginning with France in 1804.[6] Later this came to seem inadequate and detailed special legislation followed - in Belgium in 1924, in France in 1938 and again in 1965, in Germany in 1951, and so forth. Outside Europe a very large number of countries enacted legislation in the post-war period. In the English-speaking world the most influential examples have included the Conveyancing (Strata Titles) Act 1961 (New South Wales),[7] the Sectional Titles Act of 1971 (South Africa),[8] and the Uniform Condominium Act of 1977 (United States).

2.3 So far the United Kingdom has resisted this legislative tide. In Scotland this can probably be explained by the development since the 1790s of a conveyancing device, known as the real burden, by which maintenance obligations could be made to bind successive owners of property.[9] Thereafter conveyancers were able to supply what was lacking under the general law by providing in the title deeds of individual tenements a detailed regime for repair and renewal. By contrast other countries did not, and for the most part still do not, recognise the possibility of positive obligations binding successors. In

1 Stair II.7.6.

2 For example, in *Whitmore v Stuart & Stuart* (1902) 10 SLT 290 the court applied what was said to be Edinburgh custom in deciding that chimney stacks are the common property of those proprietors with flues therein, the number of flues determining the size of the *pro indiviso* share. We recommend that this rule be retained: see para 4.25 and recommendation 4(g).

3 See in particular: J G S Cameron, "The Law of the Tenement" (1959) 1 Conv Rev 105 and 240, and (1960) 2 Conv Rev 102; J M Halliday, *Conveyancing Law and Practice* vol II (1986) paras 18-20 - 18-22; W M Gordon, *Scottish Land Law* (1989) paras 15-35 - 15-45 (referred to in this Report as "Gordon"); and K G C Reid *The Law of Property in Scotland* (1996) (referred to in this Report as "Reid") paras 227-251.

4 Scottish Homes, *Scottish House Condition Survey Main Report 1996,* p 35.

5 The summary account which follows is based on van der Merwe ss 1-23.

6 *Code Civil*, art 664.

7 Now replaced by an Act of 1973.

8 Now replaced by an Act of 1986.

9 The earliest reported case is *Nicolson v Melvill* (1708) Mor 14516, which concerned an obligation to maintain the roof of a tenement. The obligation was held to be unenforceable. But by the end of the century the law was beginning to change.

England and Wales, where positive covenants are rejected for freehold land,[10] conveyancers by and large resorted to leasehold tenure for flatted property. Recently, however, proposals have been developed in association with the Law Commission for the introduction of new type of freehold ownership of flats, known as commonhold.[11] A draft Commonhold Bill was published by the Lord Chancellor's Department in July 1996 but has not yet been introduced to Parliament. The commonhold proposals were reviewed in our discussion paper where we concluded that, for various reasons, they were not a suitable model for reform in Scotland.[12] This conclusion was not challenged on consultation.

The law in outline

2.4 In Scotland, as in most other countries, the law on tenement property is no more than a background or default law. Certain basic rules are provided, but developers are then free to modify or, in many cases, to disregard those rules when preparing the conveyancing of individual buildings. The extent to which the background law is modified in practice may be taken as a rough and ready indication of the success of that law. In countries with modern legislation on sectional or strata titles (to use the terminology generally favoured in those countries) modification occurs on quite a small scale.[13] By contrast, in Scotland the title deeds almost always make substantial changes. Thus, except in the case of tenements built and conveyed before about 1800,[14] it is always necessary to take into account not only the law but also the individual titles. In practice title provisions vary widely. There are local variations and regional variations. Modern titles are much more ambitious in scope than those of 100 years ago or even of 50 years ago. Different types of building attract different solutions. To a degree which is unusual in other countries, each tenement in Scotland has its own private set of rules. There is not just one law of the tenement but rather innumerable such laws. This complex pattern of conveyancing, continued over 200 years, adds to the difficulties of law reform in this area.

2.5 The background law on tenements may be said to have three main concerns, and may be judged by how well it deals with each. In the first place, the law must provide for the division of ownership within the tenement building. In the second place, it must apportion the maintenance costs of those parts of the building which are of common benefit and on which the stability and safety of the building rests. Finally, it must provide a framework for management and for the making of decisions, particularly in relation to maintenance. In the remainder of this section we consider the existing law of Scotland in these three areas.

2.6 **Ownership.** In Scotland a tenement flat is a section of airspace bounded by four walls, a floor and a ceiling. Where the wall is an outside wall of the building, ownership extends to the full width of that section of wall.[15] In the case of walls internal to the building, ownership is to the mid-point. Thus the boundary between two flats in the same building is the mid-point of the wall which separates them. Floors and ceilings are treated in the same way. Each flat owns its floor or ceiling, and the boundary between successive flats is an imaginary line lying halfway through the joists.[16] Special rules apply to the highest and lowest flats in the building. The highest flat extends to the roof and so includes any intermediate roof-space.[17] The lowest flat extends to the solum (the ground on which the tenement is built) and so includes the foundations of the building and any intermediate space, including cellars.[18] Where there is more than one flat on the highest or lowest storeys, as there usually is, each owns that section of roof or, as the case may be, solum which lies directly above or beneath.[19]

---

10 *Rhone v Stephens* [1994] 2 AC 310.
11 *Commonhold: Freehold Flats and Freehold Ownership of other Interdependent Buildings: Report of a Working Group* (Cm 179, July 1987); *Commonhold - A Consultation Paper* (Cm 1345, November 1990).
12 Discussion Paper No. 91, paras 5.14 - 5.17.
13 See for example C G van der Merwe, *Sectional Titles, Share Blocks and Time-sharing* vol 1 (1995) p 13-7.
14 1800 marks the beginning of the use of real burdens: see para 2.3.
15 Bell, *Principles* s 1086.
16 *Girdwood v Paterson* (1873) 11 M 647; *McArly v French's Trs* (1883) 10 R 574.
17 *Taylor v Dunlop* (1872) 11 M 25.
18 *Johnston v White* (1877) 4 R 721.
19 *Sanderson's Trs v Yule* (1897) 25 R 211.

2.7 Ownership of the solum carries with it the ownership of the airspace above the building.[20] The reason for this, perhaps rather surprising, rule is that property law regards land as the main object which is capable of ownership. The ownership of airspace separate from the land is regarded as an exceptional arrangement which is permitted in the case of flats, where plainly it is unavoidable,[21] but which is not otherwise allowed. Hence the owner of the solum - the land - owns *a coelo usque ad centrum* (from the heavens to the centre of the earth) except for those sections of airspace actually occupied by flats. This rule prevents the owner of a top flat from building an extra storey[22] although not, apparently, from adding a dormer window.[23]

2.8 The common passage and stair (including the walls, roof and solum) is the common property of those flats which obtain access by it.[24] Thus main-door flats have no share of ownership unless they also have a door leading into the common passage.

2.9 Outside the building, the common law provides that any garden or other land forming part of the tenement is the property of the lowest flat. If there is more than one flat on the lowest storey, each owns that section of garden which is immediately adjacent.[25] This rule is another example of the favour shown by the law to the lowest flat.

2.10 A notable feature of the distribution of ownership is the almost complete absence of common property. The outside walls of the building are owned in individual sections corresponding to the different flats in the building. The same is true of the roof and the solum. Inside the building the boundary features separating one flat from another are not common property but are owned, on each side, to the mid-point.

2.11 **Maintenance costs.** Maintenance costs follow ownership. But while, as a matter of general law, an owner is free to neglect his property if he chooses, and hence to avoid expenditure, in a tenement certain parts are so essential to the integrity of the building that the law imposes a positive obligation to maintain. The device used to achieve this result is common interest.[26] The owner of each flat is said to have a right of common interest in those parts of the building which are not his; and the corresponding obligations imposed on each owner include an obligation to maintain any part which is needed for the shelter or support of the building as a whole. Thus the owner of the roof (at common law the owner of the highest flat) must keep it in good repair to provide shelter for the rest of the building. Similarly, each owner must attend to the repair of any wall or other feature in his flat which supports the structure of the tenement.[27] In practice the title to individual tenements will usually spread maintenance costs in a more even-handed way, either by making certain strategic parts (such as the roof) common property or by imposing real burdens of maintenance on all the owners. Sometimes both methods are employed together.

2.12 **Management and decision-making.** On this subject the common law of the tenement makes no provision whatsoever. The operative principle is one of extreme individualism. Each owner can do with his own flat as he pleases, subject only to the common interest obligation to provide support and shelter. There is almost no common property and hence there are almost no common repairs. Decisions as to

---

20 *Watt v Burgess' Tr* (1891) 18 R 766. But see also para 4.22.

21 In many countries the idea that flats might be owned separately from the land on which they were built was not recognised, and sectional or strata titles became possible - often quite recently - only as a result of legislation.

22 *Watt v Burgess' Tr* (1891) 18 R 766.

23 *Sanderson's Trs v Yule* (1897) 25 R 211. The decision here is perhaps not easy to reconcile with the approach taken in *Watt v Burgess's Tr.* Title to the airspace does not seem to have been considered, and the court's main concern may have been to homologate what had become a very common practice. According to the Lord President (Robertson) (at p 216) the owner of a top flat "is entitled to make any change on his part of the roof which does not interfere with the efficiency of the roof as a covering to the house as a whole, or with the stability of the rest of the building. What, then, of the change proposed? In its nature it is a very simple and harmless change, and one which is made every day."

24 *Anderson v Dalrymple* (1799) Mor 12831; *WVS Office Premises Ltd v Currie* 1969 SC 170.

25 Rankine, *Landownership* (4th edn, 1909) (referred to in this Report as "Rankine"), p 662. Rankine's view has come to be accepted although the point has never been litigated.

26 On common interest generally, see Reid, paras 232-9 and 354-74, and Gordon, paras 15-31 - 15-45.

27 Stair II.7.6; Bankton II.7.9; Erskine II.9.11; Bell, *Principles* s 1086; *Luke v Dundass* (1695) 4 Brown's Supp 258; *McNair v McLauchlan and McKeand* (1826) 4 S 546.

common property generally require unanimity.[28] There is no system in place which allows the appointment of a professional factor or other person to manage the tenement.

Evaluation of the existing law

2.13 **Uncertainty.** The problem of uncertainty has already been referred to. The case law on tenements is so meagre that, even after 300 years, a number of areas of doubt remain. For the most part these affect the distribution of ownership. Thus, while it is settled that the common passage and stair is the common property of all flats which have access by it, what is not settled is the manner in which that ownership is divided. Two views have been expressed. On one view each flat holds an equal *pro indiviso* share in the entire passage and stair.[29] On the other view a flat does not extend to any part of the passage and stair which does not directly serve it.[30] This view would exclude ground floor flats from ownership of the stairs, while the final section of stairs would be the exclusive property of the flats on the top floor. The issue has never been litigated. Uncertainty also affects the ownership of the walls of the passage and stair where they form a boundary with another flat. The view has variously been expressed that these are the sole property of the flat in question,[31] or that they are common property,[32] or again that the mid-point forms the boundary with sole ownership lying on either side.[33]

2.14 A problem of a different kind concerns the operation within tenements of the rules of accession.[34] Although the point has not been judicially discussed, it is taken for granted that accession does not operate through the boundaries of individual flats, at least where such boundaries are internal to the building. Thus the ground floor flat does not accede to the solum, and the first floor flat does not accede to the ground floor flat. Similarly, if the owner of a top flat adds parquet tiles to his floor, the tiles accede to that flat but not to the flat underneath.[35] The same rule applies to walls. Kitchen units accede to the flat in which they are placed and not to the neighbouring flat on the other side of the shared wall. This is a satisfactory - indeed probably an inevitable - rule. But what is unclear is whether the same rule applies in respect of boundaries which are wholly external. Do pipes accede to the outside walls of the building or do they remain separately owned, whether as heritable or as moveable property? Are satellite dishes treated in the same way as pipes or in a different way? Are the rhones part of the roof? The practical importance of this uncertainty lies mainly with pipes and cables. If pipes accede to the wall then, like the wall itself, they are owned in sections by the owners of the successive flats. If they do not accede, they are probably common property, although in what proportions is uncertain.

2.15 **Rigidity.** The common law rules on ownership are specific and narrow, and general principles seem almost wholly absent. This makes it difficult to accommodate innovation. A standard illustration is the introduction into tenements of entryphone systems. Where does ownership lie? Various views seem possible. The whole system may be seen as a single unit and hence the common property of all the flats that it serves; or a distinction may be made between the main system, and the individual wires and handsets serving individual flats, with the result that only the former is common property and the latter are individually owned; or again the position may be regulated by accession, with complex and unsatisfactory results.

2.16 **Unfairness.** But even where the rules of ownership are certain, they do not always seem fair. In particular, the flats at the lowest level of the building are placed in a position of privilege which seems difficult to justify. In all modern legislation on sectional or strata titles introduced in other countries the ground on which the building is constructed is treated as common property.

---

28 Reid, paras 23-5. The main exception is in relation to necessary repairs, which any one owner can instruct and recover the cost *pro rata* from the others.
29 Reid, para 231.
30 Rankine, p 677.
31 *Anderson v Dalrymple* (1799) Mor 12831; *Ritchie v Purdie* (1833) 11 S 771.
32 Rankine, pp 667-9.
33 Reid, para 231.
34 On accession generally, see Reid, paras 570-577.
35 Reid, para 585.

2.17 A lack of fairness also affects the apportionment of maintenance costs. Stair's account of the law of common interest was of a system in perfect balance. The upper proprietors maintained the roof, but in return the lower proprietors maintained the walls:[36]

> "[W]hen diverse owners have parts of the same tenement, it cannot be said to be a perfect division, because the roof remaineth roof to both, and the ground supporteth both; and, therefore, by the nature of communion, there are mutual obligations upon both, viz that the owner of the lower tenement must uphold his tenement as a foundation to the upper, and the owner of the upper tenement must uphold his tenement as a roof and cover to the lower .."

Today the bargain seems a bad one. All experience shows that roofs require more maintenance than walls. In practice title deeds almost always re-apportion roof maintenance amongst all the proprietors, and in the few cases where this has not been done the value of the flats at the top of the building is sharply reduced.

2.18 **The insolvent or absconding owner.** A related difficulty arises where a person who is liable for repair costs cannot or will not pay. That person may be insolvent, or he may have disappeared, or, most commonly of all, he may have sold his flat without leaving a forwarding address. Under the present law it is not clear where liability then falls. On consultation this was seen by professional bodies as one of the main defects of the existing law. For example the Royal Institution of Chartered Surveyors in Scotland commented that:

> "[T]here is now .. an urgent need to protect owners .. from the financial burden of their neighbours absconding from the property without paying their share of repairs. The RICS understands that the inability to enforce payment is a major obstacle to efficient property management and that it is now becoming clear that the only means of ensuring payment will be to legislate for any debts arising from the maintenance of property to be declared real burdens. This will protect proprietors and property managers from the threat of substantial loss arising from instructing repairs."

A recent decision of the House of Lords[37] concerning the liability of heritable creditors for the unpaid bills of their debtors brought the issue into sharp focus and, in the opinion of a number of consultees, has made a bad situation worse.

2.19 **Lack of a system of management.** The most serious defect has not yet been mentioned. This is the absence in the existing law of a proper system of management and decision-making. The importance of this issue was emphasised repeatedly by consultees. For example, the City of Edinburgh Council commented that:

> "[T]he main difficulty with existing arrangements is that owners must agree unanimously to carry out repairs and, setting aside the cost factor, this need for unanimous agreement has been a primary factor in the deterioration of the city's tenements."

Evidence of that deterioration was provided by a 1996 survey by the Edinburgh Council into all pre-1919 tenements (some 4,147) within its area.[38] The results are disheartening. For example, in relation to the roof alone, it was found that 10% of tenements require a new roof now or soon, while a further 30% will require a new roof within the next 20 years. More than one consultee suggested that, unless the law is changed to make repairs easier, the substantial injection of public funds which took place in the 1970s and 1980s in the form of common repair schemes for tenements will inevitably have to be repeated in perhaps as little as 20 years' time.

2.20 At the root of the problem, of course, is the requirement of the common law that decisions be made unanimously. Unless everyone is willing to agree, repairs cannot usually go ahead. But in practice

---

36 Stair II.7.6.

37 *David Watson Property Management v Woolwich Equitable Building Society* 1992 SC(HL) 21.

38 *Edinburgh Pre 1919 Tenement Condition Survey: Final Report* (prepared for Edinburgh District Council by Market Research Scotland Ltd, 1996). The report presented the key results from a comprehensive evaluation of conditions in the City of Edinburgh's pre- 1919 tenement housing stock.

unanimity is not easy to achieve, and the problem is made worse by the relatively rapid turnover of ownership of tenement property. A person who expects to sell in a year's time is unlikely to vote for a major repair to the building. One consultee[39] likened this problem to "an elaborate game of pass the parcel". A persistent failure to reach agreement on the subject of repairs can lead to tension growing within a tenement which may then spill over into unneighbourly conduct or even into violence.[40]

2.21 It is, of course, true that local authorities have statutory powers to require that repairs be carried out; and where a notice requiring repairs is not complied with the council may carry out the work itself and recover the cost.[41] But in practice the cost of work carried out in this way cannot always be recovered, and some councils are understandably reluctant to use their statutory powers. In any event, the intervention of the council ought to be the last resort and not the first. The general law should encourage people to make their own arrangements for repairs.

2.22 Later in this report[42] we make recommendations for the introduction of a mandatory management scheme for all tenements. However, it would be unrealistic to suppose that, on its own, improved efficiency in decision-making will solve the problem of deteriorating tenements. There will still be a number of reasons, sometimes peculiar to individual tenements, why necessary repairs are not in fact carried out. Furthermore, in view of the relatively high turnover in the ownership of individual flats, there is and will continue to be a tendency to avoid fundamental repairs and to seek instead temporary (and therefore cheaper) solutions. Nonetheless, the provision of a more efficient method of decision-making seems an indispensable beginning.

The role of real burdens

2.23 Mention was made earlier[43] of the use of real burdens as a means of imposing maintenance obligations on the owners of tenement flats. Such obligations bind not merely the first purchasers of flats but also their successors as owners. In this way it has become possible to supplement the rudimentary, and sometimes inequitable, rules of the common law. Real burdens are found in the titles of almost all tenements. Routinely they provide for shared liability for the maintenance of certain strategic parts of the building - the roof, the external walls, the pipes and other services. In modern titles they also impose restrictions on use in the interests of overall amenity. For example, there may be a prohibition on use for business purposes, or on the keeping of animals. Originally real burdens had to be imposed separately in the title of each individual flat but since 1874 it has been possible to register a deed of conditions containing burdens which affect the whole tenement (or other development).[44] Almost from the beginning deeds of conditions began to be used in the west of Scotland for the regulation of tenements, elsewhere they were little in evidence until the post-war period. The modern deed of conditions runs to many pages and makes detailed provision, not only for maintenance and amenity, but also for management. The Glasgow factor owes his existence almost entirely to deeds of conditions. When well drafted, deeds of conditions dispose of many of the difficulties with the common law which were identified earlier. For tenements governed by such deeds the need for reform is much reduced. Indeed deeds of conditions are tailored to the needs and peculiarities of the individual tenement and so provide a more apt regime than could ever be possible under reforming, but necessarily general, legislation.

---

39 The Property Managers Association Scotland Limited.

40 On 29 November 1996 the owner of a flat in Bruntsfield Place in Edinburgh was convicted of inciting a workmate to murder the owner of a flat in the same stair. The plan involved abseiling from the defender's top-floor flat to the victim's flat below. It seems that for over a year the intended victim had objected to all proposals for common repairs and improvements. See (1997) 1 ELR 280.

41 Civic Government (Scotland) Act 1982 ss 87(1) and 99; Housing (Scotland) Act 1987 ss 108 and 109. There are also local statutes such as the City of Edinburgh District Council Confirmation Order Act 1991, Part VI. These various provisions apply to all buildings, but in practice most statutory notices issued relate to tenements. The City of Edinburgh Council has tended to be pro-active in relation to the exercise of these powers. See Edinburgh College of Art / Heriot Watt University Research Paper No 66 (December 1997): *Collective Action and the Maintenance of Owner Occupied Flats in England and Scotland.*

42 Paras 3.15 and 3.16 and recommendation 2(a).

43 Para 2.3.

44 Conveyancing (Scotland) Act 1874 s 32.

2.24 Without real burdens the law could scarcely have survived unreformed for so long. Nonetheless real burdens are less useful than they might seem. This is because the rules of constitution are so technical and strict that, in a significant number of cases, title provisions fail to make the grade and turn out to be unenforceable. In practice there are four possible reasons why a title provision might not be enforceable against successors.

2.25 In the first place, maintenance provisions often seek to impose liability by reference to some external measure such as the rateable value of the property. However, it is settled law that the terms of a real burden must appear in full within the constitutive deed. In one well-known case a burden failed because it made reference to an Act of Parliament without at the same time repeating the actual terms of that Act in the deed.[45] Although the conclusion is unpalatable and may come as a surprise to some, it seems that a maintenance burden which is dependent on an external measure is subject to similar objections. However, it should be emphasised that the issue has not been the subject of express decision and it may be that some point of distinction could be found.

2.26 Secondly, the burden may take the form of an (indirect) obligation to pay for a repair, as opposed to a (direct) obligation to carry out a repair. The effect of a burden in this form is controversial and the case law is in some disarray.[46] On one view, however, such an obligation is not enforceable, on the basis that it imposes an obligation to pay a sum of money which is not sufficiently specified.

2.27 Thirdly, a burden may be invalid because of its content. In particular it seems likely that some at least of the provisions which are commonly found in relation to management and decision-making are unenforceable because they are insufficiently "praedial" in character.[47] Possible examples include provisions relating to the composition and conduct of residents' associations, and provisions conferring rights and imposing obligations on factors.

2.28 Finally, even if a burden is properly constituted, there may be no one with a title to enforce it. This is a particular problem in relation to burdens created in dispositions.[48] Here the granter has no continuing relationship with the property, and, except where express provision is made (which is unusual), the co-disponees can enforce only if they fall within the rules for implied *jus quaesitum tertio*.[49] These rules are complex, illogical and, in some cases, uncertain.

2.29 We are currently reviewing the law of real burdens and expect to issue a discussion paper for comment in the course of 1998. But for present purposes it seems plain that the deficiencies of the common law of the tenement are not always cured by the conditions which appear in the titles.

Summary: the case for reform

2.30 The existing background law - the common law of the tenement - is defective in a number of respects. It is sometimes uncertain. It is sometimes unfair. Above all, it fails to provide a proper mechanism for decision-making and for management. We should, of course, recognise its longevity and its vigour. The courts and conveyancers have, between them, produced a system which has lasted for 300 years. For the most part that system has worked reasonably well. Nonetheless the case for reform now seems overwhelmingly strong. In our discussion paper we advanced the proposition that a new law of the tenement should be enacted,[50] and on consultation this idea was warmly supported. In the rest of this report we set out our proposals for a modern law of the tenement.

45 *Aberdeen Varieties Ltd v James F Donald (Aberdeen Cinemas) Ltd* 1939 SC 788 (revsd on a different point, 1940 SC(HL) 52).

46 Reid, para 418(4).

47 Reid, para 391. The rule is that a real burden must regulate, or otherwise burden, one piece of land (which can include a flat in a tenement) for the benefit of another piece of land.

48 Whether directly, or in deeds of conditions incorporated into dispositions.

49 In this context *jus quaesitum tertio* refers to the right of a third party, such as a neighbour in a tenement, to enforce real burdens which were originally created for the benefit of someone else. See further Reid, paras 399-405.

50 Discussion Paper No 91, paras 3.1 - 3.8 and proposition 1(i).

Part 3 Approaches to Reform

The approach in the discussion paper

3.1 In our discussion paper we suggested that a legislative code might be introduced setting out a new law of the tenement.[1] The proposed new law would be characterised by a decisive shift from individual ownership to common ownership. In the future, it was suggested, the main parts of a tenement building should be the common property of everyone. More particularly, common property should extend to the roof, external walls, common passage and stair, solum and foundations of the building, and to internal structural devices such as walls, beams and joists.[2] To the extent that they were not included in this list, walls and other boundary features dividing any two flats should be the common property of the flats in question. Individual ownership would be confined to the stratum of airspace occupied by the flat and to internal non-structural walls and other parts. In putting forward this model we were adopting, and extending, an approach found both in modern titles and in the legislation of other countries. Its advantage is that it solves, in a neat way, the problem of maintenance. Property which is owned in common will automatically be maintained in common. Moreover, common property provides not only a mechanism for common maintenance but also a justification. Under the suggested new code there would be a move away from the individualism of the common law to a more community-based distribution of rights and obligations.

3.2 Our proposal was that the new law should apply to all tenements coming into existence once the legislation was in force, subject to such variation as individual titles might make.[3] However, the law should not apply to existing tenements unless all the owners agreed or, in appropriate cases and on application, the Lands Tribunal for Scotland so ordered.[4] The overwhelming majority of consultees took issue with the last part of this proposal. They argued that the value of legislation would be greatly reduced unless it applied to all tenements, both old and new. It was in fact with older tenements that most of the problems arose. Modern tenements were usually governed by deeds of conditions which made sufficient provision for management and maintenance. For such tenements a new code was barely necessary, although it might be helpful on some points of detail. The real difficulty, it was suggested, lay with existing tenements. In general, the older the tenement, the less adequate the title provisions were likely to be. In the case of some very old tenements there were no title provisions at all and the common law applied without modification. It was here that help was needed most.

3.3 We are persuaded by these arguments. On a careful reconsideration of the issue we have concluded that the new law should apply to all tenements, regardless of age. But this decision has important implications for our overall approach. A code which is to apply to existing tenements must, so far as possible, respect existing rights. In particular it must respect existing rights of ownership. If the new law were to follow the proposals set out in the discussion paper it would result, for existing tenements, in a substantial redistribution of ownership. The proprietor of the top flat would lose ownership of the roof. The proprietor of the bottom flat would lose ownership of the solum. All proprietors would lose exclusive ownership of the walls bounding their flats. To some extent, of course, losses and gains would be in balance, but the proprietor of the ground flat in particular might feel that he had been deprived of

1 Discussion Paper No 91, see in particular Part III.
2 Discussion Paper No 91, para 4.3.
3 Discussion Paper No 91, para 3.5.
4 Discussion Paper No 91, paras 3.5 - 3.7, and proposition 1(ii), (iii).

property rights without adequate compensation. Arguably, there would be a contravention of the European Convention on Human Rights.[5]

3.4 We have investigated the issue of compensation and concluded that no readily workable scheme is available. It is unrealistic to suppose that publicly-funded compensation might be paid. And any scheme which involved one owner in a tenement paying compensation to another would give rise to formidable difficulties in practice. For how would the creditors and the debtors be identified? How much should be paid? When would it be due? From the point of view of the debtor, the legislation would have the effect of thrusting on him a "benefit" which he may not have wanted, for which he may not be able to pay, and which may not result in any increase in the value of his property.

3.5 There is also a second reason for a change in approach. We have come to have misgivings about a radical extension of common property. The benefits which common property brings, particularly in relation to maintenance, seem in some cases to be outweighed by disadvantages. This is particularly true in the case of the walls surrounding a flat. We now doubt whether the aspirations of home ownership are properly served by a rule which makes external and structural walls common property. A flat-owner might be surprised to learn that the rights of his neighbours in "his" wall were no less than his own. Nor is the point merely one of human psychology. Under the rules of common property the flat-owner could not paint the wall without the unanimous agreement of his fellow owners, while anything which he attached to it - a Victorian fireplace, for example - would by accession become the common property of everyone else. The practical difficulties which too liberal use of common property can cause were highlighted in a recent case,[6] where Lord Justice-Clerk Ross commented that:[7]

> "It is somewhat ironical that if, instead of making these elaborate provisions regarding common property, the granter had allowed the more usual law of the tenement to prevail,[8] many of these difficulties would not have arisen."

Of course it would be possible to alter the rules of common property by legislation so as to meet the various difficulties which might occur. A flat-owner could be given an exclusive right of use of the internal decorative surface of any wall; he could be allowed to make vents in the wall; the normal rules of accession could be suspended; and so on. But such elaborate provisions could be justified only if there were important reasons for making walls common property. If the only reason for common property is to ensure that the walls are commonly maintained, then it is much more straightforward to make direct provision to that effect and to leave the rules of ownership alone.

Four principles of reform

3.6 In Part 2 we identified the main weaknesses of the present law as being uncertainty, unfairness, and the absence of a proper system of management and decision-making. In devising a new law of the tenement which, so far as possible, addresses these weaknesses, we have been guided by four key principles. These are:

(i) that the rules of ownership provided by the existing law should be left undisturbed, and such doubts as exist should be resolved;

(ii) that it should be possible to vary the new law in the titles of individual tenements;

(iii) that the new law should be at a sufficient level of generality to allow for the extraordinary variety of buildings which qualify as tenements; and

(iv) that, so far as possible, there should be continuity between the old law and the new.

---

5 Article 1 of the First Protocol provides that: 'Every natural or legal person is entitled to the peaceful enjoyment of his possessions. No one shall be deprived of his possessions except in the public interest and subject to the conditions provided for by law and by the general principles of international law.'

6 *Rafique v Amin* 1997 SLT 1385.

7 At p 1387F.

8 Of course, under the "more usual" law of the tenement there is very little common property indeed: see para 2.10.

3.7 **Ownership undisturbed.** If it is accepted that existing rights of ownership are not to be interfered with, then any new law of the tenement must re-state the previous rules unchanged.[9] But the opportunity can be taken to clear up the doubts in the existing law and to produce rules of sufficient generality to cope with technological innovation in the future.

3.8 **Free variation.** The present law of the tenement is a background or residual law, and applies only to the extent that it has not been altered in the titles. We accept the principle of free variation as a sound one. No set of general rules could provide solutions which apply with equal appropriateness to every single case. Nor can general rules safely supply the level of detail which efficient tenement management often requires. Like the old law, therefore, the new law should be a background law only, freely variable by conveyancers. Moreover, this principle should be retrospective as well as prospective. For the new law will apply to old tenements, which will already have title provisions in place, and should take effect only where the title does not otherwise provide. Subject to what is said in the next paragraph, nothing in the new law is intended to affect the enforceability of existing real burdens.[10]

3.9 However, title provisions should not apply where they are incoherent. Maintenance real burdens which fail to account for 100% of liability would be a standard example.[11] At one time we were tempted to add a second exception. Considerations of fairness suggest that the roof of a tenement ought to be commonly maintained, and later in this report we recommend that a rule to this effect be incorporated into the new law.[12] But what if the title expressly provides otherwise? Although the situation is not common, it can occasionally happen that real burdens apportion the full cost of roof repairs amongst some only of the flats. Sometimes this was because the original builder was retaining one of the flats for his own use and wished to ensure that it was free of roof burdens. At our second seminar[13] we put forward the suggestion that real burdens which divided liability in an inequitable fashion should cease to have effect. This idea was challenged. As one participant[14] pointed out, owners will sometimes agree among themselves that liability should be distributed in a way which is inequitable. A typical example is where the owner of the top flat is given exclusive rights over the roof space on condition that he assumes full liability for roof repairs. Our proposal, if enacted, would re-write a bargain which had been freely entered into. We are persuaded by this argument. At root it is based on the principle that owners should be bound by the terms of their titles. Flats are freely bought and sold on the basis of particular title provisions. The law should not interfere with those provisions without very good reason.

3.10 **Sufficient generality.** A Victorian house which has been divided into two is a tenement. So is a seventeenth century "land" in Edinburgh's High Street, or a building erected this year and containing 95 separate flats. Only the most general of general rules are possible where the raw material of tenement life is so varied. A background law can provide for the ownership and maintenance of roofs and walls; but it should not seek to provide rules for underground car parks or swimming pools. Conveyancers in Scotland are well used to making special provision in cases where special provision is required.

3.11 **Continuity.** Provisions in existing titles were drafted against the background of the common law of the tenement. To some extent they are a reaction to that common law. Our recommendations, if enacted, will provide a new background law, and unless that law is close to the old, at least in form, there is a danger that existing title provisions will come to bear a meaning other than the one which was originally intended. As part of our reform exercise we have examined the titles of numerous tenements, but we have not examined the titles of all the tenements in Scotland. Thus we do not know, and cannot discover,

---

9 The only way of avoiding this conclusion would be to have two sets of ownership rules, one for existing tenements (which would simply repeat the existing law) and one for new tenements. For reasons given at paras 4.11 ff we are unable to recommend this approach.

10 We do not, however, consider that it is necessary for the legislation to give formal expression to a principle which seems self-evident.

11 See rule 1 of recommendation 13(a).

12 See paras 5.10 and 5.63 - 5.65, and rules 4 and 5 of recommendation 13(a).

13 See para 1.1.

14 Mr G P Fletcher, solicitor.

the full range of title provisions which currently exist. The only statement we can make with any confidence is that the content of title provisions is highly variable. This argues for a degree of caution. In fact we have no difficulty in building on the structure of the existing law. With its mixture of ownership and common interest, the existing law is soundly conceived. In the next section we discuss how this structure can best be used for the new law.

3.12 Summing up, we recommend that:

1(a) The rules of ownership laid down by the common law of the tenement should be clarified and substantially[15] re-stated.

(b) The new law of the tenement should be freely variable.

(Clauses 1 - 3)

Our new approach

3.13 Before we embark on a detailed account of our recommendations for a new law of the tenement, it may be helpful to begin with a summary.

3.14 A preliminary point is that the new law, like the law which it is intended to replace, is exclusively concerned with the network of rights and duties which arise within a tenement. It deals with the owners of flats in their internal relations and not in their relations with third parties. If an owner employs a tradesman to carry out a repair, their relationship is governed by the law of contract and not by the law of the tenement. Similarly the statutory rights and duties of local authorities in relation to tenements and other buildings are excluded from our remit.[16] Further, the new law is not intended to affect liabilities in respect of damage to tenement property which might arise under the law of negligence or nuisance.

3.15 At present the law of the tenement comprises two main elements. First, there is a set of rules which apportions ownership within the tenement; and secondly, there is a set of maintenance obligations founded on the principle of common interest. The maintenance scheme is rather narrow in scope and is based on ownership: the roof must be maintained by its owner for shelter while the walls and other structural parts of the building must be maintained by their owners for support.[17] Our recommendations for a new law of the tenement retain both of these existing elements, more or less in their existing form,[18] but add a third. The new element is a set of rules providing for decision-making, management, and the apportionment of liability for maintenance and certain other costs. For convenience we have collected these rules together into a self-contained management scheme contained in a schedule to the draft Bill and known as Management Scheme A.[19] The scheme has been drafted in language which is as simple as possible, consistent with legal certainty, in the hope that it might be used by owners with the minimum of professional help. It is accompanied by explanatory notes written in lay language and which are designed to guide the reader through the scheme.[20] Scheme A contains many of the rules which are already found in well-drawn deeds of conditions. The inclusion of rules apportioning liability for maintenance means that, in the normal case, maintenance is likely to be carried out under Scheme A rather than under common interest. Thus under our proposals common interest occupies a less important role than under the existing law, but it will remain as a residual mechanism for ensuring that fundamental repairs are not neglected.

---

15 The restatement is not absolutely complete. For example, we do not think it necessary to re-state the rule that a stratum of airspace may be owned separately from the surface of the earth.

16 Some of these rights and duties were mentioned earlier, at para 2.21. It has not been suggested to us that they are in need of reform.

17 See paras 2.4 - 2.10.

18 See Part 4 for the rules of ownership and Part 7 for the rules of the replacement for common interest.

19 For Management Scheme A, see Part 5.

20 The explanatory notes can be found in Appendix 1, on the pages facing Schedule 1 to the draft bill. It is suggested that where a developer decides that Scheme A should apply to a tenement, either with or without amendment, he may care to reproduce these notes, amended as appropriate, in the deed of conditions which applies to the tenement.

Choosing a management scheme

3.16 The intention is that, like the rest of the new law, Management Scheme A should apply automatically to all tenements, both old and new. But it is to be a background law only, subject to the terms of individual titles. It should be possible for the titles to amend Scheme A or to reject it altogether in favour of some other management scheme. There seems no good reason for forcing tenements to use one particular scheme rather than another. The principle is merely that some kind of management structure should be in place. Scheme A will apply unless some other choice is made, but a developer or other owner or owners of a tenement should be able to disapply that scheme and opt for some other arrangement. This could most simply be done by a deed of conditions, duly registered in the Land Register or Register of Sasines.

3.17 In order to increase the available choice we have included in our recommendations a second management scheme, known as Management Scheme B.[21] We have done this with some diffidence. We are well aware that developers, or conveyancers, may often have a favoured style of deed of conditions of their own. They may be unwilling to abandon this for Scheme B, and indeed there is no reason why they should do so unless Scheme B is felt to be better than the existing style. That is a matter for the judgment of the developer or conveyancer concerned. Scheme B is much more elaborate than Scheme A. The tenement is to be governed by an owners' association headed by a single manager. The association will be a body corporate. Provision is made for annual budgeting and, where desired, for the building up of a reserve fund. The scheme has been devised mainly with larger tenements in mind. It is offered as an example of what we consider to be good practice. The drafting has been kept as simple as possible, and we have avoided the disfiguring convention often found in deeds of conditions by which all the provisions are encompassed within a single sentence, usually of inordinate length. We hope that Scheme B will at least be understandable.

3.18 While the principle of choice will be available for all tenements, we imagine that in practice it will be exercised mainly in the case of tenements which are newly built. Under our recommendations the developer of a new tenement has various options. If he does nothing, Management Scheme A will apply automatically. For simple developments that might be a perfectly satisfactory outcome. Alternatively he can execute and register a deed of conditions providing (i) that Scheme A applies subject to such variations as are specified in the deed or (ii) that Scheme B applies or (iii) that Scheme B applies subject to such variations as are specified in the deed or (iv) that some other management scheme applies. In relation to (iv) a developer would be fully at liberty to use a deed of conditions of the kind which is in current use. The doubts which are sometimes expressed as to the enforceability of management conditions at common law[22] would be removed under our proposals where such conditions would take effect by force of statute.

3.19 In practice the deed of conditions which provides for the management scheme is likely also to contain real burdens regulating use and conduct. As a matter of drafting, there would be obvious merit in dividing the deed into two parts, with one part dealing with the rules of management and maintenance in the form of a management scheme, and the other regulating use by means of real burdens. One practical effect of our proposals is that, in the future, provisions as to maintenance[23] are likely to be included as part of a management scheme rather than, as at present, as real burdens. The juridical nature of the rules of management schemes and their relationship to real burdens are discussed later in this report.[24]

3.20 Once individual flats have been sold and the tenement is a going concern there will rarely be reason for changing the existing arrangements. In cases where a change is thought to be needed, we regard it as unrealistic to require unanimity of the owners. Instead we propose that, in the case of tenements subject to Scheme A or Scheme B, the owners of a majority of flats should be able to take the relevant

---

21 For Management Scheme B, see Part 6.

22 See para 2.27.

23 ie, provisions on the model of rule 5 of Scheme A and rule 11.1 of Scheme B.

24 Para 5.87.

decision. A change of schemes would require a registered deed of conditions, but it would be sufficient if the deed is executed by a majority of owners or, in the case of a Scheme B tenement, by the manager. On registration such a deed would then bind all the owners and - removing a doubt under the existing law - all heritable creditors and others holding subordinate real rights in the tenement. We do not consider that a change in scheme would be prejudicial to heritable creditors, and in relation to individual owners judicial challenge would be available in cases of unfair prejudice.[25]

3.21 Summing up, we recommend that:

2(a) As a general rule Management Scheme A should apply to all tenements.

(b) However, the owners should be able to provide, by deed of conditions, that the tenement is instead to be governed by

(i) Management Scheme A as varied by the deed, or

(ii) Management Scheme B, or

(iii) Management Scheme B as varied by the deed, or

(iv) some other management scheme specified in the deed.

(c) A deed of conditions should take effect on registration in the Land Register or Register of Sasines or on such later date as the deed may specify, provided that no deed should taken effect before the tenement comes into existence.

(d) In the case of a tenement which is already governed by Management Scheme A or Management Scheme B, a decision to change management schemes should be capable of being taken by the owners of a majority of flats.

(e) A deed of conditions in implement of a decision under (d) which is executed by the owners of a majority of flats or, in a case where Management Scheme B applies, by the manager of the owners' association should, once it has taken effect, bind all the owners and any other person who has a real right in the tenement.

(Clauses 4, 5 and 6; Scheme A, rule 2.2(g) and 2.4; Scheme B, rule 12.1(a))

Strata titles in other jurisdictions

3.22 As part of our work we carried out a review of the legislation on strata or sectional titles in a number of other jurisdictions.[26] However, while interesting in a general way, this proved to be of only limited assistance in formulating our recommendations. One reason for this is that, quite often, the legislation in question was introducing the apartment ownership for the first time, and previously it had not been possible for a section of airspace to be owned separately from ownership of the ground. Thus the devisers of the legislation had a free hand. There was no need to adapt to the needs of pre-existing tenements governed by a pre-existing law. Thus it is not surprising that we have found the example of other countries of greatest use in relation to Management Scheme B, which is an optional scheme and one which will not in the normal case apply to existing tenements.

25 Later we recommend a general right to seek judicial annulment of any decision made under Scheme A or Scheme B. See paras 5.19-5.25 and recommendation 7. In view of the informality of Scheme A, and hence of the possibility of appeal deadlines being missed, we further recommend that a decision to vary or discharge Scheme A is not valid if it increases an owner's liability for scheme costs unless that owner voted in favour of the decision. See para 5.76 and recommendation 14(iv).

26 Some of the leading examples of such legislation are mentioned at para 2.2.

Part 4 Ownership

Meaning of "tenement"

4.1 Since the new law, like the old, is to regulate only those buildings which are "tenements", the way in which tenement is defined is of crucial importance. But as one consultee observed,[1] "tenements are more easily identified than defined". In the mind's eye the standard tenement is a four or five storey stone building, erected around 1890, with a slate roof axnd a "close" or common passage and stair. But the legal definition is much wider and includes, for example, both tower blocks and converted Victorian villas. In 1841 Lord Fullerton offered, as a working definition "sufficient for all practical purposes", the following:[2]

> "a single or individual building, although containing several dwelling-houses, with, it may be, separate means of access, but under the same roof and enclosed by the same gables or walls."

But while this definition has been widely used, it suffers from a number of shortcomings. In the first place, it seems to confine tenements to dwelling-houses and so would exclude buildings where the use was commercial or where there was a mix of commercial and residential use. As a number of our consultees pointed out, there can be no good reason for excluding a building on grounds of type of use. Secondly, it requires "several" dwelling-houses, which seems too numerous. Thirdly, the reference to "under the same roof" is in some cases too narrow and in others too wide. It is too narrow because single buildings sometimes have more than a single roof, for example if they are built at more than one level, and it is too wide because several separate buildings may share the same roof. Fourthly, there is no reference to the fact that the dwelling-houses should be in separate ownership. A building owned by a local authority and consisting of sixteen flats all of which are leased to tenants is not a tenement within the normal meaning of the law. Fifthly, the definition fails to incorporate one of the defining characteristics of a tenement, namely that the division of ownership should be horizontal. Lord Fullerton's words seem sufficiently wide to include semi-detached or terraced houses where the division of ownership is vertical.

4.2 A more helpful definition, although of "flat" rather than of "tenement", is found in s 338(1) of the Housing (Scotland) Act 1987:[3]

> "'flat' means a separate and self-contained set of premises, whether or not on the same floor and forming part of a building from some other part of which it is divided horizontally."

If to this there is added the idea of separation of ownership, then we are close to a definition which is suitable for our purposes. There seem four key elements in any such definition. A tenement is (i) a single building (ii) which comprises two or more flats (iii) which are in separate ownership and (iv) which are divided from each other horizontally.

4.3 **A single building.** While certain additional buildings - outhouses and the like - may perform a subordinate function and so may attach as pertinents, it is of the essence of a tenement that it is a single building. On this point Lord Fullerton's definition is beyond reproach: "a single or individual building .. enclosed by the same gables or walls". It is this sharing of a single building - its walls, roof, and foundations - which colours the whole nature of tenement life and gives rise to its distinctive problems.

---

1 Professor W M Gordon.

2 *Scott v Police Commissioners of Dundee* (1841) 4 D 292, 303.

3 This definition was drawn to our attention by the Scottish Consumer Council.

4.4 In a small number of cases it may not be absolutely clear where one building ends and the next begins. Modern tenements usually stand on their own and are physically separate from any other building, and even with Victorian tenements, which were often built in terraces, there is usually no difficulty. Victorian buildings are joined together by common gable walls[4] and, by a well-settled rule, the boundary is the mid-point of the gable.[5] Each tenement was built separately, on a separately feued plot of ground, and often by a separate builder. Each has its own separate close and it own separate identity. Inevitably, though, there are difficult cases. Where a tenement is built at a corner site, it may have a single roof but two or even three closes. A more exotic example is the country house conversion, where the owner may have kept a whole wing for himself but divided the rest of the house into flats. Is the retained wing then part of the tenement or is it a separate building? No general rule can deal adequately with difficult cases and indeed is likely to do more harm than good. The demarcation of buildings is a question of fact and much will depend on individual peculiarities. Plainly the method of construction - the use of roofs, gables, closes and so on - will be of considerable importance, but so too will the division of responsibilities narrated in the titles. Tenements are demarcated as much by conveyancers as by builders. If flats served by two separate closes are subject to a common maintenance regime for the roof and the walls, then it is difficult to avoid the conclusion that there is one building and not two; and in the country house example the crucial consideration is likely to be whether the retained wing is maintained together with, or separately from, the part of the building which is flatted.

4.5 **Two or more flats.** In order to qualify as a tenement, a building must consist of at least two flats. The idea of a "flat" is sufficiently well understood not to require further definition other than to make it clear that it includes premises which are used for commercial and other non-residential purposes.

4.6 **In separate ownership.** The law of the tenement regulates rights and duties within a building which is in multiple ownership. If a building has only a single owner, no rights and duties require to be regulated and the law of the tenement does not apply. Hence a building is not a tenement unless there are at least two owners or, more precisely, unless at least two flats are in separate ownership. This means that a flatted building which has just been constructed is not a tenement until the first flat is sold.

4.7 In some areas the practice grew up of disposing of flats by long lease rather than by disposition, although overall numbers do not appear to be large. Usually the leases are of extremely long duration, running to hundreds of years, so that the tenant can be viewed virtually as an owner; and in practice the law of the tenement is applied by analogy. We considered whether we should formalise the position by extending our proposals to flats which are held on exceptionally long lease but concluded that the issue is best approached as part of our long-term project on leasehold tenure.[6]

4.8 **Divided horizontally.** Some legal systems apply the law of sectional or strata titles wherever a building is in multiple ownership, regardless of whether the division of units is horizontal or vertical.[7] By contrast in Scotland the law of the tenement has traditionally been confined to cases of horizontal division. There are of course some common issues. Houses which are terraced or semi-detached share common walls, and there is often a continuous roof line. In our discussion paper[8] we invited views on whether elements of the law of the tenement might usefully be applied to terraced property. Consultees were evenly divided and there was no strong support for extending the law. We have decided that the law should be left as it is. Apart from anything else, an extension of the law would sit uneasily with conveyancing practice, which tends to treat each house in a terrace as a separate building and to avoid provision for common maintenance.

4 Or sometimes by a double gable.
5 Reid, paras 218 and 223.
6 *Fifth Programme of Law Reform* (Scot Law Com No 159) (1997) paras 2.36 and 2.37.
7 Indeed some systems go further still and apply the law to developments comprising several buildings.
8 Discussion Paper No 91, para 3.10.

4.9 **Garden and other ground.** One further matter requires mention. Tenements are often surrounded by garden and other ground. Most Victorian tenements have back greens. Some have small front gardens. In modern blocks of flats there is often shared amenity ground. Sometimes the ground contains outhouses or garages or other buildings. The law of the tenement applies not merely to the tenement building itself but to any land pertaining to the building, and this requires recognition in any general definition.

4.10 We recommend that:

3(a) "Tenement" be defined to mean a building which comprises two or more flats in separate ownership and divided from each other horizontally, together with the solum and any other land pertaining to that building.

(b) "Flat" be defined to mean a dwelling-house or any business or other premises in a tenement.

(Clause 30(1))

One set of rules or two?

4.11 For reasons given earlier,[9] we do not feel able to recommend a redistribution of ownership rights within existing tenements. Hence, so far at least as existing buildings are concerned, the new law can do no more than re-state the rules of ownership provided by the old. Naturally, the same difficulties do not apply in relation to new tenements, and it would be possible to have a different set of rules which applied, prospectively, to new tenements only.

4.12 There is much to be said for making separate provision for new tenements. The existing rules on ownership are not wholly satisfactory. No one devising a completely new law of the tenement would come up with some of the rules currently found in our common law. One should not legislate for the twenty first century by reproducing rules from the seventeenth. The main changes which could usefully be made are to increase the parts of the tenement which are owned in common. Here the rules adopted by modern legislation in other countries form a useful model. In particular, it seems clear that the solum, the roof and the airspace above the building ought to be common property.

4.13 The arguments just mentioned are arguments of principle. The counter-argument is essentially one of convenience. To have separate sets of provisions would complicate the law without bringing about much actual benefit. Today developers invariably make their own provisions about common property, and they would continue to do so even if the background law were changed. The effect of modern conveyancing practice is to make the background law relatively unimportant.[10]

4.14 When the question was put at our second seminar on the law of the tenement, the response was strongly hostile to the idea of having two different sets of rules. In a paper delivered on that occasion Professor Robert Rennie commented:

> "The Commission ask for views on the feasibility of running two separate systems, one for tenements in existence before the passing of the Act and one for those which are erected after. I am implacably opposed to such a divisive scheme .. In any event, I consider ownership something of an academic matter so far as tenement property is concerned. What matters is who has to maintain the roof not who owns it and while I accept that there are problems with air space and the like - especially the top flat, dormer and attic extensions - I do not think that there should be different rules .. Lawyers find great difficulty in deciding what burdens are real and what burdens are not. I do not think we should add another imponderable in relation to different ownership schemes."

9 Paras 3.3 and 3.4.
10 See para 3.2.

We are not all equally persuaded by such arguments but, with some hesitation, we do not recommend that separate rules of ownership should be enacted for new tenements.

The rules of ownership

4.15 We consider that the restatement of the rules of ownership should apply both to existing and also to new tenements, but subject in both cases to the terms of individual titles[11] and to any enactment. The caveat repeats the pattern of the present law. In practice the enactment most likely to be of relevance is the Prescription and Limitation (Scotland) Act 1973. So for example if the owner of a top floor flat extends from his own roofspace into the roofspace of a neighbouring property then, assuming an appropriate title registered in the Register of Sasines,[12] ownership of the roofspace is acquired after ten years by positive prescription.

4.16 The restatement gives the opportunity to clear up doubts and uncertainties in the existing law, and to express that law in modern statutory language. In formulating the restatement we have had regard to the practice of conveyancers, in split-off deeds, in making the distinction between the flat itself and the various other rights which attach to the flat as pertinents. This model has a number of attractions. It is intrinsically neat. It takes into account the fact that a flat and its pertinents are not merely physically distinct but also in many cases physically separate. It would allow the new law to be read more easily with the individual titles to which that law is to be subject. And finally it has the technical advantage that, for the future, a conveyance of the flat would carry automatically the statutory pertinents without the need for special enumeration.[13]

4.17 **Boundaries of flats.** So far as the flats themselves are concerned, the main task of any restatement is to give an indication of boundaries. Under present law and practice boundaries are not always clear. The formula standardly used by conveyancers is to give the address of the tenement coupled with no more than a rough indication of the position of the flat within the building:[14] for example

> "ALL and WHOLE that flatted dwelling-house entering by the common passage and stair number Ten Main Street, Kirkcaldy, being the southmost dwelling-house on the second floor above the street or ground floor .."

This traditional method of description has been carried over into the Land Register. Although the Register is plan-based, and is as a general rule very successful in indicating boundaries, no boundaries are shown for tenement flats, and the title plan merely shows the solum of the tenement building together with any adjacent ground over which common rights exist.[15] At one stage in this exercise we considered the possibility of introducing to the Land Register plans which would show tenement buildings in sections. Sectional plans are used in a number of other jurisdictions and have obvious benefits. However, following consultation with the Keeper of the Land Register we concluded that the practical difficulties outweighed any advantages which might accrue.

4.18 In the absence of sectional plans, it is at least possible to lay down a set of general rules as to boundaries. Indeed this task is not confined to flats, for a tenement may also contain a close or roofspace or cellars, or, more unusually, an underground car-park or a laundry room. A useful generic name for separate parts of a tenement (including flats) is a "unit"; and any restatement requires to set out the rules which determine the boundaries between one unit and the next.

4.19 Under the common law the horizontal boundaries of a unit are the mid-point of the dividing structure, while the vertical boundaries are uncertain and controversial.[16] Partly for reasons of consistency

---

11 This is an application of the principle of free variation mentioned at para 3.8.

12 Positive prescription operates for titles registered in the Land Register only where the Keeper has excluded indemnity: see Prescription and Limitation (Scotland) Act 1973 s 1(1)(b).

13 Reid, para 204.

14 For a discussion of descriptions of this kind, see *Beneficial Bank PLC v McConnachie* 1996 SC 119.

15 Registration of Title Practice Book, para E.14.

16 The common law is summarised at paras 2.6 - 2.10.

and partly to avoid the difficulties associated with common property,[17] we propose that the boundaries in all cases should be the mid-point of the dividing structure. Thus the boundary between two flats on the same level would be the mid-point of the common wall, while the boundary between an upper and a lower flat would be the centre line of the joists. Similarly, the wall separating the common passage from an individual flat would be owned on each side to the mid-point. The overall effect is that a flat or other unit would consist of a section of airspace bounded by four walls, a ceiling and a floor. The boundary features would generally be owned to the mid-point but where they formed the outer surface of the building (as with external walls or the roof) the entire feature would be counted as part of the unit.

4.20 Sometimes a common boundary contains something which is wholly or substantially for the benefit of one only of the units. The front door of a flat leading into the close is a standard example. In cases like this we suggest that the door or other feature should be the sole property of the unit which it serves.

4.21 We propose to follow the special rules which, at common law, apply to the flats on the highest and lowest levels of the building. This means that the top flat extends to include the roof and the intermediate roofspace while the bottom flat extends to include the foundations and solum.

4.22 At common law the airspace above the building is the property of the owner of the solum.[18] However, the triangle of airspace lying between the surface of a pitched roof and the top of the building is treated separately. That was settled in *Sanderson's Trs v Yule*[19] where the owner of a garret was allowed to construct a storm window notwithstanding the objections of other owners in the building.[20] It seems that the owner of each part of a roof has the right to build into the triangle of airspace directly above that part. If the roof is common property, then the airspace is common property also. In practice, as the Lord President pointed out in *Sanderson's Trs,*[21] dormer windows are commonplace in tenements. Hence the attribution of ownership is founded on practice and convenience, and should be re-stated in the proposed new law.

4.23 **Pertinents.** The parts of the tenement which do not comprise individual flats require to be apportioned amongst those flats, as pertinents. But at this point the common law lets us down. For while there are one or two specific rules, for example in relation to the close or the garden ground, there is wholly lacking any general principle which can be applied to the miscellaneous other parts commonly found in tenements. These parts include rhones, pipes, conduits, cables, tanks, chimney stacks, chimney flues, entry-phone systems, television aerials, common heating and lighting systems, paths, and outside stairs. In our discussion paper[22] we suggested that the most appropriate basis for a general principle lay with the idea of benefit or service. The ownership of a part would depend on which flats it served. If it served all the flats in the building, then it would be universal common property. If it served some flats only, then it would be the common property only of those flats. Finally, if it served only one flat, then that one flat would have sole ownership. On this basis the rhones and down pipes would be the common property of all those sheltered by the roof which they drain,[23] a chimney stack would be owned by all those with flues leading into it; and a path would be owned by all those to whose flats it gives access.

4.24 On consultation this suggestion was well received and we recommend its adoption in the new law. Of course it is not beyond criticism. In marginal cases there may be difficulties in deciding whether the service test has been fulfilled in relation to a particular flat. A more serious objection is that service implies a structural or functional relationship which may not exist in the case of some parts of the tenement

17 See para 3.5.
18 Para 2.7.
19 (1897) 25 R 211. But the window must not impair the efficiency of the cover provided by the roof. And nor must it significantly increase the loading on the walls. See *Sharp v Robertson* (1800) Mor App *sv* Property no 3.
20 However, there is no right to add an additional storey, for that would encroach into the airspace above the building. See *Watt v Burgess' Tr* (1891) 18 R 766.
21 (1897) 25 R 211 at 216.
22 Discussion Paper No 91, paras 4.30 - 4.37 and propositions 17-19.
23 However the roof itself, while serving all the flats which it covers, is treated as part of the individual top flats and so cannot be owned as a pertinent.

- for example, garages or swimming pools or garden ground. A practical difficulty[24] is that it might sometimes be difficult to determine quickly which group of flats was served by a particular pipe. We think that these objections can be lived with. The only sure means of avoiding them would be to make all parts of the tenement the common property of everyone; but this would be unprincipled, unfair, and, in relation to existing tenements, bring about a substantial and unwarranted redistribution of ownership.

4.25 Since the effect of the service test will usually be to create common property, it is necessary to make provision for the relative sizes of the *pro indiviso* shares. This is important, not in relation to use of the property - because all co-owners can use common property regardless of the size of their shares[25] - but in relation to liability for maintenance. Except where the titles provide otherwise, co-ownership means co-maintenance, and liability is determined by size of shares. Apportioning shares by reference to the use made of the pertinent, whether actual or potential, would be attractively equitable but unattractively vague. The only case where we suggest this approach is in relation to chimney stacks, where we recommend the adoption of the common law rule that ownership is proportional to the number of flues.[26] Less equitable but more certain would be to apportion shares by reference to the relative sizes of the flats, using either floor area or volume as the measure. However, in our view the complexity of this approach is out of scale with the relative triviality of many of the items to which it would apply. The only approach which is simple and at the same time relatively fair is equality of shares. This means that each flat would have an equal share in all parts which were of service to it. We concede an element of rough justice. On the other hand, the service test of itself gives rise to a reasonable correspondence between use and liability for maintenance. An example makes the point. A pipe which runs the full height of a building and which serves all the flats will be owned at different stages by different flats. All flats will own the lowest section of pipe, but as it ascends the building the flats on the lower levels will gradually drop out so that the final section is owned only by the flats on the top storey. Furthermore, the branch pipes leading off into individual flats will be in the exclusive ownership of the flats in question. Hence if the pipe leaks and requires to be repaired, liability for repair will be confined to those owners who use the pipe at the relevant point.

4.26 In three cases the service test is either inapplicable or inappropriate.

4.27 Mention was made earlier of parts of the tenement which cannot be said to be of service to individual flats. The examples are relatively exotic and are likely to be found only in modern buildings: swimming pools and other recreational facilities, basement car parks, laundry rooms, and so on. In cases like this it is inconceivable that the titles will not make provision for ownership. The background law need not and should not be drawn into areas such as this.[27]

4.28 A second type of case is where the part in question is shared by more than one tenement, or by a tenement and by other non-tenemental property which together comprise a common development. Examples include recreational areas and common hot water systems. Again these are confined to modern buildings where it may be assumed that ownership will be fully regulated by the titles. In the very unlikely event that the titles fail to make adequate provision the service test would be of assistance at least to the extent that the hot water system or other item can be treated as a part of the tenement.

4.29 Finally there are the cases where special rules exist in the common law which require to be repeated in the restatement. There are only two. At common law the garden and other ground attached to the tenement is the property of the bottom flat or flats most nearly adjacent. This is several ownership and not ownership in common: where there is more than one flat on the lowest storey, each has its own section of garden ground. The rule may not seem very fair, and in practice is almost always displaced by a title provision making some or all of the garden common property. But it has at least the merit of providing a clear rule for a case which could not easily be covered by a service test.

---

24 Emphasised to us by the Property Managers Association Scotland Limited.
25 Reid, para 24.
26 *Whitmore v Stuart & Stuart* (1902) 10 SLT 290.
27 This is the principle of sufficient generality discussed at para 3.10.

4.30 The other special rule concerns the close, by which we mean the system of passageways, corridors, stairs and landings internal to a tenement building. At common law the close is the common property of those flats which obtain access by it, but the manner in which shares are allocated is disputed.[28] One version of the law would apply a strict service test, so that the lower flats would have no share of ownership in any part of the close which lay at a higher level. The other version states that the whole close is owned by all the flats in equal shares. The second version is much the simpler of the two, while at the same time paying proper regard to the central importance of the close, both to the structure of the building and as a means of access. We are content that paths and stairs external to the building should be governed by the service test,[29] but in our view the whole close should be treated as a single unit and should be owned by all the flats to which it gives access.

4.31 Unsurprisingly, the common law makes no provision for lifts but the functional and structural similarities suggest that lifts should be treated in the same way as closes. Consultees were generally supportive of the view that lifts should be common property in equal shares, at least of those flats which make use of them. Only ground floor flats would not share in ownership. In the discussion paper we suggested that it might be appropriate for ground floor flats to own in cases where there were common facilities which could be reached by the lift,[30] but on reflection we feel that refinements of this kind are best left to individual sets of titles.

4.32 We recommend that:

4(a) **The boundary between a flat or other unit and any contiguous flat or unit should be the mid-point of the structure which separates them; but any door or other item which wholly or mainly serves a particular flat or unit should be wholly part of that flat or unit.**

(b) **Where the boundary of a flat or other unit is an external surface of the building, the flat or unit should be taken to include the full thickness of that boundary.**

(c) **A top flat should extend to and include the roof over that flat.**

(d) **A bottom flat should extend to and include the solum under that flat.**

(e) **Ownership of a sloping roof (or part of the roof) should carry with it ownership of the triangle of airspace lying between the roof (or part) and the highest point of the building.**

(f) **Ownership of the solum (or part of the solum) should carry with it ownership of the airspace directly over the solum (or part) and above the tenement building.**

(g) **Except where (j) or (k) apply there should attach to each flat as a pertinent a right of property in any part of the tenement which serves that flat.**

(h) **To the extent that a part serves one flat only, the right of property mentioned at (g) should be a right of sole property.**

(i) **To the extent that a part serves two or more flats, the right of property mentioned at (g) should be a right of common property held in equal shares; except that where the part is a chimney stack the share allocated to each flat should be proportional to the number of flues.**

(j) **Any land pertaining to the tenement should attach as a pertinent to the bottom flat most nearly adjacent to the land.**

(k) **Any close or lift should attach as common property, in equal shares, to any flat to which it gives access.**

---

28 See para 2.8.
29 See para 4.23.
30 Discussion Paper No 91, paras 4.33-4.35.

(l) **The rules given above should be subject to the title to the tenement and to the effect of any enactment.**

(Clauses 1 - 3)

Separation of pertinents

4.33 In the discussion paper we suggested, although without giving reasons, that common property attaching as a pertinent to a flat should be inalienable except on alienation of the flat itself.[31] A majority of consultees supported this suggestion, also without giving reasons. A similar rule is found in a number of other jurisdictions. None the less we have come to have second thoughts. Freedom of alienation is a fundamental right which should not be interfered with without compelling reason. It is not clear why alienation of pertinents should be regarded as unacceptable. In theory there might be a danger that, through sale of a share in some strategic part of the building, a third party wholly unconnected with the tenement might come to hold the owners to ransom. In practice the situation is likely to be ruled by market forces. A flat owner will not sell a pertinent which is necessary for the enjoyment of his own flat, because to do so would impair its marketability. But if a pertinent is not necessary for enjoyment of the flat it is unlikely to be of crucial importance to the building. The more serious danger is that an owner might sell, not his whole share in the pertinent, but a fractional part of it. It is a feature of common property that it can be divided up into an infinite number of shares.[32] Hence in theory a flat owner who holds a one eighth *pro indiviso* share in, say, the close could divide that share in two and, while retaining one share, could convey the other one sixteenth share to a third party. In practice the risk seems fanciful. It is not suggested that the present law, which appears[33] to allow alienation, has led to difficulties; and it is difficult to see how the one sixteenth share held by the third party offers much in the way of prejudice to the other owners. By virtue of his share the third party could make use of the close, but then so can the other owners. From the point of view of a third party the attractiveness of a right to use is likely to be diminished by the correlative obligation to pay for maintenance.

4.34 There are practical problems also, some of which were mentioned by consultees. It may be assumed that any restriction on alienation should not prevent owners from conveying pertinents to one another. For example the owners in a tenement where the roofspace is common property might agree that the roofspace should become the sole property of the owner of the top flat. Other schemes for reorganising rights within a tenement can easily be envisaged. There can be no reason for discouraging or preventing such schemes. But sometimes alienation even to third parties may be an acceptable and sensible arrangement. Certainly this is true of pertinents outside the actual tenement building. For example the owners might wish to sell a part of the garden ground for redevelopment. But even within the tenement there may be cases where alienation is justified. East Kilbride Development Corporation gave the example of blocks of flats with integral garages belonging to third parties. The sheer variety of tenement life is such that any provision restricting alienation would require to be drawn with the utmost care and would run the risk of frustrating the reasonable wishes of owners. In our view the scale of the problem does not justify the potential complexity, and the potential risks, of legislative intervention.

Subdivision and amalgamation

4.35 Sometimes the boundaries between flats are altered. The typical case is where two flats are knocked into one, but it also sometimes happens that a large flat is divided into two smaller ones. From the point of view of our proposals the main impact of subdivision or amalgamation is to alter the number of flats in the tenement. This has certain implications. The size of shares in common property is determined by the number of flats in the building. So, under Management Scheme A, is liability for certain costs,[34] and

---

31 Discussion Paper No 91, para 3.17 and proposition 2(iv).

32 *Menzies v Macdonald* (1854) 16 D 827 affd (1856) 2 Macq 463.

33 In *Michael v Carruthers* 1997 SCLR 1005–1008 Lord Hamilton suggested that flat owners might not have "an unqualified right" to dispose of their shares in pertinents. There was, however, no discussion as to the type of qualification which might possibly exist.

34 Paras 5.59 - 5.67, 5.79 and 5.83; recommendations 13 and 15(a). But maintenance costs are apportioned by reference to floor area in the case of any tenement where the largest flat is more than one and a half times the size of the smallest.

the right to take part in decision-making. Two approaches seem possible here. If no special provision is made, the legislation will at any given time apply to the tenement as it actually is at that time. A tenement which in the year 2010 consisted of eight flats might, by the year 2020, consist of ten. In 2010 each flat will have a one eighth *pro indiviso* share in the common parts and a one eighth liability for certain costs. By 2020 the size of the *pro indiviso* share will have diminished to a one tenth share, with a corresponding reduction in liability. The alternative approach is to treat the internal organisation of the flat as fixed as at the date when the legislation first comes into force or, if later, on the date when the tenement is first created. For the purposes of counting *pro indiviso* shares or votes or liability, later subdivisions and amalgamations would then simply be ignored.

4.36 There is a certain awkwardness in the idea that *pro indiviso* shares can be reallocated merely by changes in the internal organisation of a building. In our law real rights in heritable property are not usually transferred by knocking down a wall.[35] But property law purism should not stand in the way of a solution which in every other respect is much the superior. To ignore alterations in the number of flats would be artificial, inequitable (at least in relation to liability for maintenance), and, with the passage of time, impractical. Fifty years later changes may well be impossible to detect. We conclude, therefore, that our recommendations should apply to the tenement as it actually is without regard to its previous internal organisation.

4.37 Finally, mention may be made of additional storeys. Unlike the laws of some other countries,[36] Scots law makes no special provision for additional storeys. In fact in Scotland the adding on of a further complete storey or storeys is extremely unusual. The owner of the existing top storey could not normally add to the building because he is unlikely to have sole ownership of the airspace above the top of the roof line.[37] At common law the airspace belongs to the owner of the ground flat, while most titles make it common property.[38] Furthermore, anyone seeking to add a further storey would be regarded as increasing the loading of the building and hence as interfering with the common interest obligation of support.[39] In practice, therefore, it is difficult to see how an additional storey could be built without the consent of all the owners and without a certain amount of conveyancing. Any necessary adjustments to common rights and liabilities could then be included as part of the conveyancing. Our proposals are neutral on this whole issue, and it does not seem that special provision is required.

35 However in the law of accession physical acts change real rights.

36 eg, Italian Civil Code art 1127; French law of 1965, art 3.

37 *Watt v Burgess' Tr* (1891) 18 R 766.

38 This is achieved, indirectly, by making the solum common property.

39 *Sharp v Robertson* (1800) Mor App *sv* Property no 3. We recommend later that the common law obligation of support be preserved: see paras 7.4 - 7.13 and recommendation 30.

Part 5 Management Scheme A

Scope

5.1 We explained earlier[1] that our proposals for management and maintenance are collected together into a self-contained management scheme, known as Management Scheme A. In principle Scheme A will, like the rest of the proposed legislation,[2] apply to all tenements; but it will be possible for the owners of a tenement to vary Scheme A, or to disapply it altogether and replace it with some other management scheme.[3] Furthermore Scheme A is designed to supplement, and not to replace, existing title provisions, and is perhaps best regarded as a shadow deed of conditions. Its function is to provide model rules on key topics. Where a particular topic turns out to be covered by a provision in the titles, the title provision applies in place of the model rule. But where the title is silent, or seriously inadequate, the relevant model rule will apply. It follows that Scheme A will not apply to all tenements equally. Where a tenement is already governed by a well-drawn deed of conditions, there is little for Scheme A to add. But where the titles make little or no provision for management and maintenance, the background law as set out in Scheme A will come fully into operation.

5.2 A small number of rules in Scheme A apply regardless of the content of the individual titles. The most important are the rules which list the subjects on which owners may make decisions[4] and the rule which deals with emergency repairs.[5] In practice there will not usually be a matching provision on these subjects in the titles, but any matching provision which did exist would remain enforceable in its own right[6] and would provide owners with an alternative basis for action.

5.3 Scheme A is deliberately limited in scope. That mandatory should mean modest seems unavoidable: rules which are intended to be both universal and compulsory could scarcely be otherwise. In Scheme A we have sought to provide what we consider to be the minimum framework necessary for the proper administration of a tenement. More elaborate provisions are of course possible and, in the case of some tenements, highly desirable. Sometimes such provisions will already be in place, in the form of a sophisticated deed of conditions. For tenements not in this position we offer an off-the-peg alternative to Scheme A in the form of Management Scheme B.[7] Scheme B is optional and requires the execution and registration of a deed of conditions by a majority of owners. But except where Scheme B or some other management scheme is brought into operation in this way, the tenement will be governed by Scheme A.

Meaning of "scheme property"

5.4 Scheme A provides for the collective management and maintenance of "scheme property". The scope of this term is of crucial importance. Not all of a tenement should be scheme property. On the whole, owners expect to manage, and to maintain, their own flats without reference to or interference from their neighbours. Scheme property is, in a non-technical sense, merely the common parts of a tenement - that is to say, the parts which are either used in common or which are so fundamental to the building as a whole that they require to be maintained in common.

---

1 Para 3.15.
2 Other than Management Scheme B.
3 Paras 3.16 - 3.21, and recommendation 2.
4 Scheme A, rule 2, discussed at paras 5.70 - 5.78.
5 Scheme A, rule 7, discussed at paras 5.54 - 5.58.
6 Paras 3.8 and 3.9.
7 Management Scheme B is discussed in Part 6.

5.5 **Common property.** For the most part, scheme property is self-selecting. The essential distinction is between property which is owned in common and property which is held in individual ownership. Hence as a minimum, scheme property includes all those parts of a tenement which are owned in common by the owners of two or more flats.[8] Under our recommendations the incidence of common property depends mainly on the application of a service test.[9] Leaving aside individual flats and their boundary features (such as roofs and walls), which are in individual ownership, other parts of a tenement are treated as the common property of those flats which they serve. Depending on the tenement the list of common property might be quite a long one including rhones, down pipes, soil pipes, entry-phone systems, the close, common lighting and heating systems, external pathways, fire escapes, and so on. Of course in many cases title deeds will add quite substantially to this list, from which it follows that the precise content of scheme property will vary from tenement to tenement.

5.6 **Strategic parts.** We would not confine scheme property to property which is owned in common. Certain parts of a tenement building are of such strategic importance that they ought to be scheme property regardless of ownership. For unless these parts are adequately maintained the building as a whole would cease to be viable and ownership of individual flats would count for nothing. In our view such parts are properly the concern of everyone, and ought to be maintained by everyone. The parts which fall into this category include all the external surfaces of the building - the outside walls and the roof - together with the solum and the foundations. Inside the building there should also be included load-bearing walls. Taken together these account for all of the parts which provide shelter against the weather, as well as the most important parts which contribute to structural stability. Although none of these parts is common property in terms of our recommendations, many of them may be common property under the titles and hence already qualify as scheme property on that ground.

5.7 It would of course be possible to go further. For example, there is an argument that scheme property ought to include any part of the building which is of structural significance, regardless of its nature. This might bring in items such as floors and joists and columns. However, we have concluded that scheme property ought not to be so extensive. Partly this is to avoid disputes. If a broad view is taken, there are many parts of a tenement which might be regarded as structurally significant. We are not confident that owners would be able to operate on the basis of a definition on which experts are quite likely to hold different views. But the main reason for restricting scheme property is the mandatory nature of Scheme A. Developers and owners are free to make their own arrangements to suit the peculiarities of their own buildings, but a scheme which is both mandatory and universal should do no more than the indispensable minimum.

5.8 Some qualifications are necessary to the list of strategic parts. A ground floor offshoot from the main building should be the sole responsibility of the flat of which it forms part. Standard examples are rear kitchen extensions and protruding shop fronts. The same rule should apply to chimney stacks, except where they are common property.[10] Doors, windows and vents should be the sole responsibility of the flats which they serve and should be scheme property only where they belong to the close or some other part of the building which is owned in common. The position of roof lights is more difficult. The Property Managers Association Scotland Limited commented that:

> "On the one hand we see no reason why a roof light should be treated any differently from a window in a wall. It could be argued that if the roof light serves a common area then it should indeed be subject to common ownership and all that that entails, whereas if it serves an individual unit then it could be argued that it should be treated as being part of that individual unit. On the other hand, however, it could be argued that the consequences of lack of maintenance are greater in the case of roof lights than they are in the case of windows in a wall and that the roof lights should indeed be regarded as part of the roof."

---

8 But excluding any parts owned along with a third party: Scheme A takes no account of third party interests and it would be inappropriate for the Scheme A rules to apply in a case such as this.

9 Paras 4.23 - 4.32, and recommendation 4(g)-(k).

10 A chimney stack which serves two or more flats will be common property and hence scheme property on that ground.

On balance, the Property Managers took the view that roof lights ought to be commonly maintained, while the Royal Institution of Chartered Surveyors in Scotland thought that maintenance should be a private matter except where the lights serve common areas. Departing from the view expressed in the discussion paper,[11] we are now inclined to favour the latter position, mainly in the interests of consistency with the position for ordinary windows. Dormer windows would fall to be treated in the same way. Consultees were not wholly agreed on the position of the roof, sides and related guttering and flashing which surround a dormer window. Most of those who commented challenged our provisional view[12] that the roof part of the window should be individually maintained. It was suggested that dormers were sometimes original to the building and that in any event, while the window itself benefited only the individual flat, the roof surrounding the window was for the benefit of everyone in the tenement. We are persuaded by these arguments, and consider that the roof surrounding a dormer window ought, like the rest of the roof, to be scheme property.

5.9 **Collective maintenance.** Under our proposals scheme property will not only be collectively administered but will also be collectively maintained.[13] The principle of collective maintenance is of great importance. So vital are the component elements of scheme property to the building as a whole that the individualism of the common law seems badly out of place. Those who live in a tenement should be bound to contribute to the cost of maintaining its essential fabric. Of course in a large majority of cases this result is already achieved under the title deeds, but sometimes there are gaps and, in the case particularly of older tenements, the titles may be silent or extremely inadequate.

5.10 For tenements with silent or inadequate titles our proposals will have the effect of rearranging maintenance liabilities. At common law the owners on the top storey must maintain the roof while those further down the building must maintain the walls, foundations and other structural parts.[14] Under our proposals, which will replace[15] the common law, all owners will share liability for all scheme property. To some extent these changes balance out. The owner of a lower flat will take on some liability to maintain the roof but he will also lose some liability to maintain the walls. Inevitably, however, the exchange may not always be regarded as a fair one, especially where it involves acquiring liability for the roof.[16] But the imposition of liability for future repairs is not, in our view, unreasonable in itself, and indeed legislation often imposes new liabilities. Moreover, our proposals do not affect existing title provisions.[17] A person who bought a flat on the basis of a maintenance regime set out in the titles will continue to have the benefit or burden of that regime. The object of our proposals is merely to replace a background law which was universally seen as unfair with a new background law in which maintenance costs are equitably distributed. We accept that our proposals, if enacted, will lead to an increase in the value of the small number of top floor flats currently governed by the common law rule which imposes sole liability for roof maintenance. We would be very surprised if there were a corresponding reduction in the value of flats lower down the building. Surveyors do not normally consult the title deeds before deciding on the value of a flat, and prospective purchasers usually expect to have to pay a fair share of maintenance costs. Our proposals will ensure that that expectation is properly met.

5.11 We recommend that:

5(a) Scheme property should include any part of a tenement, including any garden or other ground, which is the common property of some or all of the owners.

(b) Scheme property should also include the following parts of a tenement-

(i) the solum;

(ii) the foundations;

---

11 Discussion Paper No 91, para 4.22.
12 Discussion Paper No 91, para 4.22.
13 The details of collective maintenance are given below, at paras 5.40 - 5.53.
14 See paras 2.11 and 2.17.
15 But the common law obligations of support and shelter will survive in a slightly different form. See Part 7.
16 See para 5.68, example 3.
17 See para 3.8.

(iii) the external walls;

(iv) the roof;

(v) if the tenement is separated from another building by a gable wall, the part of the gable wall that is part of the tenement building; and

(vi) any other wall that is load-bearing.

(c) However there should be excluded from (b) -

(i) any offshoot which forms part of one flat only;

(ii) any door, window, skylight, vent or other opening; and

(iii) any chimney stack or chimney flue.

(Scheme A, rules 1.2 and 1.3)

Majority decision-making

5.12 Probably the most serious single defect in the present law is the requirement that decisions be reached unanimously.[18] In practice unanimity is often impossible to achieve. One of the owners may be abroad or otherwise unavailable; or the ownership of a particular flat may be uncertain; or again one or more owners may consistently refuse to sanction any form of expenditure. Experience shows that where maintenance requires unanimity it will very often not get done at all. In cases where the common law rule is disapplied, the replacement rule in the titles is almost always for majority decision-making, and in our discussion paper[19] we suggested that the background law should now follow this lead. On consultation our proposal was warmly welcomed as an indispensable first step in improving the management of tenements.

5.13 Simplicity suggests that one vote be allocated to each flat, and that a simple majority should be sufficient to bind all the owners.[20] If there is a tie, then no majority is achieved and the decision is not carried.

5.14 In some cases not all of the owners may be liable for a particular expenditure. An example is a repair to a pipe (or section of a pipe) which serves only two of the flats. Under our recommendations such a pipe would be the common property of the two flats and hence scheme property; but, unless the titles provided otherwise, sole liability for the repair would rest with the owners of the flats in question.[21] In a case like this it seems wrong in principle that the remaining owners should have a vote in deciding on a repair for which they do not have to pay. While it is difficult to engineer a precise relationship between voting rights and liability for costs,[22] there should at least be some relationship. Thus we suggest that, in the case of decisions concerning maintenance, the number of votes available should be determined by the number of flats which are liable for the cost of the repair. The decision is then made if it achieves a majority of the votes available.

5.15 There is no reason why a vote need be cast in person, and it should be possible to authorise someone else to exercise the vote. We do not suggest a formal requirement of writing, although in some cases writing would clearly be prudent. Where a flat is owned by two or more people, any one of the co-owners should be entitled to exercise the vote allocated to that flat. Any other rule would be unworkable. A person going from door to door seeking to assemble a majority for a particular proposal should not have

---

18 Paras 2.12 and 2.19-2.22. However in the case of common property any one owner can instruct necessary repairs and recover the cost. This rule is not easily compatible with majority decision-making and we recommend later that it should cease to apply in the case of scheme property. See para 10.30 and recommendation 45.

19 Discussion Paper No 91, para 5.7, and proposition 22(ii), (iii).

20 However, for some qualifications to this rule, see paras 5.26 - 5.32.

21 See rule 2 of recommendation 13(a).

22 This issue is pursued at paras 5.28 and 5.29.

to ask an assenting owner whether his wife (or her husband) is of the same mind. However, even after the vote has been cast for a particular flat, another co-owner should be entitled to express a dissenting view and, provided that this is done before the decision-making process is complete, the dissent should have the effect of cancelling the previous vote. No vote will then be entered for that flat.[23]

5.16 Only an owner (or his representative) has the right to vote. In doubtful cases a person seeking to assemble a majority may have to carry out some detective work as to the true identity of the owners. A person who to all outward appearances owns a flat may turn out to be only a tenant; or again of two people sharing a flat, only one may be the owner. This is not a new problem. Indeed the removal of the requirement of unanimity is likely to make matters considerably easier. For in cases where the apparent majority for a decision is high, the proposer can feel relaxed at the prospect that one, or even two, of those voting in favour may turn out not to have been owners. The position is different where the voting is close or where the amount of expenditure authorised is very substantial. In cases like this the proposer might wish to make absolutely sure that there is a majority. The answer will usually be found, at a cost, in the Land Register or Register of Sasines. However, while both Registers are reasonably up-to-date, there remains the difficulty that a person who has received delivery of a conveyance but has not yet registered is treated, under our proposals, as if already the owner.[24] In most cases, though, it will be known within a tenement if a flat has recently changed hands. Apart from the Registers no other source of information is readily available. For flats in residential use a valuation list is maintained for the purposes of the council tax[25] and is open to public inspection free of charge.[26] But there is currently no obligation for the list to include names,[27] and in any event council tax is payable by tenants as well as by owners.[28] For flats in commercial use a valuation roll is maintained for rating purposes, but once again the tax is payable by tenants as well as by owners. It is difficult to see how the situation can be further improved. In our discussion paper[29] we expressed doubt as to the utility and practicability of requiring incoming owners to make formal notification to the other owners in the tenement, and our doubts were shared by a number of consultees.[30] However, in cases where tenements are factored our recommendations on transmission of liability[31] are likely to encourage an incoming owner, or his solicitor, to contact the factor to inquire about any outstanding liabilities of the seller.

5.17 There is no reason for forcing our proposals for decision-making on tenements which already have their own arrangements. Accordingly, where the title to a tenement contains appropriate procedures, these procedures should take effect to the exclusion of our proposals. It should not matter for this purpose if the title provisions are not, as a matter of strict law, real burdens.[32] For ease of exposition decisions made in accordance with our recommendations or in accordance with the titles may be referred to as "scheme decisions".

5.18 We recommend that:

6(a) Decisions under Management Scheme A should be taken by a simple majority, one vote being allocated to each flat.

(b) However, where the decision relates to the maintenance of scheme property, no vote should be allocated to a flat whose owner is not liable for the cost of such maintenance.

(c) An owner should be able to authorise a person to vote on his behalf.

(d) Where two or more persons own a flat, any one owner should be able to vote, but if the owners disagree as to how the vote is to be cast the vote should not be counted.

---

23 This proposal is modelled on the Condominium Act 1990 s22, which applies in Ontario.
24 Para 8.25 - 8.29, and recommendation 36.
25 Local Government Finance Act 1992 s 34.
26 Local Government Finance Act 1992 s 91.
27 Council Tax (Contents of Valuation Lists) (Scotland) Regulations 1992, SI 1992/1330.
28 Local Government Finance Act 1992 s 75(2).
29 Discussion Paper No 91, para 5.13.
30 However, in the much more formal Management Scheme B we recommend that a person selling a flat should have a duty to notify the manager. See para 6.59 and recommendation 26(b).
31 Paras 8.9 - 8.24, and recommendations 34 and 35 .
32 For some of the difficulties here, see para 2.24.

(e) **Where the title to a tenement provides its own procedures for the making of decisions, those procedures should apply in place of the rules given above and in recommendations 8 and 9.**

(Scheme A, rules 1.5, 2.1, 3.1-3.6)

Annulling decisions

5.19 It is a reasonable proposition that, within a tenement, individual wishes should in certain cases give way to the wishes of the majority. But a majority may not always act either wisely or fairly. Some kind of check seems to be required.

5.20 In our discussion paper we suggested[33] that a decision of the majority might be made subject to review by the Lands Tribunal for Scotland. On consultation, however, the Lands Tribunal was unenthusiastic about this proposal, pointing out that it was "hardly appropriate that this small specialised Tribunal situated in Edinburgh should be involved in local maintenance disputes all over Scotland". We accept these comments. On reflection the more appropriate forum for review is the sheriff court. The sheriff is already empowered to consider appeals against statutory repairs notices,[34] a jurisdiction which seems broadly analogous. As with the statutory notices procedure, there would be a further appeal, on a point of law, to the Court of Session.[35]

5.21 There are two kinds of review. Decisions made under Scheme A are always positive in nature - as for example to carry out maintenance or to employ a factor. Hence the outcome of a successful application for review is that the decision is judicially annulled: the maintenance cannot be carried out, or the factor is not to be employed. But there may also be a failure to reach a decision at all. For example, a proposal to carry out a particular repair may not achieve the requisite majority. Departing from the view expressed in the discussion paper, we do not think that the failure to reach a decision should be subject to review. Courts should prevent expenditure but not authorise it. A court has neither the information nor the expertise to embark on a programme of maintenance on behalf of the owners of a tenement. The court cannot be expected to act as property manager. If an owner is unable to persuade his fellow owners of the wisdom of a repair, it seems an acceptable result that the repair will not get done. Later, however, we propose certain safeguards where a repair is essential for the support or shelter of the building as a whole,[36] and in an emergency work can always be carried out.[37]

5.22 A sheriff should be able to annul a scheme decision where either it is not in the best interests of the owners taken as a whole or where it is unfairly prejudicial to one or more of the owners. If the application for review is in respect of a decision to carry out maintenance, the sheriff should have particular regard to the age and condition of the tenement, to the likely cost of the work, and to whether the cost of the work is reasonable. Thus, if a tenement has deteriorated to the point where it can no longer be economically repaired,[38] the court may readily conclude that to carry out any maintenance at all is to throw good money after bad. Similarly the perfectionism of the majority in insisting on a repair being carried out to the highest possible standard may seem unreasonable, particularly if a cheaper repair would produce a result which was almost as durable.

5.23 Appeals against statutory repairs notices must be made within either 14 or 21 days.[39] 21 days is also the statutory default period for summary applications.[40] We consider that 21 days is the appropriate

---

33 Discussion paper No 91, para 5.9.

34 Civic Government (Scotland) Act 1982 s 106; Housing (Scotland) Act 1987 s 111.

35 We considered whether further appeals should be to the Sheriff Principal, but decided that the appeal provisions should be based on those which apply to statutory notices for repairs.

36 Paras 7.4 - 7.13 and recommendation 30.

37 Paras 5.54 - 5.58.

38 Later we recommend that the obligation on all owners to maintain their property should cease to apply once this threshold is crossed. See para 7.8 and recommendation 30(a).

39 Civic Government (Scotland) Act 1982 s 106(3); Housing (Scotland) Act 1987 s 111(1).

40 Act of Sederunt (Sheriff Court Summary Application Rules) 1993 (SI 1993/3240) r 6.

period for applications to the sheriff for annulment. Any appeal period must be sufficiently long to allow owners time to reflect and to take legal advice, but sufficiently short to prevent repairs from being unduly delayed. The 21-day period would start running from the date of the relevant meeting or, in a case where an owner was not present at the meeting or where no meeting was held, from the date of notification of the decision. If different owners are notified on different days there will be different appeal periods for each. During the whole appeal period the decision would be frozen and no expenditure could be incurred. An owner who jumped the gun and incurred expenditure in implement of a decision which was subsequently annulled would be unable to make recovery under the rules of the Scheme. However, work which is genuinely urgent should be allowed to proceed even during the appeal period.[41] If the 21 days has expired without notification to the owners of an appeal having been made, the owners are free to give effect to the scheme decision. Work should not be held up for longer than this. An owner who appeals timeously but who fails to inform his fellow owners[42] will run the risk of the work having been completed before his appeal can be heard.

5.24 We considered whether there should be some kind of threshold requirement before application to the sheriff is permitted. A pecuniary limit would be random and might easily be avoided by authorising expenditure in stages rather than by a single decision. A rule which required a certain percentage of owners to concur in any application would fail to protect individual owners who had been unfairly treated. We do not, therefore, recommend a threshold requirement. In practice we imagine that the potential cost of an application will act as a deterrent except in cases where quite substantial sums are at stake. Moreover, owners are able to prevent trivial applications by agreeing to sanction in advance any repair up to an agreed figure.[43] We understand that appeals against statutory repairs notices are made very infrequently,[44] and we would not expect applications for annulment of scheme decisions to be any more common.

5.25 We recommend that:

7(a) **Where any vote allocated as respects a flat is not cast in favour of a scheme decision, the owner of that flat should be able, by summary application, to apply to the sheriff for an order annulling that decision.**

(b) **An application should be made no later than 21 days after (i) the date of the meeting at which the decision was made or (ii) where no meeting was held or where the applicant did not attend the meeting, the date on which the notification of the decision was sent to him.**

(c) **During the appeal period mentioned at (b) it should not be competent to incur any expenditure in implementation of a scheme decision except in a case where work requires to be carried out urgently.**

(d) **If during the appeal period the owners receive notice of an application, the bar on expenditure should continue until the application has been disposed of or abandoned.**

(e) **The sheriff should be empowered to annul a scheme decision in whole or in part if he is satisfied that (i) it is not in the best interests of all the owners or (ii) it is unfairly prejudicial to one or more of the owners.**

(f) **In determining whether he is satisfied under (e) in relation to a decision to carry out maintenance, improvements or alterations the sheriff should have regard to—**

(i) **the age and condition of the tenement;**

---

41 We have in mind here work which, while urgent, does not qualify as an emergency in the sense discussed in paras 5.54 - 5.58.

42 Other than by service of the initial writ outwith the appeal period.

43 Para 5.73, and recommendation 14(i).

44 In each of the last two years the City of Edinburgh Council issued around 25,000 individual statutory notices, but only 14 or so were appealed to the sheriff. We are grateful to the Property Services Department of the Council for providing us with this information.

(ii) **the likely cost of carrying out the work; and**

(iii) **whether the cost of the work is reasonable.**

(Clause 8 and Scheme A, rule 4)

Special protections

5.26 A general right to apply for annulment may not always be a sufficient or an appropriate safeguard. Majority decision-making gives rise in a predictable way to situations in which a minority might come to be unfairly treated. On one view a minority owner placed in such a situation should have automatic protection without the inconvenience, expense and risk of an appeal to the sheriff. There seem to be three main cases where some kind of special protection might possibly be justified.[45]

5.27 **Small tenements.** Where a tenement is very small, say two or three flats, majority decision-making is both less necessary and also more susceptible to abuse. It is less necessary because unanimity is more easily achieved with small numbers. It is more susceptible to abuse because personality clashes and idiosyncratic views can have a decisive impact in a case where only two votes are required for a majority. There is much to be said for a rule which requires unanimity where the number of votes eligible to be cast is three or less. Such a rule would be mainly for small tenements but would also apply to a repair in a larger building which was the responsibility of the owners of only two or three flats.[46]

5.28 **Imbalance of voting power and liability.** A number of consultees urged that voting power should be tied to liability to pay. On this view a person who has 30% liability for the cost of repairs should also command 30% of the votes. We accept the justice of this principle, at least in the majority of cases, and we adopt it for Management Scheme B.[47] But under Scheme A each type of scheme cost is treated differently, for reasons which are not avoidable, and there is no general formula on liability which could be used for the purposes of allocating votes.[48] The question remains of whether some special protection is required. Serious discrepancies between voting power and liability will be unusual but not unknown. The standard cases of substantial liability falling on individual flats occur where the flat is used for commercial purposes or where it is much larger than the other flats in the building. Under Scheme A such a flat would continue to have only a single vote. The Property Managers Association Scotland Limited pointed out some of the difficulties here:

> "It is fairly common in practice in traditional tenements to find mixed commercial and residential use (the familiar situation of a tenement of dwelling-houses with shops on the ground floor). It is frequently found that the owners of the shops are made responsible for a very substantial proportion of common charges. We are able to cite one particular case in Glasgow where a tenement consists of dwelling-houses on the upper floors and a public house on the ground floor. The basis of apportionment as defined in the existing Deed of Conditions is that it should be on the basis of rateable value but the voting rights are one vote for each house or unit owned in the property. The result of that is that the public house has only one vote out of fourteen in the property but is liable to pay 87% of all common charges. This does not seem equitable. On the other hand, however, for the owner of the public house, because he pays 87% of the common charges to have himself 87% of the voting powers would not in our view be equitable either as one owner could then dictate policy for the whole building."

5.29 Where liability and voting power are seriously out of line, a majority of owners might cheerfully support a repair in the knowledge that it is one of the dissenting voices who must pick up most of the bill. The danger seems sufficiently serious to merit a degree of protection. We are not inclined to interfere with the rules of voting as such. In particular we are not in favour of introducing a double threshold, so

---

45 A fourth is mentioned at para 5.76 and recommendation 14(iv).

46 Only those responsible for a repair have voting rights: see para 5.14.

47 Scheme B, rules 9.1 and 11.1. In many other countries voting rights are tied to liability to pay.

48 See paras 5.40 - 5.53 and para 5.78.

that decisions would require to be passed by a second majority, expressed in terms of liability to pay. Not only would such a system be unduly complex but, in view of the disparate pattern of liability under Scheme A, it would present owners with the serious practical difficulty of having to determine the precise basis of liability in advance. We propose a simpler solution. Decisions would continue to be taken by a majority calculated by number of flats; but for a limited period such a decision would be open to veto by those owners who together are liable for 75% of the cost. In the case of a narrow vote, this would mean that a decision was challengeable if the 51% voting in favour were liable for only 25% of the cost. If a higher majority in favour were obtained, the prospect of a challenge would be correspondingly reduced. The period in which a challenge might be made should be the same as the period for appeals, normally 21 days from the date of the decision. The veto should require to be notified to the other owners in writing. The decision would be annulled from the date of notification, but not with retrospective effect.[49]

5.30 **Majority of flats in single ownership.** Occasionally a majority of the flats is owned by the same person.[50] A typical case is where the original owner of a building has sold some flats but continues to rent out others. The right-to-buy legislation[51] has made this pattern more common, with local authorities quite often retaining a majority stake in tenements where some of the flats have been sold. If the tenement consists of three flats or fewer there is no difficulty, for under our recommendations any decision would require to be unanimous.[52] But in the more usual case of a larger building, the person holding a majority of flats would be in a position of complete control and could, if he wished, proceed without the agreement of any of the other owners.

5.31 We have found this a difficult issue. We do not under-estimate the risk of oppression of the minority. Nonetheless we have concluded that this is not a case where a special protection should be put in place, for a number of reasons. First, the principle of majority rule is based on the idea that those holding a majority of flats have the majority stake in the building. That principle is not impaired merely because a majority of flats happen to be held by one person and not by several. Secondly, the fact that a majority of flats is in the hands of one person is accidental rather than structural. It is likely to change over time. As more tenants exercise their right to buy, the holding of the local authority will be correspondingly reduced. This distinguishes the problem from the other problems identified earlier in this section. Thirdly, any special provision which we might recommend could readily be evaded in practice. A majority owner could lose his majority status by transferring an appropriate number of flats to a nominee. But he would retain effective control of the tenement.

5.32 Summarising the discussion in this section, we recommend that:

8(a) If in relation to a particular decision the number of votes allocated does not exceed three, that decision should require to be reached unanimously.

(b) Where a decision which requires the expenditure of money is duly made but is not supported by those owners who are liable for 75% of the cost of such expenditure, those owners should be able to annul the decision by sending a notice to that effect to the other owners not later than the period for appeal mentioned in recommendation 7(b).

(Scheme A, rules 3.7, 3.12 and 3.13)

Mechanics of decision-making

5.33 In devising rules for how decisions are to be made we have been concerned above all with ease of use. Since most owners are neither lawyers nor professional property managers, the rules must be as straightforward as possible. Two principles have influenced us in particular. In the first place, it is better

49 Thus any money which had already been expended on urgent repairs under rule 4.2(b) of Scheme A would be fully recoverable.

50 The facts of *McNally and Miller Property Co v Mallinson* 1977 SLT (Sh Ct) 33 are an example.

51 Now contained in the Housing (Scotland) Act 1987.

52 Para 5.27 and recommendation 8(a).

that the rules be simple than that they cater for every possible situation. Our rules contain a number of omissions. At a certain point common sense becomes a surer guide than yet another detailed rule. In the second place, the rules should demand only the minimum in the way of formality. Repairs often involve small amounts of money, and agreement is obtained by knocking on individual doors. Legislation must recognise reality. There is no point in providing in Scheme A for regular meetings, preceded by long written notice, and followed up by written minutes. Some tenements would comply but many would not. Nor is informality necessarily a bad thing. Different methods work best in different tenements.

5.34 Our proposals envisage that decisions may be taken either formally, at a meeting, or informally, without a meeting. In either case contact should be made with all the owners. Thus a formal meeting should be preceded by proper notice of at least 48 hours. Where there is no meeting, the person putting forward the proposal should not be allowed to stop once he has secured his majority but should go on to consult all the owners except where this is impracticable, for example because of long-term absence. All owners need to know about proposals being put forward for decision, and all should have a chance to express their views and to influence the views of others. Consultation would normally be face to face but might also be in writing. It should be sufficient to consult with an owner's representative, such as a letting agent, and in the case of flats owned in common, one co-owner should be considered as representing the others.[53] Once a decision has been made it should be notified to all the owners as soon as practicable. In the case of a decision taken as a meeting there is of course no need to notify those who attended the meeting.

5.35 Writing is not mandatory. Notice of a meeting can be given by telephone or by knocking on doors. So can notification of a decision. But of course writing may often be prudent, especially in cases of substantial expenditure.[54] Without writing there may be disputes as to precisely what was decided and when, and it may be impossible to prove if or when a particular decision was notified. Under Scheme A dates can be important. In a case where a flat is sold, the liability of the outgoing owner depends on the date on which the relevant decision was made or on the date of notification.[55] Similarly, the 21-day period for appeals to the sheriff runs from either the date of the decision or the date of notification.[56]

5.36 Where a notice is given in writing there is a question as to how it is to be delivered. Clearly it should be sufficient if it is put through the letter-box of the owner's flat. Alternatively it could be posted to that address or to such other address as he is known to have. This would allow proof of date of posting if the letter is sent by recorded or registered mail. We also think that it should be possible to send the notice electronically, whether by fax or by electronic mail. Most businesses have fax machines and an increasing number use e-mail. Domestic use of both is increasing rapidly. In 20 years' time it may be unthinkable to communicate in any other way. One advantage of putting the notice through the letter box is that it absolves the sender of the need to ascertain in whose name the title to the flat is held.[57] In cases of doubt the notice can be addressed to "Mr and Mrs X or the owner of flat Y" or even just to "the owner of flat Y".

5.37 The procedural requirements outlined above are relatively simple and informal. Yet they will not always be complied with. Owners may be unaware of the law, or unable to understand it, or they may simply forget to do something. In our view it would be wrong, and also scarcely practical, if scheme decisions were automatically invalidated merely because of a minor irregularity in procedure. Suppose for example that an owner wishes to carry out a repair to scheme property. He convenes a meeting which is well-attended and at which the repair is agreed. He instructs the repair and pays for it. He then asks his fellow owners for reimbursement. At this point it turns out that, due to an oversight, he forgot to give one of the owners the required notice of the meeting. In this situation it seems insupportable that the

53 Just in the same way as one co-owner can vote for the others: see para 5.15 and recommendation 6(d).

54 Consultees who attended the seminar in September 1996 advocated a requirement for a written record of all scheme decisions. We do not recommend that level of formality as part of the statutory scheme.

55 Para 8.5 and recommendation 33(a).

56 Para 5.23 and recommendation 7(b).

57 This problem is discussed at para 5.16.

original decision should simply be considered invalid with the result that the repair costs cannot be reimbursed, except by means of a fresh decision.[58] Those who attended the meeting should not escape liability on a technicality. The defect in procedure did not affect them. However, the person who was not notified may be in a different position. Certainly if he did not know of the meeting, and did not learn of the subsequent repair, there are reasonable grounds for saying that he should not be liable. The other owners should then make up the difference. On the other hand, if he knew of the repair but took no steps to question it, then it seems just that he should have to pay with the others. In effect the situation should be ruled by personal bar: an owner directly affected by an irregularity should escape liability except where he is personally barred from claiming the exemption.

5.38 It should be emphasised that we are dealing here with minor irregularities of procedure. The leniency would not extend to a failure to obtain a proper majority, even where that failure was accidental in the sense that one or more of the votes counted on turned out to be cast by a person who was not in fact the owner.

5.39 We recommend that:

9(a) It should be possible to make a scheme decision without a meeting being held.

(b) If an owner wants to call a meeting, he should have to give 48 hours notice of its date, time, location and purpose.

(c) Where a meeting is not held, the person proposing the decision should consult all the owners (or representatives of the owners) except where it is impracticable to do so.

(d) A decision should be notified to all the owners as soon as practicable.

(e) Any notice which requires to be given to an owner under the Scheme may be given in writing by-

(i) delivering the notice to his flat;

(ii) posting it to that address or such other address as he is known to have; or

(iii) transmitting it to him by electronic means.

(f) An irregularity in procedure should not of itself invalidate a decision; but an owner who is directly affected by the irregularity should be relieved by the others of liability for any costs relating to that decision unless he was aware that they were being incurred and did not immediately object.

(Scheme A, rules 3.8 - 3.11, 6.3, 8.5 and 8.6)

Maintenance of scheme property

5.40 A majority should not be able to decide whatever issues it wants. The principle of majority decision-making would be unacceptable unless accompanied by a fixed, and limited, list of subjects on which decisions can competently be made. The content of the list fixed for Scheme A is discussed later.[59] For the moment we mention only the most important item on that list, namely decisions as to maintenance. Under Scheme A the owners may make a scheme decision to carry out maintenance to scheme property.[60]

5.41 An important preliminary question is the meaning of "maintenance" for this purpose. Clearly maintenance must include repairs. In our discussion paper[61] we sought to make a distinction between (i) essential repairs carried out to the minimum standard which would be acceptable to a prudent proprietor

---

58 Rule 2.2(f) of Scheme A permits a scheme decision authorising maintenance which has already been carried out.
59 Paras 5.70 - 5.77.
60 For the meaning of "scheme property", see paras 5.4 - 5.11.
61 Discussion Paper No 91, paras 5.6 - 5.10.

(ii) essential repairs carried out to a higher standard, and (iii) non-essential repairs.[62] We suggested that while category (i) repairs might be authorised by a majority decision, repairs falling into the latter two categories should possibly require unanimity. On further reflection we would not wish to place so much weight on the narrow and troublesome distinctions between these three categories.[63] Instead we prefer the broad and simple rule that a majority of owners should be able to decide on a repair - of whatever kind - to the scheme property. It seems reasonable to assume that the power will be exercised with good sense and prudence. A decision to repair means a decision to pay out money. Owners are unlikely to agree to a repair which is obviously unnecessary, or to insist on it being carried out to a standard which is extravagantly high. Such a repair could in any event be challenged before the sheriff.[64] Indeed the risk seems mainly the other way around. Tenements are not usually over-repaired. It is much more likely that owners will refuse to sanction a repair which is necessary than that they will clamour for one which is unnecessary.

5.42 "Maintenance" should not include out-and-out improvement. A majority of owners should not be able to insist that a tennis court be built on the grounds or that the cupboard under the common stair be turned into a sauna. For improvements of this kind the common law should continue to apply. In the case of common property this imposes a requirement of unanimity, while for scheme property which is individually owned the owner is at liberty to carry out the improvement, but at his own expense.[65] In fact out-and-out improvements are rare in tenements. Most improvements are in the form of betterment arising in the course of repair or replacement of a pre-existing facility. On consultation the view was strongly expressed that betterment should be considered as a normal part of repair. We agree with that view. Advances in technology and changes in building methods mean that a replacement part may often be different from, and better than, the original. Indeed the availability of a better, and safer, alternative may sometimes be of itself sufficient ground for change even if the original is still capable of functioning. Thus in our view it is maintenance of a tenement to replace lead piping with copper, or to replace Victorian pull-bells with an entryphone system.

5.43 Maintenance may involve replacement and re-building. If a floor of a building is gutted by fire it will need to be re-built. But where a tenement is wholly or substantially destroyed the issues are different and more complex, and any decision to re-build should be taken unanimously and not by a bare majority. Similarly a majority should not be able to sanction the demolition of the tenement or of a part of the tenement. We discuss later the rights and duties of the owners in the event of destruction.[66]

5.44 Cleaning and painting are part of maintenance. So is gardening. Maintenance may also involve the day-to-day running of the tenement.

5.45 Under Scheme A maintenance is a right but it is not a duty. We do not suggest that owners be placed under a positive obligation to maintain the tenement. The building is theirs, and what they do with it is a matter for their own collective decision. In any event, a positive obligation to maintain is difficult to reconcile with the principle of majority decision-making. The freedom of the majority to decide becomes illusory if, because of the existence of a positive obligation, they must always decide in a particular way. That freedom should not, however, be wholly unfettered. The condition of the housing stock is a matter of public interest, at least to some degree, and within a tenement is always a matter of private interest to the owners of the individual flats. Under Scheme A there is a danger that repairs which ought to be done are not done because it proves impossible to assemble a majority. In practice, however, four factors operate to minimise the problem.

---

62 We also canvassed views on whether it was desirable to alter the existing rule of common property that non-essential repairs require unanimity. This was primarily in the context of an individual owner who wished to carry out a non-essential repair without expecting reimbursement from his fellow owners. The importance of this suggested change falls away with the decision (described at para 3.5 of this report) not to extend common property.

63 On this see eg *McNally and Miller Property Co v Mallinson* 1977 SLT (Sh Ct) 33.

64 See paras 5.19 - 5.25 and recommendation 7.

65 However, the improvement must not interfere with the support or shelter provided to or by the building. See para 7.10 and recommendation 30(c).

66 Paras 9.15 - 9.35.

5.46 The first factor is common interest. At common law each proprietor is under a positive obligation, arising out of common interest, to repair any part of the tenement in his ownership to the minimum standard necessary to safeguard support and shelter. This is both sensible and effective. Support and shelter are the two elements fundamental to the integrity of a building. Unless they are properly secured, individual owners are prevented from the full use and enjoyment of their own property. Majority decision-making is appropriate for maintenance in general, but where support or shelter are at issue any single owner should be entitled to require that the necessary work be carried out. In Part 7 of this report we recommend a statutory restatement of common interest. As under the present law, this is intended as a right to be held in reserve and used only rarely. In the normal course of events an owner who wishes to have a repair carried out will put the matter to the vote. If a majority is achieved, the repair can then be carried out under Scheme A. However, the existence of the reserve powers will no doubt assist in obtaining a majority in cases where the repair relates to support or shelter. If a majority cannot be achieved, the owner can then seek to enforce against the relevant person or persons the statutory obligations of support and shelter.[67]

5.47 Secondly, titles quite frequently contain real burdens which impose a positive obligation of maintenance. Enforcing a real burden[68] is an alternative to proceeding under Scheme A, although once again such a right is likely to be held in reserve for cases where a majority cannot be assembled.

5.48 Thirdly, local authorities have statutory powers to require the carrying out of maintenance to buildings, and in practice these powers are exercised mainly in relation to tenements. Thus a council may by statutory notice require the owners to rectify such defects as are required to bring the building into a reasonable state of repair, regard being had to its age, type and location.[69] The council may also require the owners to paint the common passage and stair.[70] Lighting in the common passage and stair must be provided and maintained except where this is already provided by the council.[71] Finally, the occupiers of flats owning or using the common passage and stair, the back green and certain other common parts are under a statutory obligation to keep these areas clean to the satisfaction of the council.[72] These last two are free-standing obligations which do not require a statutory notice to bring them into play.

5.49 In form these are public interest provisions, but they also have an important role in protecting private interests, for in practice statutory notices are often issued as a result of a flat-owner complaining to the council. However, councils vary in their willingness to issue statutory notices. This is partly because of the administrative costs involved but more particularly because of the risk of bad debts in the event that the notice is not complied with and the council is forced to instruct the work and try to recover the costs. We hope that the introduction of Scheme A might make statutory notices less necessary but at the same time more effective. Statutory notices should be less necessary because, with majority decision-making, owners will more often succeed in reaching agreement among themselves; and they should be more effective because the extra stimulus provided by a statutory notice is quite likely to persuade the majority to act ahead of any possible action by the council, with a consequent reduction in the problem of bad debts.

5.50 Finally, every part of the tenement is owned by somebody, and an owner of property is always free to see to its repair. This remains true even with common property, any *pro indiviso* owner being entitled to carry out necessary repairs.[73] Thus an owner who is unable to achieve a majority has always the option of carrying out the repair himself, at least where the property is his. Indeed if the disrepair is a danger

67 If the property to be maintained is scheme property, the relevant owner or owners can recover the cost from the other owners under rule 5 of Scheme A. See para 7.7 and recommendation 30(b).
68 The enforceability of real burdens is not affected by our proposals: see para 3.8.
69 Civic Government (Scotland) Act 1982 s 87(1). Similar provisions are contained in s 108(2) of the Housing (Scotland) Act 1987. Section 24 of the City of Edinburgh District Council Order Confirmation Act 1991 empowers the council in Edinburgh to require repairs to the structure of any building.
70 Civic Government (Scotland) Act 1982 s 92(6).
71 1982 Act s 90(4).
72 1982 Act s 92(2).
73 Reid, para 25; Gordon, para 15-19.

to others he may have no choice if he is to avoid a future claim in negligence or nuisance.[74] An owner who has granted a standard security is obliged to maintain his property in good and sufficient repair to the reasonable satisfaction of the creditor.[75] In all such cases the owner would be solely liable for the cost.[76]

5.51 Summing up, we recommend that:

10(a) The owners should be entitled to make a scheme decision to carry out maintenance to scheme property.

(b) "Maintenance" should include repairs and replacement, cleaning, painting, and other routine works, gardening, the day-to-day running of a tenement and the reinstatement of a part (but not most) of a tenement; but it should not include demolition, alteration or improvement unless reasonably incidental to the maintenance.

(Scheme A, rules 1.4 and 2.2(a))

5.52 Once a repair has been decided on, certain other decisions may then have to be taken. Estimates will have to be considered and a choice made. A contract or contracts will have to be entered into. If the tenement is not already factored, it may be thought desirable to appoint someone - whether a professional manager or one of the owners - to manage the particular repair. Above all else there is the question of money. Except where the repair is very small, a contractor might not be willing to start work unless he has a firm assurance of payment. He is unlikely to be satisfied by the signature on the contract of a single owner, or even perhaps of a bare majority of owners; and for their part individual owners are likely to be reluctant to sign unless the other owners sign also. Sometimes the best method of proceeding is simply to collect the whole money in advance and to hold it in a bank account pending completion of the work; but under the present law this is not possible except by unanimous agreement, and attempts at repairs may fail because such agreement cannot be reached. Under Scheme A we propose that a majority should be able to require payment in advance of the estimated cost of a repair.[77] There seems little point in providing for majority decision-making for the instruction of maintenance if the majority cannot then regulate the means by which the work is to be financed. The question of access for repairs is discussed later.[78]

5.53 We recommend that:

11 If the owners decide under recommendation 10 to carry out maintenance to scheme property, they should thereafter be able to make a scheme decision to -

(i) appoint a person to manage the work;

(ii) instruct or arrange for the carrying out of the work;

(iii) require each owner to deposit an amount of money representing a reasonable estimate of that owner's share of the cost of the work; and

(iv) take such further steps as are necessary to ensure that the work is carried out to a satisfactory standard and completed in good time.

(Scheme A, rule 2.3)

---

74 *Sedleigh-Denfield v O'Callaghan* [1940] AC 880; *R H M Bakeries (Scotland) Limited v Strathclyde Regional Council* 1985 SC(HL) 17.

75 Conveyancing and Feudal Reform (Scotland) Act 1970 Sched 3, standard condition 1(a).

76 At common law a *pro indiviso* owner can recover the cost of necessary repairs from his fellow owners. But while we would not wish to interfere with the right of a *pro indiviso* owner to carry out repairs, we recommend later that he should not be allowed to recover the cost. See para 10.30 and recommendation 45.

77 Interest earned on this sum would be treated for taxation purposes as the income of the individual owners in proportion to the size of their contributions.

78 Paras 10.10 - 10.21.

Emergency work

5.54 In an emergency there will be no time for consultation, and some provision must be made for individual owners to instruct or carry out all necessary work and to recover the cost. A key issue is the definition of "emergency". The definition must be sufficiently wide to allow prompt action to avoid injury to the tenement, but at the same time sufficiently narrow to prevent owners who are pessimistic about the chances of obtaining majority approval from carrying out ordinary repairs under cover of an emergency. In the discussion paper[79] we suggested that

> "an 'emergency repair' is a repair which would require to be effected immediately to prevent deterioration of a common part".

Consultees felt that the definition was too narrow. It was wrong to concentrate on the deterioration of the common part to the exclusion of the possible effect of such deterioration on the rest of the building. Furthermore, it was necessary to include considerations of health and safety, in relation both to the occupiers of the tenement and to the public at large.[80] The real emergency might be, not that the building itself was vulnerable to damage, but that a loose part of the stonework might fall on a passer-by. Similarly, blocked drains might not be an immediate risk to the building but would pose an immediate risk to the health of its inhabitants.

5.55 We accept the force of these comments, and agree that the definition should be widened. We also now think that "work" is a more apt word than "repair". If the roof of a tenement is seriously damaged in a storm, the first thing - indeed probably the only thing - which needs to be done at once is to provide some kind of temporary covering. But, strictly, that would not be a repair. In one respect, however, we think that the definition should be narrower. Under Scheme A it will normally be possible to consult other owners, and hence to seek a scheme decision, within 24 hours. In our view an emergency arises only where the repair cannot wait the few hours necessary for consultation.

5.56 The cost of emergency work should be recoverable as if the work had proceeded on a scheme decision. But the emergency must have been genuine. If there was no true emergency the person carrying out the work would not be able to recover. Occasionally this may lead to harsh results. An owner might panic and instruct work which did not need to be done at once. Even though he was acting for the best, he would finish up with sole liability for the repair. We think that in cases like this a majority of owners should be able to ratify the work. Indeed there seems to be need for a more general power to adopt work which has already been carried out, with the consequence that the work is then paid for under Scheme A. Another example of where this might be necessary is if the scheme decision on which the work originally proceeded turned out to be invalid for some procedural or other reason.[81]

5.57 We recommend that:

12(a) Any owner should be entitled to instruct or carry out emergency work to scheme property.

(b) The owners should be liable for the cost of any emergency work as if it had been authorised by a scheme decision.

(c) "Emergency work" should mean work which requires to be carried out at once and before a scheme decision can be taken in order (i) to prevent damage to any part of the tenement or (ii) in the interests of health or safety.

(d) The owners should be entitled to make a scheme decision to adopt and pay for maintenance which has already been carried out.

(Scheme A, rules 2.2(f) and 7)

79 Discussion Paper No 91, para 5.11 and proposition 23(ii).

80 Section 87(3) of the Civic Government Act (Scotland) 1982 empowers local authorities to carry out work, without prior notice, where it appears to be necessary "in the interests of health or safety or to prevent damage to any property".

81 See paras 5.37 and 5.38.

5.58 Our recommendations are not intended to affect the statutory right of local authorities to intervene in cases of emergency.[82] Nor are they intended to affect the common law of *negotiorum gestio*.[83] Indeed the scope of the common law is wider. A *gestor* need not be a fellow owner, and in cases where intervention is justified he is not confined to scheme property but can carry out work on an individual flat. Private property may be entered in an emergency without trespass being committed.[84]

Liability for maintenance costs

5.59 Once maintenance has been agreed upon and the work carried out, the question then arises as to the apportionment of the costs. In an ideal world there should be a single rule of liability which would apply in all cases. For example, Scheme A might provide that maintenance costs are to be borne equally on the basis of one share per flat, or alternatively that liability is apportioned by reference to the respective floor areas of the flats. However, despite its obvious attractions, we are not able to recommend this approach. It would have considerable merit if Scheme A were confined to new tenements only. But for existing tenements it would often have the unacceptable effect of overruling existing title provisions. Such provisions deserve to survive, not merely because they form the basis on which individual flats have been bought and sold in the past, but because they are specially designed for each individual tenement and are likely to provide, far better than any general rule, a properly sensitive basis for distributing liability.[85]

5.60 Where titles make provision for maintenance costs they may do so either directly or indirectly. Direct provision is made by means of a real burden. Indirect provision is made through the mechanism of common property, in reliance on the rule that property which is owned in common must be maintained in common, in proportion to the size of the respective *pro indiviso* shares.[86] As between these two methods the direct outranks the indirect. Hence if titles provide that the roof is owned in common, in equal shares, but that it is to be maintained in accordance with rateable value, maintenance costs are apportioned by rateable value and not equally. Occasionally different methods are found in the titles of flats within the same tenement, particularly if the split-off deeds were granted over a long period. For example, in a tenement of eight flats, the titles to the first four might impose an express obligation to pay a one eighth share of the cost of roof repairs, while the titles to the other four might simply convey the roof as common property. Each flat would then have liability for one eighth of the cost of roof maintenance, but for different reasons.[87] We do not propose to disturb those various title arrangements. Accordingly, the basic rule under Scheme A is that where the title makes provision for maintenance costs, whether directly or indirectly, that provision will prevail.

5.61 We are, of course, aware that in some cases a direct provision for maintenance may, for technical reasons, fail as a real burden and hence, strictly, be unenforceable.[88] We have no concern with such matters here. Under our proposals maintenance costs will be recovered under the rules of Scheme A and not under the common law of real burdens. The title provisions are relevant, not for their own sake, but only because they provide a convenient apportionment of liability which is likely to be more suited to the tenement than any general measure of liability that could be provided by law. It is simply a matter of incorporating by reference into Scheme A the figures given in the titles. We suspect that this pragmatic approach is not very different from that adopted in practice at the moment, whereby title provisions are followed without much regard as to whether they fully satisfy the strict rules on constitution of real burdens.

5.62 Existing title provisions may rely on methods of apportionment which are becoming obsolete. We have in mind particularly feuduty and rateable value. The vast majority of feuduties have now been

82 Civic Government (Scotland) Act 1982 s 87(3); City of Edinburgh District Council Order Confirmation Act 1991 s 24(2).
83 For which see *Stair Memorial Encyclopaedia* vol 15 para 99.
84 Reid, para 181(5).
85 See paras 3.8 and 3.9.
86 Reid, para 25.
87 Sometimes, though, the effect of using different methods is to produce an inequitable result. See para 5.68, example 6.
88 See paras 2.23 - 2.29.

redeemed under the provisions of the Land Tenure Reform (Scotland) Act 1974, and in a forthcoming report we will recommend the redemption of all remaining feuduties as part of the abolition of the feudal system. We doubt whether this matters very much. The feuduty figures continue to be readily available. In the case of titles on the Land Register the practice is to include a note of feuduties on the title sheet in all cases where they are used to apportion maintenance costs. The amount of feuduty is usually loosely related to the size and value of the individual flats and thus continues to provide an equitable basis for apportioning liability. Much the same may be said about rateable value. Domestic rates were abolished with effect from 1 April 1989, but the old valuation rolls continue to be available.[89] In the case of tenements with residential or mixed use, statute provides that maintenance costs tied to rateable value are to be apportioned on the basis of the entries on the valuation roll in force immediately before abolition.[90] Of course both with feuduty and with rateable value there is a danger of the figures becoming inappropriate through the passage of time. Many feuduties were fixed in the nineteenth century or even earlier; and, except in the case of tenements used exclusively for non-domestic purposes, rateable values are now frozen as at 1989. The problem is perhaps not a very serious one. On the whole flats do not change very much in relative value, if only because it is impossible in most cases to build on an extension. But in any event it is difficult to see what can usefully be done to improve matters. A system which apportions by reference to value would require to be replaced by an equivalent system. Rateable value, in particular, loads a heavy premium on to non-domestic properties, and it would not be acceptable to replace this by a system (for example floor area) which makes no distinction according to type of use. There is no obvious equivalent system. It is true that council tax, the current replacement for domestic rates, operates by reference to value, albeit in rather a crude way, but the tax is confined to dwelling-houses[91] and the valuations would not be available for mixed use tenements. In theory it would be possible for statute to provide that in all cases where apportionments are calculated by feuduty or by rateable value they should in future be calculated by the respective market values of each flat; but the expense and the difficulties involved in obtaining valuations could not be justified by the relatively minor nature of the problem to be solved. On the whole we incline to the view that no action can usefully be taken.

5.63 Titles may not provide for all items of scheme property. Real burdens might deal with the roof, rhones, downpipes and chimney stacks but not with the foundations or with the internal structural walls. Clearly some kind of default rule is necessary for lacunae. A default rule is also required for cases where the title provisions do not add up - for example, where they allocate only 87% of the total liability. In our discussion paper[92] we suggested that floor area might be an appropriate measure of liability, but on consultation this proved controversial. A substantial minority of consultees put forward the attractively simple alternative that each flat should bear an equal share of the costs of maintenance. Two consultees argued that volume was a fairer measure of liability than floor area. Even the majority who supported floor area did so without much enthusiasm and emphasised the potential expense involved and the possibility of disputes.

5.64 Despite the obvious attractions of equality of liability, we do not feel able to recommend this as a universal rule. It would work well where all flats in the building are of roughly the same size. But tenements are extremely diverse in nature. Equality would not be an acceptable rule in the case of a Victorian villa on three floors where the attic storey had been sold off as a separate flat. However, a compromise seems possible here. We suggest that equality be accepted as the general rule, but that in cases where differences in size would make such a rule obviously unfair, liability should be determined by floor area. In the interests of certainty "obvious unfairness" should be measured by a formula and not left open to argument. The choice of formula is, necessarily, somewhat arbitrary, but we think that a reasonable definition of unfairness is where the floor area of the largest flat is more than one and a half times that of the smallest flat. Except in marginal cases it will be obvious to the eye whether or not this formula has been satisfied.

89 Abolition of Domestic Rates Etc (Scotland) Act 1987 s 5(8).
90 1987 Act s 5(1).
91 Local Government Finance Act 1992 s 70.
92 Discussion Paper No 91, para 3.16 and proposition 2(iii).

5.65 As a number of our consultees noted, floor area will require to be carefully defined. We are concerned here only with the floor area of individual flats, under exclusion of pertinents such as balconies or cellars or garages. Adapting a formula suggested to us by the Royal Institution of Chartered Surveyors in Scotland, we recommend that floor area should mean the total area within the boundary walls of a flat, including all areas occupied by internal walls and partitions.[93] We are informed by surveyors that it is easier to include internal walls and partitions than to exclude them. Any basement or loft which is used as part of the habitable accommodation of a flat should be included in the calculation of floor area. For example, where a double upper flat extends into the roof space there can be no reason for not taking account of the upper level. However, the position seems different if the loft or basement are used only for storage, and in that event they should be disregarded for the purposes of the calculation.

5.66 More needs to be said about the costs which the above rules are intended to cover. It was explained earlier[94] that "maintenance" includes, not only repairs, but also cleaning, painting and day-to-day running costs. Hence all costs of this kind fall under the general heading of maintenance costs. If a person is appointed to manage a particular repair, the expenses of and any remuneration paid to that person should likewise be treated as maintenance costs. An issue requiring special consideration is statutory repair notices issued by a local authority. Repair notices contain a time limit within which the work must be carried out. If the work is duly carried out by the owners, this would then count as a normal Scheme A repair. But if the time limit is not complied with and the council intervenes to carry out the work, the question then arises as to liability for the council's costs. So far as the council is concerned, there is an entitlement to apportion the costs among the owners without regard to the title deeds provided that the chosen method of apportionment is not in itself unreasonable.[95] In practice councils often charge all owners the same amount.[96] If the council's apportionment is different from that provided by the title deeds, owners have - in theory at least - a right of relief among themselves. However, where a repair is covered by Scheme A but is not provided for by the titles, it may be in the interests of some of the owners to obstruct the normal decision-making process and to induce a statutory notice. This is because the basis of apportionment used by the council may be more favourable than that provided under Scheme A; and since the Scheme A liability is not repeated in the titles there would be no automatic right of relief. In our view it would be wrong to encourage reliance on statutory notices, particularly where this is used as a means of avoiding Scheme A liability. The problem seems easily solved. We propose that maintenance costs should include the cost of any work to scheme property carried out by the council. Hence, following recovery by the council from individual owners, the rules of Scheme A would be available to allow the exercise of a right of relief.

5.67 Summing up the discussion in this section, we recommend that:

13(a) Maintenance costs of scheme property should be apportioned amongst the owners in accordance with the following rules (the first applicable rule being the relevant one and excluding any later rule):

***Rule 1.* Costs are apportioned according to any express provision made in the title to the tenement; but this rule does not apply where part only of a particular cost is provided for.**

***Rule 2.* If the property being maintained is common property, costs are apportioned according to the respective sizes of the shares held by the owners.**

***Rule 3.* If (i) the express provision made in the title to the tenement deals with part only of a particular cost and (ii) the property being maintained is common property,**

93 This recommendation bears some relation, in a highly simplified form, to the concept of gross internal area: see p 10 of the *Code of Measuring Practice* (4th edn, 1993) published by the Royal Institution of Chartered Surveyors and the Incorporated Society of Valuers and Auctioneers.

94 Paras 5.41 - 5.44, and recommendation 10(b).

95 *R S and D Elliot Ltd v City of Edinburgh District Council* (Edinburgh Sheriff Court, 10 August 1988) (unreported but summarised in Reid, para 248, note 9).

96 For Edinburgh s 27(2) of the City of Edinburgh District Council Order Confirmation Act 1991 authorises recovery in equal shares.

the title provision is followed as far as possible and the balance of the cost is apportioned according to the respective sizes of the shares held by the owners.

Rule 4. **Except where the floor area of the largest flat is more than one and a half times that of the smallest flat, costs are apportioned equally among the flats.**

Rule 5. **Costs are apportioned in accordance with the respective floor areas of each flat.**

(b) **"Maintenance costs" should mean (i) the cost of such maintenance as has been authorised under Scheme A and (ii) any cost due to or recovered by a local authority following the service of a statutory repairs notice.**

(c) **"Floor area" should mean the total floor area measured within the boundary walls, including the area occupied by internal walls and partitions, but excluding (i) any balcony or other pertinent and (ii) any basement or loft which is used only for storage.**

(Clause 30(3); Scheme A, rules 5.1(a) and (d) and 5.2 - 5.5)

5.68 The rules set out in recommendation 13(a) are not as complicated as they seem. Rules 1-3 implement the policy that the title provisions should prevail. Indeed they are no more than re-statements of the present law. Rules 4 and 5 are default rules for where there are no relevant title provisions, and for where the scheme property is not otherwise common property. The default rules will apply only infrequently because most scheme property will be common property and will fall within rule 2 where it does not already fall within rule 1. The following examples illustrate how these rules would operate in a tenement of eight flats, all of approximately the same size.

Example 1

A repair is carried out to the roof. The split-off disposition of each flat imposes a one eighth liability for roof repairs.

Rule 1.[97] The titles prevail. Each flat is liable for a one eighth share. There is no change from the present law. This is a "direct" provision for maintenance costs.[98]

Example 2

A repair is carried out to the roof. The split-off disposition of each flat conveys a right of common property in the roof along with the other proprietors in the tenement, but does not provide directly for maintenance costs.

Rule 1 does not apply because there is no express provision for maintenance. Hence Rule 2[99] applies and once again the titles prevail: this is an "indirect" provision for maintenance costs.[100] Each owner holds a one eighth *pro indiviso* share in the roof and each is liable for one eighth of the cost of maintenance. There is no change from the present law.

Example 3

A repair is carried out to the roof. The titles are silent both as to ownership of the roof and as to liability for the cost of repairs.

Rule 4.[101] The roof is not common property under the general law[102] and it is not common property under the titles. Each flat is liable for a one eighth share. This changes the law. Under the existing

97 Scheme A, rule 5.2.
98 See para 5.60.
99 Scheme A, rule 5.5(a).
100 See para 5.60.
101 Scheme A, rule 5.5(b)(ii).
102 Under the general law it is part of the topmost flat which it covers. See draft Bill, clause 2(3) and (5).

law sole liability would fall on the flat directly underneath the section of roof being repaired.[103] (If the flats had been of markedly different sizes the relevant rule would have been rule 5.)

Example 4

A repair is carried out to the roof. In the case of six of the flats the split-off disposition imposes a one sixth liability for roof repairs. The split-off dispositions of all eight flats convey a right of common property in the roof along with the other proprietors.

Rule 1.[104] The titles prevail. The six burdened flats are liable for a one sixth share. The other two flats escape liability altogether. The same, slightly inequitable,[105] result would occur under the present law. It is uncommon in practice.

Example 5

A repair is carried out to the roof. In the case of four of the flats the split-off disposition imposes a one eighth liability for roof repairs. In the case of the other four flats the split-off disposition imposes liability for roof repairs in proportion to relative rateable value. When the rateable value proportions are calculated and added together with the four shares of one eighth liability, the whole adds up only to 92%. No provision is made as to ownership of the roof.

Rule 4.[106] The titles are disregarded.[107] Rule 1 cannot apply because the titles fail to apportion the full liability. Rule 2 cannot apply because a roof is not common property under the general law and it is not common property under the titles. Each flat is liable for a one eighth share. This solves in an equitable way a problem which is insoluble under the present law.[108]

Example 6

A repair is carried out to the roof. In the case of four of the flats the split-off disposition imposes a one eighth liability for roof repairs. The split-off dispositions of all eight flats convey a right of common property in the roof along with the other proprietors.

Rule 3.[109] The titles prevail. The four flats with the real burden are liable for a one eighth share. The "missing" one half share is then divided amongst all eight owners equally (since each has an equal *pro indiviso* share in the roof). Hence the first four flats must each pay three sixteenths of the cost while the remaining four flats pay only one sixteenth of the cost. The present law would produce the same result. This situation is unusual but not unknown.[110]

Example 7

A repair is carried out to one of the rhones. There is no mention of the rhones in the titles.

Rule 2.[111] Under the general law introduced by our proposals the fact that the rhones serve all the flats means that they are the common property of all the owners in equal shares.[112] Each flat is liable for a one eighth share. This clarifies the present law on this point which is disputed and uncertain.

Example 8

A repair is carried out to the entryphone system. There is no mention of the entryphone system in the titles.

---

103 See para 5.10.
104 Scheme A, rule 5.2.
105 The reasons for carrying this inequity over into the new law are set out in para 3.9.
106 Scheme A, rule 5.5(b)(ii).
107 This is the only case in our entire proposals where title provisions are not given effect to: see para 3.9.
108 In practice, however, public-spirited owners may each agree that their shares be grossed up to achieve a total of 100%.
109 Scheme A, rule 5.3.
110 For a case where rule 3 operates to produce an equitable result, see para 5.60.
111 Scheme A, rule 5.5(a).
112 This is because the rhones "serve" all of the flats. See para 4.23 and draft Bill, clause 3(4)(b) and (5).

Rule 2.[113] Under the general law introduced by our proposals the entryphone system is the common property of all the owners in equal shares. Each flat is liable for a one eighth share. However individual handsets and the wiring leading to individual flats are the sole property of the flats in question and hence not scheme property at all.[114] Repairs to those parts of the system must be paid for by the owners of the flats concerned. The present law on this whole issue is disputed and uncertain.

5.69 A number of conclusions may be drawn from these examples. First, the methodology for determining liability is unchanged from the present law. Under that law owners reach first for their titles, and if the titles are silent they then have recourse to the background law. This combination of titles and background law can be criticised as unduly complex. But it is the price of allowing title deeds to vary the background law and to provide rules adapted to the needs of individual tenements.[115] Secondly, under our recommendations the background law is much more comprehensive than at present. This means that where the title deeds fail, there will be an appropriate rule of liability. Owners will not be left uncertain as to how to divide up the cost of repairs.[116] Thirdly, a crucial feature of the new background law is the rule which allocates ownership of pertinents by reference to a service test.[117] This has the effect of making into common property many items the ownership of which, under the present law, is uncertain; and once an item is discovered to be common property, maintenance costs are governed in a straightforward way by rule 2. Fourthly, the distribution of liability resulting from our recommendations is almost unchanged from the present law. The main point of difference relates to scheme property which is neither common property[118] nor provided for in the titles. The roof can occasionally be an example.[119] The current law would place liability for maintenance solely on the owner, while our recommendations would apply one of the two default rules (rules 4 or 5). Finally, the one rule which is complex to operate - rule 3 - will almost never apply. It is included only because it restates the effect of a particular mix of title provisions which is sometimes, if infrequently, encountered in practice.[120]

Scheme decisions on other subjects

5.70 Owners should be able to take scheme decisions on subjects other than maintenance. However, the list should not be a long one. In the context of an imposed management scheme, individual owners should be required to submit to the will of the majority only in relation to matters which are of demonstrable importance to the well-being of the tenement as a whole. We suggest only five matters for inclusion.

5.71 **(1) Appointment of property manager or factor.** The professional management or factoring of tenements is common in Glasgow and surrounding areas, but far less common in the rest of the country. Opinions vary as to the value of factoring. Some regard factors as expensive and ineffectual, or at any rate prefer to attend to repairs themselves. Others regard the appointment of a property manager as money well spent. As with other professional services much depends on the individuals or firms concerned. We offer no view here as to whether tenements ought or ought not to be factored; but we think that the question of whether to appoint a factor should be open for decision by the owners. Under the present law a factor can be appointed only when the titles so provide or when all the owners agree. Obtaining the agreement of everyone is usually very difficult and, since contracts often run from year to year, owners have recurrent opportunities to change their minds. Furthermore an incoming owner is not bound by the agreement of the person from whom he bought the flat. Sometimes individual owners refuse to agree to factoring arrangements which have been in place for many years. Usually the factoring then continues but the owner in question does not pay any share of the charges. This is unsatisfactory. A property manager cannot factor nineteen flats in a tenement but not the twentieth. In practice he factors the whole

113 Scheme A, rule 5.5(a).
114 Para 4.25 and draft Bill, clause 3(4) and (5).
115 See para 3.8.
116 As they currently would be in examples 7 and 8.
117 Paras 4.23 - 4.25 and draft Bill, clause 3(4).
118 The list of scheme property which is not (or not necessarily) common property is given in rule 1.2(b) of Scheme A.
119 See example 3.
120 See example 6.

tenement, and the dissenting owner receives the benefit without paying the cost. If there is more than one dissenting owner in the building factoring arrangements may begin to break down. We propose, therefore, that the decision to appoint a property manager or factor should be capable of being taken as a scheme decision, by a majority vote.[121] Once the decision is made the minority is bound and dissenting owners must pay their share of the charges. Incoming owners are also bound.[122]

5.72 Titles sometimes provide that a named person is to be appointed as factor. This is perhaps most common in the case of sheltered housing. There is reason to doubt whether a provision of this kind is enforceable in a question with successors of the original owners,[123] but no doubt owners will take such provisions into account before deciding to make their own separate arrangements for factoring.

5.73 On consultation it was strongly urged by the Property Managers Association Scotland Limited that the owners should be able to delegate the task of attending to minor repairs without the need for further consultation:

> "A wealth of practical experience has shown that it is an expensive and time consuming exercise to obtain the agreement of proprietors to repairs ... To seek to extend this time consuming procedure to routine jobbing operations would be totally unworkable in practice and would simply clog up the whole management function and would delay simple repairs to the complete detriment of all the owners. It is essential that there be built into the proposed law of the tenement some form of delegation of responsibility."

We are persuaded by this line of argument, and we suggest that, in cases where a manager has been appointed, it should be possible by scheme decision to delegate the right to carry out maintenance up to a certain value. The value might be expressed either in terms of the cost of individual repairs (eg, no repair over £200), or in terms of the total amount which could be spent over a stipulated period, such as a year.

5.74 **(2) Common insurance.** Later we recommend the introduction of compulsory insurance for tenement flats.[124] Insurance can be obtained either on a flat by flat basis or, collectively, for the tenement as a whole. While there seems little doubt that the second is preferable to the first, common insurance can be obtained only if individual owners are willing to co-operate with one another. To assist the prospects of co-operation we recommend that owners should be able to make a scheme decision about common insurance. Hence if a majority of owners is persuaded of its virtues, an appropriate policy can be negotiated and obtained. A decision to take out common insurance should be accompanied by a decision apportioning the premium among the flats. Since circumstances will vary from tenement to tenement, it does not seem possible to say more than that any apportionment must be defensible and equitable. If the flats are of roughly the same size and are all in residential use, the premium should presumably be the same for each flat. In cases where the title provides for a common policy it may also provide for an apportionment of the premium, and such apportionment would then be binding.[125]

5.75 **(3) Relief from scheme costs.** Circumstances may occur in which an individual owner deserves to be relieved from some or all of his liability to pay repair or other costs incurred under Scheme A. We say more about this subject later.[126] We suggest that this is a matter on which owners should be able to make a scheme decision.

---

121 Factors are very often self-employed. But if a professional factor is not used, the person appointed as manager will probably be an employee, and in such a case consideration will have to be given to the proper identification of the employer (all of the owners? or some only?), and to compliance with the obligations imposed on an employer by fiscal and employment law. Of course these issues arise under present law and practice.

122 Para 5.84 and recommendation 16(b).

123 *Tailors of Aberdeen v Coutts* (1840) 1 Rob 296, 319 per Lord Corehouse. See further Reid, para 391.

124 Paras 9.1 - 9.8 and recommendation 37.

125 Para 5.79 and recommendation 15(a)(i).

126 Para 5.82.

5.76 **(4) Variation or disapplication of Scheme A.** Earlier we recommended that a majority of owners should be able to vary Scheme A or to replace it with Management Scheme B or some other management scheme.[127] This would be achieved by an appropriate scheme decision followed by the execution and registration of a deed of conditions. It is sufficient if the deed is executed by a majority of owners. We do not imagine that this power would often be used. But it provides owners with the flexibility to change schemes if the mandatory Scheme A does not fit well with the title provisions or the layout of the building, or if a more sophisticated scheme seems desirable and appropriate. In order to avoid the slight danger that a majority of owners would choose a new scheme which increased the liability for costs of the dissenting minority, we recommend that a scheme decision should not be valid unless it is supported by any person whose liability for costs is thereby increased.

5.77 **(5) Modification or revocation of a scheme decision.** A scheme decision binds owners and their successors as owners.[128] But it should not be irrevocable. Owners should be able to change their minds. Decisions may be made on the basis of incomplete or inaccurate information. Circumstances may alter. In the case of decisions which have long-term consequences, such as the appointment of a property manager or factor, a change in the composition of the owners may lead to a wish to review the original decision. Accordingly, we suggest that an earlier scheme decision should be capable of modification or revocation by a later scheme decision.

5.78 We recommend that:

14 The owners should be entitled to make a scheme decision to -

(i) appoint a person including a firm[129] to manage the tenement, and, if desired, to delegate to that person the right to carry out or instruct maintenance of scheme property up to a stipulated amount;

(ii) arrange for the tenement a policy of common insurance in accordance with recommendation 37 and against such other risks as the owners may decide, and to determine on an equitable basis the liability of each owner to contribute to the premium;

(iii) determine that an owner is not required to pay all or part of scheme costs for which he would otherwise be liable;

(iv) determine that Management Scheme A should be varied, or disapplied and replaced with some other management scheme, but subject to the consent of any owner whose liability for costs would be thereby increased; and

(v) modify or revoke any scheme decision.

(Scheme A, rules 2.2 and 2.4)

Liability for scheme costs

5.79 **Other scheme costs.** Scheme decisions often lead to the incurring of costs. Earlier we gave our recommendations in relation to the most important of these, the cost of maintenance.[130] The scheme costs which remain are (i) remuneration payable to a property manager or factor for the tenement (ii) premiums on a policy of common insurance, and (iii) a small residual category of any other costs incurred in the management of scheme property. We suggest that liability for these costs should follow broadly the pattern proposed for maintenance costs, but subject to two simplifications. First, the special rule which applies to the maintenance of property which is owned in common has no place. There is no reason for distinguishing scheme property of one type from scheme property of any other type. Secondly, the refinement which introduces an alternative default rule in cases where the floor area of the largest flat in

127 Paras 3.16 - 3.21 and recommendation 2.
128 Para 5.84 and recommendation 16(b).
129 In terms of Schedule 1 to the Interpretation Act 1978 "person" is defined to include "a body of persons corporate or unincorporate". It is not clear that this would cover partnership.
130 Paras 5.59 - 5.69, and recommendation 13.

the tenement is more than one and a half times that of the smallest seems unnecessary and out of place in relation to the relatively small sums of money with which we are concerned. In any case, it is not clear that a factor renders a lesser service to the owner of a small flat than to the owner of a large one. We recommend therefore that liability for these other scheme costs should be determined by only two rules. First, where provision is made in the titles, that title provision should apply. Secondly, where no provision is made in the titles, liability should be shared equally among the flats, except in relation to premiums on common insurance policies. We recommended earlier that the apportionment of premiums should be a matter for the owners to determine by scheme decision.[131]

5.80 **Liability of co-owners.** On the whole, the rules for scheme costs (including maintenance costs) apportion liability by reference to flats. For example, the standard default rule is that scheme costs are shared equally among the flats. The owner of course must pay, but if there is more than one owner the question arises as to where precisely liability lies. A practical difficulty is that co-owners may be in an unequal financial position. One owner may work and have substantial savings while another may be unemployed and have few assets other than co-ownership of the flat itself. From the point of view of the other people in the building it is important that co-owners should be jointly and severally liable for the full debt allocated to the flat. Many co-owners are married or cohabiting, and an affluent co-owner should not be able to shelter behind his (or her) impecunious partner. However, in a question with each other, co-owners should be liable in the proportions in which they own the flat. Where one co-owner pays the full debt, there would be a right of relief against the other co-owner or co-owners.

5.81 **Owners in default.** Sometimes an owner either cannot pay or will not pay. If he will not pay he can be sued, although owners in tenements are naturally reluctant to sue one of their own neighbours. If he cannot pay, the money is not recoverable, at least in the short term. The usual reason why someone cannot pay is that he is insolvent. Under the present law it is unclear what happens where part of the cost proves irrecoverable. Title deeds usually restrict the liability of individual owners to a fixed share of the total cost, and they cannot be made to pay more. Of course, sometimes the owners may agree to divide up the missing share; but where they do not the outcome is determined by the law of contract, liability resting with the owners (or factor) who happened to sign the agreement with the contractor. This is not satisfactory. We suggest that in cases where a share proves irrecoverable it should be divided amongst the other owners in the same manner as the rest of the scheme cost. But the owners who have to pay extra should then have a right of relief against the owner who pays nothing. Unless there is a miraculous return to solvency, a right of relief is unlikely to be worth much against the original owner. But if the flat is sold, perhaps as a result of insolvency proceedings, the incoming owner would inherit the outstanding liabilities of his predecessor[132] and the right of relief could be duly enforced.

5.82 We recommended earlier that owners should be able to make a scheme decision exempting one of their number, in whole or in part, from liability for a share of a scheme cost which would otherwise be due.[133] This power could be exercised on compassionate grounds, or perhaps for practical reasons. For example, it might be more sensible to accept a percentage of the total share from an impecunious owner than to attempt to sue him for the full amount. Where a decision to exempt is taken, the owner's liability falls away and there can be no question of a right of relief in the event of a return to financial health.

5.83 We recommend that:

15(a) Scheme costs (other than maintenance costs) should be apportioned amongst the owners in accordance with the following rules:

(i) Scheme costs are apportioned in accordance with any express provision made in the title to the tenement, except that this rule does not apply where part only of a particular cost is provided for; and

131 Para 5.74 and recommendation 14(ii).
132 See paras 8.9 - 8.17 and recommendation 34.
133 Para 5.75 and recommendation 14(iii).

(ii) **where no express provision is made in the title to the tenement, scheme costs are apportioned equally among the flats, except that the premium on a policy of common insurance is apportioned by scheme decision under recommendation 14(ii).**

(b) **Co-owners of a flat should be jointly and severally liable for scheme costs (including maintenance costs), but as between themselves they should be liable in the proportions in which they own the flat.**

(c) **Where any share of a scheme cost (including the cost of maintenance) is irrecoverable or where a scheme decision is taken under recommendation 14(iii) to exempt an owner, whether in whole or in part, from liability for his share, that share should be paid by the other owners in the same proportions as the remainder of the cost; but in the case of an irrecoverable share there should be a right of relief against the defaulting owner.**

(Scheme A, rules 5.1(e)-(g), 5.2, 5.4, 5.6 - 5.8, 6.1 and 6.2.)

Enforcement

5.84 Except where it is disapplied by deed of conditions, Scheme A applies automatically to all tenements.[134] Hence the owners for the time being of flats are subject to its terms. Just as important as the actual rules of the scheme are the decisions reached under these rules. Accordingly, we suggest that scheme decisions should be binding on the owners and on their successors as owners. This would mean that an incoming owner is bound by a prior decision to carry out a repair, or to take out a policy of common insurance, or to employ a property manager. No doubt in practice he might wish to make enquiries, at least in relation to outstanding repairs, before committing himself to the purchase.[135] However, as mentioned earlier, existing scheme decisions can be modified or reversed.[136]

5.85 In Scheme A there should be reciprocity of right and obligation. All owners are bound by the rules of the scheme and by decisions taken under it; but they should have a corresponding right to enforce both the rules and the decisions. This hardly needs to be justified. It seems self-evident that a person who in implement of a scheme decision instructs and pays for a repair should then be able to recover the cost of that repair in accordance with the rules of the scheme. Otherwise Scheme A would be unworkable. Sometimes it might be convenient for enforcement to be carried out in the name of a property manager or other agent. A standard case would be where a majority of owners wishes to recover money due under the scheme from a recalcitrant minority. Under present law and practice, property managers sometimes raise actions in their own names on behalf of the owners,[137] and we suggest that this should be possible under the new law also. The manager should require to receive written authorisation.

5.86 We recommend that:

16(a) Management Scheme A should bind the owners for the time being of flats.

(b) **A scheme decision should be binding on the owners and their successors as owners.**

(c) **Any obligation imposed by Management Scheme A or arising from a scheme decision should be enforceable by any owner or by a person authorised by an owner in writing to act on his behalf.**

(Scheme A, rules 8.1 - 8.4)

---

134 Para 3.16 and recommendation 2(a).

135 See further paras 8.18 - 8.23.

136 Para 5.77 and recommendation 14(v).

137 An example is *David Watson Property Management v Woolwich Equitable Building Society* 1992 SC(HL) 21.

Juridical nature of management schemes

5.87 The rules of Scheme A and of other management schemes are not real burdens. They are created by, or by virtue of,[138] statute and they do not conform to the strict rules provided by the common law for the constitution of real burdens.[139] Nonetheless they resemble real burdens. They perform a task which, under the present law, is usually performed by real burdens. Furthermore, they have a close relationship with actual real burdens. In the titles of existing tenements real burdens often regulate management and maintenance, and also use and conduct; and Scheme A makes close use of the former,[140] if not of the latter. In the future, management and maintenance provisions are more likely to appear in titles as part of a management scheme,[141] with real burdens in the strict sense being confined to conduct rules; but in practice both will probably appear in the same deed of conditions, and, depending on the drafting, may not be very clearly distinguished.[142] The most apt way of characterising the rules of management schemes is to say that they are real conditions, in the wide sense of rights and obligations attaching to and binding persons in their capacity as owners of property.[143] As real conditions, they[144] would seem to satisfy the definition of "land obligation" for the purposes of the jurisdiction of the Lands Tribunal of Scotland:[145]

> ".. an obligation relating to land which is enforceable by a proprietor of an interest in land, by virtue of his being such proprietor, and which is binding upon a proprietor of another interest in that land, or of an interest in other land, by virtue of his being such proprietor".

This would mean, in theory at least, that an application could be made for their variation or discharge. We have considered whether the rules of management schemes ought to be excluded from the Lands Tribunal jurisdiction. Schemes A and B can already be varied by agreement of a majority of owners. Further, the three grounds on which the Lands Tribunal is permitted to vary or discharge obligations[146] seem remote from the typical content of a management scheme. On balance, however, we think it is better to leave matters as they are, if only because management rules and real burdens may sometimes be so closely intertwined within a single deed that it may be difficult to separate them, or even to distinguish them.

138 This applies to a management scheme which is neither Scheme A or B but which is created by virtue of clause 5(1)(c).
139 Reid, paras 386-396.
140 By incorporating some of their terms: see eg para 5.60.
141 ie, either as a variation of Scheme A or Scheme B, or as an alternative management scheme: see clause 5.
142 Para 3.19.
143 Reid, paras 344 ff.
144 It might even be argued that scheme decisions satisfy the definition also.
145 Conveyancing and Feudal Reform (Scotland) Act 1970 s 1(2).
146 1970 Act s 1(3).

Part 6 Management Scheme B

Structure and scope

6.1 Management Scheme A is to apply automatically to all tenements. But, as was explained earlier,[1] Scheme A can be disapplied and replaced with another management scheme of the owners' - or, more usually, the developer's - choice. In this part of the report we describe Management Scheme B, which is offered as a possible model for an alternative scheme. In practice it will be rare for the owners of flats in existing tenements to change from Scheme A to Scheme B, and we anticipate that the main use of Scheme B will be for new tenements. Scheme B is brought into operation by a deed of conditions executed and registered by the developer or other owner,[2] a conveyancing device which replicates current practice for new tenements.

6.2 We have set out Scheme B in three parts. Part I contains a number of basic provisions about the establishment of an owners' association, its powers, its internal governance, and its winding up. The detailed rules of the scheme are then given in Part II. Part III deals with questions of interpretation. We suggest that the Secretary of State should be empowered to alter Scheme B by statutory instrument, although this would not affect tenements to which the scheme already applied. In addition, it is possible to vary Scheme B in its application to individual tenements,[3] and in practice we imagine that it will very often be varied in the initial deed of conditions, at least to the extent of giving a fuller definition of the property to which it applies and, perhaps, of varying the rules as to liability for maintenance. However, we suggest that it should not be possible to vary Part I, which sets out and regulates the special privileges which apply to owners' associations. We recommend therefore that:

17(a) The Secretary of State should have the power to alter Scheme B by statutory instrument, but such alterations should not apply to applications of Scheme B by a deed of conditions executed before the coming into force of the instrument.

(b) In varying Management Scheme B in terms of recommendation 2(b)(iii) it should not be possible to vary Part I of the scheme.

(Clauses 5(1)(b)(ii) and 7)

Variation is effected by making appropriate provision in the deed of conditions. Depending on the number of changes being made, this might take the form of particular alterations to particular rules, or alternatively, and preferably, the deed of conditions might reprint Scheme B in full with the variations duly incorporated.

6.3 Earlier we mentioned the constraints which affected the making of Scheme A.[4] With Scheme B there have been no such constraints, for the scheme will apply only by choice, and it can be freely varied. Thus we have felt able to provide a degree of elaboration which was not possible in the case of Scheme A. Scheme B is much the longer of the two schemes. The idea was to provide a contrast, and hence a choice. While Scheme A will generally be suitable for small tenements, Scheme B is aimed at larger developments where a more formal management structure is appropriate.[5] It is also likely to be suitable

1 Paras 3.16 and 3.17.
2 Paras 3.16 - 3.21, and recommendation 2.
3 Para 3.8 and recommendation 2(b)(ii).
4 Para 5.3.
5 There may be tax reasons for not using Scheme B in the case of tenements consisting of five or fewer flats: see para 6.69.

for sheltered housing.[6] There is, of course, no reason why a developer should use either scheme in its enacted form. Scheme A might be developed and expanded, or Scheme B might be shortened. Another option would be to create a wholly new scheme, but using some elements from one, or both, of the statutory schemes. In cases where a development comprises separate dwelling-houses as well a tenement or tenements, there is no objection to applying one of the statutory schemes, appropriately amended, to non-tenemental buildings.[7] But of course a developer would always remain free to disregard both schemes and to persevere with a deed of conditions in the form which is in current use.

6.4 Like Scheme A, Scheme B is confined to matters of management and maintenance and makes no provision as to the conduct of the owners or the use to be made of the property. The omission is deliberate. Tenements vary so much in size and in character that there seemed little advantage in drawing up a set of model conduct rules which developers might find to be of little or no assistance. We expect that in the future, as in the past, developers will wish to include in the deed of conditions real burdens regulating conduct and use, and, in cases where Scheme B is being used, these burdens could conveniently be included in an additional Part IV of the scheme.[8]

6.5 In drawing up Scheme B we have derived considerable help both from deeds of conditions in current use, and from the statutory management schemes which have been introduced in many other countries over the past thirty or forty years.[9] A review of these sources shows extraordinary variety in both length and complexity. There is almost no legal problem, or so it seems, which might not arise in the course of tenement life and, if the will is there, almost no lengths to which the draftsman might not go for its solution. The influential New South Wales scheme consists of 43 rules and is appended to an act on strata titles which consists of 160 sections and runs to 158 printed pages.[10] Much closer to home, the draft legislation on commonhold which has been proposed for England and Wales consists of 141 printed pages and comprises 56 clauses and 12 schedules.[11] By contrast, the deeds of conditions employed by Scottish conveyancers, though often wordy, are much less ambitious in scope. On the whole we have preferred the local model. Partly this is for the practical reason that a long and complex scheme is unlikely to commend itself to conveyancers and might lie on the statute book unused. Partly too it is because of the belief that a secure set of general principles is sometimes better than intricate elaboration. The common sense of owners will then do the rest. Finally, we doubt whether a long and detailed scheme is sufficiently accessible to ordinary owners of flats. Scheme B comprises only 16 rules. It is longer than most deeds of conditions used in current practice but not, we hope, unacceptably long. As with Scheme A, an attempt has been made to use language which is as simple as is consistent with legal certainty, although we are conscious that we may not always have succeeded. The intention is that the scheme should be no harder to use than the rules of a golf club, and that owners should be able operate it with the minimum of legal or other professional assistance. The text is accompanied by explanatory notes written in non-technical language.[12]

6.6 A number of provisions are common to both Schemes A and B, the most important being: the definitions of "scheme property"[13] and "maintenance",[14] joint and several liability of co-owners,[15] the redistribution of liability in certain circumstances,[16] and emergency repairs and other works.[17] We simply

---

6 Doubtless with some modifications. The full executive authority given to the manager under Scheme B mirrors the powers given to the manager in many sheltered housing developments.
7 Draft Bill, clause 5(3). This could also be achieved by using a completely different management scheme, but a possible advantage of using Scheme B is that the facility of a body corporate is available.
8 See para 5.87.
9 See paras 2.2 and 2.3.
10 Strata Titles Act 1973.
11 The draft bill was published by the Lord Chancellor's Department in July 1996.
12 These will be found in Appendix 1, on the pages facing the text of Scheme B.
13 Scheme B, rules 16.1 and 16.2: see paras 5.4 - 5.11.
14 Scheme B, rule 16.3: see paras 5.41 - 5.44.
15 Scheme B, rule 11.5: see para 5.80.
16 Scheme B, rules 11.2, 11.6 and 11.7: see paras 5.81 and 5.82.
17 Scheme B, rule 13: see paras 5.54 - 5.58.

note these here but do not discuss them again. We would, however, draw attention to the concept of "scheme property". Scheme B does not apply to the whole tenement but only to those parts which are scheme property. Scheme property is defined as meaning (i) all parts which are owned in common and (ii) (where they do not already fall under (i)) certain other parts, such as the roof and external walls. It is expected that a developer would very often wish to add to this list. This could be done either indirectly, by increasing the number of parts of the tenement which are owned in common, or directly, by adding to the second part of the definition. Sometimes both methods will require to be used, because there may be parts of a tenement which ought to be maintained in common but which could not appropriately be made common property.[18]

Owners' association

6.7 We propose that the management of the scheme property should be entrusted to an owners' association consisting of all owners of flats in the tenement. This is not, of course, a novel suggestion. Owners' associations are a standard feature of management schemes in other countries, and they are often found in the more sophisticated of the deeds of conditions used in this country. The idea is that the association comes into existence at the same time as Scheme B, and that all owners are automatically members.[19] On ceasing to be owner they lose their membership, and the incoming owner becomes a member in turn. In cases where a flat is co-owned (for example, by a husband and wife), all co-owners are members.

6.8 In Scotland owners' associations are always unincorporated associations. In theory it would be possible for them to be constituted as companies under the Companies Acts, but the degree of formality and regulation involved are out of scale with the relatively humble functions performed by the association. By contrast, in most countries with modern legislation in this field the owners' association is a body corporate *sui generis*, incorporated under the legislation and regulated with a minimum of formality. The commonhold scheme which has been proposed for England and Wales similarly makes use of a body corporate. The idea is to bestow the advantages of incorporation but without the formality which would be imposed by company law. The advantages of incorporation arise from the fact that, unlike an unincorporated association, a corporation is a separate legal person. Thus it can enter into contracts, owe and be owed money, sue in its own name, and so on; and there is a clear division in law between the association on the one hand and the owners of the flats, who are its members. The technical superiority of incorporation seems clear enough. But we recommend it here not only for that reason but also to give developers a choice. Under the present law incorporation is not, in practical terms, available. Under our proposals a developer would be able to opt for incorporation and Scheme B. Alternatively he could, in effect, use Scheme B but without incorporation by detaching Parts II and III of the scheme and using them as the basis of a different management scheme.[20]

6.9 A body corporate requires functions and powers, and any act lying beyond these powers is *ultra vires* and void. In our view the functions and powers of an owners' association should be narrowly defined. An owner should have the reassurance that the association will not embark on the manufacture of ball bearings or on a career of property speculation; and the special informality which we are proposing for owners' associations should not be available for corporations which are engaged in trade. We suggest that the function of an association should be no more than to manage the scheme property of the tenement for the benefit of the owners. A long list of supporting powers seems not to be required. As a juristic person the association would have all powers which are necessary in order to carry out its designated function. Thus for example the association could enter into contracts and enforce them in its own name. Nonetheless it is convenient and, for the owners, perhaps reassuring, to give a non-exhaustive list of the powers which the association might normally wish to exercise. First and foremost, the association will wish to maintain the scheme property. In certain limited circumstances it might also wish to carry out

18 For some of the difficulties in using common property, see para 3.5.

19 For the meaning of "owner", see paras 8.25 - 8.29 and recommendation 36.

20 Technically this different scheme would not be Scheme B because Part I (which deals with incorporation) is a mandatory part of Scheme B.

improvements.[21] It might want to insure the tenement,[22] and for that purpose would require to be given an insurable interest. It will sometimes be necessary to hire employees or agents - gardeners, cleaners and the like. From time to time some item of moveable property may need to be purchased - a lawnmower, for example, or cleaning materials. In order to pay for those costs the association will require to levy money from the owners. A bank account will require to be opened and, in appropriate cases, money may need to be invested so as to generate income. Occasionally the association may need to borrow money, if only in the form of a temporary overdraft pending payment by the owners of their next instalment of service charge. The deed of conditions bringing Scheme B into operation might add to this list, but we suggest that it should not be possible to include a power to acquire land or to carry on any trade. As already mentioned, the list of powers is not exhaustive,[23] but the list includes those powers which we regard as central to the association's role and which we would expect to be used most frequently.

6.10 We recommend that:

18(a) An owners' association should come into existence on the day on which Scheme B takes effect.

(b) The association should be a body corporate but not a company.

(c) The members of the association should be the owners for the time being of the flats in the tenement.

(d) Where two or more persons own a flat both (or all) of them should be members.

(e) The function of the association should be to manage the scheme property for the benefit of the owners of the flats in the tenement.

(f) The association should have power to do anything necessary for the carrying out of its function and in particular should be able to -

(i) carry out maintenance, improvements or alterations to scheme property;

(ii) enter into a contract of insurance in respect of the tenement or any part of it (and for that purpose the association should have an insurable interest);

(iii) purchase or otherwise acquire moveable property;

(iv) require owners to contribute by way of a service charge to association funds;

(v) open and maintain in the name of the association an account with any bank or building society;

(vi) invest in the name of the association any money held on its behalf;

(vii) borrow money;

(viii) engage employees or appoint agents; and

(ix) act in accordance with any other powers conferred under the scheme.

(g) In varying Management Scheme B in terms of recommendation 2(b)(iii) it should not be possible to confer on the association the power to acquire land or the power to carry on any trade.

(Clause 5(6)(c); Scheme B, rules 1, 2.1 and 2.2)

Manager

6.11 The enemy of good management is apathy. Experience shows that owners of flats are often reluctant to attend meetings or otherwise to play an active part in the management of the building. Such reluctance

21 See paras 6.44 and 6.45.

22 That is to say, the whole tenement and not merely the scheme property. This is the one case where the association's powers should extend beyond the scheme property.

23 For example, as part of its management the association might wish to devise rules governing the use of scheme property.

is understandable; but it suggests that the owners as a body should not be given a day-to-day role in the running of the tenement. In our view Scheme B is unlikely to work efficiently unless one person - and one person alone - is charged with executive responsibility for the management of the tenement. Such a person may be designated as the "manager". The manager would be the executive arm of the association and hence the equivalent of the board of directors in a company. He could be one of the owners or he could be an outside professional, such as a property manager or indeed a firm of property managers. If the manager was an owner he would be able to appoint an outside professional to assist him.[24] The manager would normally be appointed by the association at a general meeting of its members. He would serve for such period of time as the owners wished. Usually he would be paid. In order to cover the period between the creation of the tenement and the first general meeting, it should be possible for the deed of conditions to nominate the first manager. But to avoid possible abuse by the developer, the first manager should serve only until the first annual general meeting, although he would be eligible for reappointment. In the absence of any agreement to the contrary the first manager would be entitled to reasonable remuneration for his period of office, which is unlikely to be longer than a few months.[25]

6.12 The manager would exercise the powers vested in the association.[26] But he would also be subject to a number of duties. Above all he would have the duty of managing the scheme property for the benefit of the owners of the flats in the tenement.[27] We imagine that it would be helpful both to the owners and also to the manager if some specific duties were also listed, and these are mentioned later.[28] Additional duties may of course be laid down in any contract entered into between the manager and the association.

6.13 The validity of a manager's actings should not be affected by a technical irregularity in the appointment process.[29] In order to satisfy contractors and other third parties, provision should be made for the manager's appointment to be evidenced by a formal certificate signed both by the manager and by a member acting on behalf of the association. Like a director of a company, the manager would be an agent of the association. This both empowers and restrains him. On the one hand he can incur liabilities and acquire rights on behalf of the association. But on the other hand he owes fiduciary duties to the association. Thus he must exercise his powers in good faith and in the best interests of the association. He must not make a secret profit. He must not, for private reasons, favour one contractor at the expense of others who might do the work just as well and at a lower cost. A manager who breached his fiduciary duties would be liable in damages to the association.

6.14 The manager will usually be appointed for a fixed period of time, although his appointment would be renewable and in practice might often be renewed. But we think that it should be possible for the members to dismiss a manager at any time by a vote taken at a general meeting and without the need to satisfy any particular criteria.[30] If a manager is thought not to be performing satisfactorily, or if he is abusing his power, there should be no delay in replacing him. However, a dismissal which could not be justified would attract a claim by the manager under his contract.

6.15 We recommend that:

19(a) In an owners' association executive responsibility should be vested in a manager, who may but need not be a member of the association.

(b) A person including a firm[31] should be appointed as manager by the association at a general meeting, and on such terms and conditions as the association may decide.

---

24 Under recommendation 18(f)(viii).

25 The first general meeting must take place within a year of the establishment of the association, and in many cases will take place sooner: see para 6.25.

26 See para 6.19.

27 This is the counterpart of the function of the association, as set out in recommendation 18(e), which function is exercised on behalf of the association by the manager.

28 See in particular paras 6.21, 6.28, 6.31, 6.40, 6.42 and 6.59.

29 This suggestion is modelled on s 285 of the Companies Act 1985.

30 An equivalent right exists in company law: see s 303 of the Companies Act 1985.

31 In terms of Schedule 1 to the Interpretation Act 1978 "person" is defined to include "a body of persons corporate or unincorporate". It is not clear that this would cover partnership.

(c) However, it should be possible to nominate in the deed of conditions the person who is to act as the first manager of the association, and such person should serve until the first annual general meeting, be entitled to reasonable remuneration, and be eligible for reappointment.

(d) The actings of a manager should be valid even if there is an irregularity in the way he was appointed.

(e) Not later than a month after a manager's appointment a certificate should be prepared recording the making of the appointment and its duration, and the certificate should be signed by the manager and, on behalf of the association, by a member.

(f) The manager should have the duty to manage the scheme property for the benefit of the members.

(g) The manager should be an agent of the association.

(h) The association should be empowered to dismiss the manager at a general meeting before his term of office has expired.

(Scheme B, rules 3.1 - 3.5, 6.1, 6.2 and 7)

Advisory committee

6.16 Under our proposals executive power rests, not with a committee of members and still less with the members as a body, but rather with a single manager. But while doubting the value of management by committee, we accept that there may still be a role for a committee of members to act in an advisory capacity. We have in mind an informal arrangement whereby a small group of members would be nominated as advisers to the manager. They would meet from time to time with the manager and offer advice on current issues. The manager would be bound to listen to the advice tendered although he would not be bound to follow it, for in the end the manager is answerable to all of the members and not merely to a small number of them, who may not turn out to be representative. However, any member of the advisory committee should be entitled to requisition a general meeting at which, if necessary, the manager could be taken to task.

6.17 We do not think that an advisory committee should be mandatory. Owners may think it is not worth the trouble, and in small tenements at least there may be no need for a separate group of members. But in a larger tenement the manager, especially where he is an outsider, may be grateful for the opportunity to discuss matters informally with a number of the owners.

6.18 We recommend that:

20(a) At a general meeting the association should be entitled to elect an advisory committee of members to provide advice to the manager.

(b) If an advisory committee is appointed, the manager should be bound to consult it from time to time, but should not be bound to follow its advice.

(c) Any member of the advisory committee should be entitled to requisition a general meeting.

(Scheme B, rules 8.3(c) and 14)

Internal governance

6.19 The two organs of the association are the members in general meeting and the manager. Both should be entitled to exercise all the powers of the association, subject, of course, to the other rules of the scheme.[32] But since general meetings will usually take place only once a year, executive power will

32 Thus for example, the general power to raise money from members conferred by rule 2.2(d) is qualified by the procedural safeguards contained in rules 10 and 11.

in practice be exercised by the manager, and the general meeting is likely to need its powers only in cases where, for some reason, there is no manager in place. However, ultimate authority should lie with the general meeting. We have already recommended that the general meeting should be able to dismiss the manager even before the expiry of his term.[33] Furthermore, the general meeting should be empowered to give the manager instructions or to impose restrictions on his authority.[34] Later we recommend specific controls by the general meeting in relation to financial matters.[35]

6.20 Under our proposals for Scheme A a decision reached by a majority of the owners is subject to the possibility of judicial annulment.[36] A disaffected owner can apply to the sheriff within 21 days of the decision or, if he did not attend the meeting, within 21 days of notification of the decision.[37] The sheriff may then annul the decision if satisfied that it is not in the best interests of all the owners or that it is unfairly prejudicial to one or more owner. We suggest that this annulment procedure be carried over into Scheme B. While oppression of the minority is likely to be unusual in the larger tenements to which Scheme B will typically apply, there is obvious value in providing a review procedure of some kind. In Scheme A a decision by owners is usually the prelude to the carrying out of maintenance, and special provision is made to prevent expenditure in implement of a decision during the days of appeal. No equivalent provision seems necessary for Scheme B. Most decisions made at a general meeting will have no immediate financial consequences, and acts of maintenance are usually carried out by the manager acting on his own authority and without recourse to a general meeting.[38]

6.21 The rules of Scheme B are, and should formally be declared to be, binding on the association, its members and on the manager.[39] An incoming owner becomes a member automatically and hence is bound by the scheme and by decisions already taken on behalf of the association by its manager or the general meeting.[40] Under Scheme A enforcement rights are conferred on individual owners, but under Scheme B enforcement should normally be left to the manager, acting on behalf of the association. Indeed we consider that the manager should be under a positive duty to enforce both the provisions of the scheme, and also any obligations owed by any person to the association, whether under the scheme or otherwise. Thus if an owner does not pay his service charge, it is the duty of the manager to take appropriate measures for its recovery.

6.22 Under Scheme B a heavy burden of responsibility rests on the manager. If the manager is efficient, the tenement will run well. But some managers may not be efficient because they are too busy or too disorganised. Occasionally a manager may behave dishonestly. For cases of inadequate performance it is necessary to decide where the title to complain should lie. We see no reason why the various duties placed on the manager by the scheme should not be owed to the individual members as well as to the association. It is true that in company law directors generally owe duties to the company rather than to its members, and further that the Scottish equivalent of the rule in *Foss v Harbottle*[41] will usually prevent individual members from enforcing the rights which the law vests in the company. But we shrink from introducing *Foss v Harbottle*, a difficult and elaborate rule,[42] into the law of the tenement. The usual justification for *Foss v Harbottle* is that it prevents the multiplication of law suits, but the danger seems slight in the case of an owners' association. Owners are lethargic rather than litigious. Where a breach of duty affects the tenement as a whole, they will be all too willing to leave enforcement to collective action, decided on at a general meeting. Individual action is likely only where the general meeting declines to take matters further, and the owner is not satisfied with the decision. Such cases will not be common. The position is different where the breach affects a particular owner individually and uniquely.

33 Para 6.14 and recommendation 19(h).
34 As in company law: see the Companies (Tables A to F) Regulations 1985 S I 1985/805, Table A, article 70.
35 See paras 6.33 - 6.41 and recommendation 23.
36 Paras 5.19 - 5.25 and recommendation 7.
37 Under Scheme B decisions require to be notified to owners within 21 days: see para 6.31 and recommendation 22(q)(iii).
38 For maintenance under Scheme B, see paras 6.42 - 6.46.
39 For the parallel provision in company law, see s 14 of the Companies Act 1985.
40 See Part 8 for a discussion of the liability of an incoming owner for costs incurred or to be incurred under the scheme.
41 (1843) 2 Hare 461.
42 The Law Commission for England and Wales has recently recommended the replacement of the rule by a new statutory remedy for shareholders: see *Shareholder Remedies,* Law Com No 246 (October 1997).

A standard example would be where the manager falls down on his duty of regular inspection,[43] and an individual flat is damaged because of the resulting deterioration in the condition of an item of scheme property. For example, dry rot might spread from the roof timbers, or there might be water damage from a leaking pipe. In situations such as these it seems only just that the owner affected should have a direct right of action against the manager, and indeed in such cases the loss has been incurred by the owner and not by the association.

6.23 Usually, of course, it will not come to litigation. A manager whose performance is unsatisfactory can be summoned to a general meeting and required to account for himself. He can be given instructions as to his future conduct. If the members are still not satisfied he can be dismissed and replaced by someone more competent, or more trustworthy. The opportunity for members to exercise control in this way occurs with reasonable frequency. Under Scheme B general meetings must be held annually, and additional meetings may be requisitioned by any member of the advisory committee or by the owners holding 25% of the total votes for the tenement.[44] Provided that members are reasonably vigilant there is no reason why the tenement should not be managed well.

6.24 Summing up this whole discussion, we recommend that:

21(a) The powers of the association should be exercisable by the association in general meeting or by the manager, but subject in both cases to the other rules of the scheme.

(b) In the exercise of these powers the manager should be subject to any directions given by the association at a general meeting.

(c) Recommendation 7 (which confers on an owner a right to apply to the sheriff for annulment of a decision on certain grounds) should apply to decisions made by the association at a general meeting.

(d) The rules of Management Scheme B should be binding on the association, its members and on the manager.

(e) The association should be entitled to enforce any provision of the scheme and any obligation owed by any person to the association; and the manager should be under a duty to carry out such enforcement on behalf of the association.

(f) The duties imposed on the manager by the scheme should be owed to the association and to its members.

(Clause 8(1) and (8) and Scheme B, rules 2.3 and 2.4, 3.6 - 3.8 and 7(g))

General Meetings

6.25 The general meeting is the legislature of the owners' association. It appoints the manager, who is the executive, and may give him instructions or impose restrictions. It may also dismiss him. Further, the general meeting has a residual right to exercise all of the powers of the association. Often only one general meeting will be held each year; and indeed we suggest, following the rules for companies,[45] that a general meeting should require to be held annually, and that not more than 15 months should elapse between successive annual general meetings. The first annual general meeting should be held not later than 12 months after the establishment of the association.[46] The main business of the annual general meeting is likely to be the approval of a draft budget for the following year.[47]

6.26 In addition to the annual general meeting it should be possible to hold other general meetings if and when the need arises. Earlier we recommended that any member of the advisory committee should

43 For the manager's duty of regular inspection, see para 6.42 and recommendation 24(a).

44 See paras 6.16 and 6.25 - 6.27 and recommendations 20(c) and 22(a)-(c).

45 Companies Act 1985 s 366. A similar rule operates for owners' associations in many other countries.

46 The association is established on the day on which the Scheme is brought into effect: see Scheme B, rule 1.1 as read with draft Bill clause 5(4).

47 For the rules about budgets, see paras 6.33 - 6.41.

be able to requisition a meeting.[48] Similarly, the manager should be able to call a meeting whenever he wishes. Ordinary owners are in a different position. In order to avoid a proliferation of unnecessary meetings, a number of owners should require to be of like mind before a meeting can be arranged, and we suggest 25% of the total voting power as a suitable threshold.[49]

6.27 Scheme B sets out certain procedural rules for the calling and the conduct of general meetings. Since these are straightforward and, we imagine, uncontroversial, only a short summary is given here. A meeting is called by sending to each member a draft agenda and a notice of the date, time and place of the meeting. These must be sent 14 days in advance. As in Scheme A,[50] a document may be sent by personal delivery to a member's flat, by post, or by electronic transmission, such as fax or e -mail. However, an inadvertent failure to send documentation to a member should not affect the validity of proceedings at the general meeting.[51] By agreement at the meeting additional items can be added to the agenda. Thus an owner who wishes to protect his interests should take care to attend, or be represented at, all meetings.

6.28 Normally the manager will call the meeting. Scheme B places him under a duty to call the annual general meeting, and also any other meeting which is requisitioned by members in accordance with the rules just described. If the manager fails to call a meeting, or if there is no manager,[52] any member is entitled to step in and call the meeting himself.

6.29 Following the lead of many other countries,[53] we suggest that the quorum at a meeting should ordinarily be 50% of the total voting power of the association. Hence in cases where each flat has a single vote,[54] a quorum will be attained if the owners of half of the flats are present or represented at the meeting. We are attracted by the system operated in South Africa whereby the quorum is reduced as the size of the development increases. This recognises the fact that in larger developments individual owners may feel that their vote counts for little and may feel inclined to stay away, with the result that a quorum is not easily attained. Under the South African legislation the quorum is 50% for developments with 10 or fewer units, 35% for developments with between 11 and 49 units, and 20% for still larger developments.[55] We suggest a slightly simpler formula: 50% for up to 30 flats in the tenement, and 35% thereafter. Of course even with a reduced quorum there will still be cases where a meeting is inquorate. In such cases we suggest that it should be possible to postpone the meeting after 20 minutes and rearrange it for another day not less than 14 and not more than 28 days later. At the rearranged meeting business may be transacted even although a quorum is not present. Under Scheme B a quorum is necessary only for the start of the meeting. Hence if an initial quorum is present business can continue to be transacted even if the quorum subsequently falls away.

6.30 The meeting is presided over by a chairman elected by the members. A chairman may be elected for a particular meeting only or, if preferred, for a period of years. As currently drafted Scheme B gives each flat the right to a single vote, but a developer may wish to provide weighted voting, at least in a case where the flats are of markedly different sizes. We imagine that voting rights will in most cases correspond with liability for scheme costs, so that a flat which has 12% liability for costs will also command 12% of the votes.[56] An owner may vote in person or he may nominate another person to attend

48 Para 6.16 and recommendation 20(c).

49 For the equivalent position for companies, see s 368. South Africa also operates a 25% threshold: see rule 53 of Annexure 8 (made under s 35(2)(a) of the Sectional Titles Act 1986) (referred to in subsequent footnotes as "Annexure 8").

50 Para 5.36 and recommendation 9(e).

51 This adopts a rule of company law: see the Companies (Tables A to F) Regulations 1985, S I 1985/805, Table A, article 39. In the less formal Scheme A, the equivalent provision is a form of personal bar: see para 5.37 and recommendation 9(f).

52 As for example, in the case of the first annual general meeting, at which point the association may not yet have a manager, if none has been nominated in the deed of conditions applying the scheme.

53 Van der Merwe, paras 344 and 369.

54 Which is the default provision contained in Scheme B: see para 6.30. But the deed of conditions may change this rule.

55 Annexure 8 rule 57.

56 Para 5.28. Under Scheme B as set out in the draft Bill each flat has both an equality of voting power and (see para 6.39) an equality of liability.

the meeting and vote on his behalf. In order to avoid disputes, the nomination must be in writing. However, it should not be possible to nominate the manager for this purpose, since he may quite often have a special interest in the outcome of a vote. As in Scheme A,[57] in the case of co-ownership of a flat either (or any) *pro indiviso* owner may exercise the vote for that flat, but where there is disagreement among the owners the vote will not be counted. A vote is normally taken by show of hands, although the chairman has a discretion to allow a ballot to be held. In practice a ballot is important only where individual owners have significantly different voting rights. Decisions are reached, in the usual way, by a simple majority of votes cast. Hence if there is present only a bare quorum of 50%, a decision can be taken by 26% of the total voting power.[58] However, there are three cases where the issues involved seem sufficiently important - and sufficiently removed from normal management - to require that an absolute majority of all votes be obtained. These are, first, a decision to vary Scheme B or to replace it with a different management scheme,[59] secondly a decision to make a payment from the reserve fund,[60] and thirdly, a decision to carry out improvements or alterations to scheme property.[61]

6.31 The manager is placed under an obligation to attend the meeting, to take minutes, and to send a copy of the minutes to all members within 21 days. He is also bound to give effect to the decisions taken at the meeting.

6.32 We recommend that:

22(a) An annual general meeting of the association should be held every year, and not more than 15 months should elapse between the date of each successive meeting.

(b) The first annual general meeting should take place not later than 12 months after the establishment of the association.

(c) Members holding not less than 25% of the votes for the tenement should be entitled to requisition an additional general meeting at any time.

(d) The manager should be under a duty to call the annual general meeting and any other meeting which is requisitioned by a member or members. In addition, he should be able to call a general meeting at any time.

(e) Where the manager fails to call a general meeting, or where there is no manager, any member can call the meeting.

(f) A meeting should be called by sending to each member, at least 14 days in advance, an agenda and a notice of the date, time and place of the meeting.

(g) However, any inadvertent failure to send the required documentation should not affect the validity of proceedings at the meeting.

(h) At the meeting a quorum should be the members holding not less than 50% of the votes for the tenement; but where the tenement has more than 30 flats the figure should be reduced to 35%.

(i) A member should be able to be represented at the meeting by a person (other than the manager) duly nominated in writing.

(j) A quorum should be necessary for a general meeting to begin, but once the meeting has begun it should be able to continue thereafter even if a quorum has ceased to attend.

(k) If there is still no quorum 20 minutes after the time fixed for a general meeting, the meeting should be postponed until another day not less than 14 and not more than 28 days later. The postponed meeting should then be able to proceed even in the absence of a quorum.

---

57 Para 5.15 and recommendation 6(d).
58 Or even less if there are abstentions.
59 See para 3.20 and recommendation 2(d).
60 For the reserve fund, see further paras 6.36 and 6.37.
61 See para 6.44.

(l) The meeting should be presided over by a chairman elected by the members.

(m) Decisions should be taken by a simple majority of the votes cast, one vote being allocated to each flat.

(n) However, an absolute majority of the votes for the tenement should be required for any decision to -

(i) vary, disapply or replace the scheme in terms of recommendation 2;

(ii) make payments from a reserve fund; or

(iii) carry out improvements or alterations to scheme property.

(o) Where two or more persons own a flat, any one owner should be able to vote, but if the owners disagree as to how the vote is to be cast the vote should not be counted.

(p) Voting should be taken by show of hands unless the chairman decides it should be by ballot.

(q) The manager should be under a duty to -

(i) attend all general meetings (except where he is unable to because of illness or some other good reason);

(ii) take minutes;

(iii) send a copy of the minutes to all members within 21 days; and

(iv) give effect to the decisions taken.

(Scheme B, rules 7(f), 8, 9 and 12.1)

Financial matters

6.33 In most tenements money is collected as and when the need for expenditure arises. There is no financial planning as such. Each item of expenditure is discussed in isolation from all others and at the time when its need has become pressing. In a bad year owners may have to meet quite frequently to sanction individual repairs or other types of expenditure. In the case of small tenements in a good state of repair, this hand-to-mouth method of proceeding may work perfectly well. But it works less well in larger developments or in tenements where there are likely to be regular calls for expenditure, and for such cases some form of annual budgeting is likely to be an attractive alternative.

6.34 In Scheme B we propose a system of annual budgeting. It works in quite a simple way. Each year the manager must produce a draft budget and present it to the annual general meeting for approval. The draft budget sets out the projected expenditure of the association for the coming 12 months on maintenance, insurance and other matters, and estimates the amount of service charge which will require to be levied on members in order to finance that expenditure. The draft budget must be circulated in advance along with the other papers for the meeting. At the meeting the budget may either be accepted, whether in its original or in an amended form, or it may be rejected. If it is accepted the manager must then proceed to levy the service charge as agreed. If it is rejected the manager must prepare a revised draft budget for submission to a second meeting held within two months.

6.35 Sometimes the estimates of income and expenditure will prove inaccurate. If more is collected from members than is needed then the surplus will be available for the following year.[62] But if there were items of expenditure which were not anticipated we think that the manager should be able to levy an additional amount of service charge without having to seek further authority. The power, however, should not be unlimited, for otherwise a manager, having won approval for a modest budget, could proceed to raise the bulk of the association's income by means of an additional service charge. A reasonable

62 We do not recommend that an owner who sells during that year should be able to take with him "his" share of the surplus, although the existence of a surplus may have some effect on the selling price.

balance between financial flexibility and financial control would be achieved by allowing the manager to raise up to 25% of the annual budget as additional revenue. Thus in approving a total annual service charge of £10,000 members would be sanctioning the possibility that the amount actually levied might be as high as £12,500. But if the manager wished to raise more than this he would have to submit a full supplementary budget for fresh approval by the members.

6.36 One potential advantage of annual budgeting is the chance to make provision for longer term repairs. Under the existing law there is a natural tendency to avoid major repairs.[63] Owners would rather patch and mend in the hope that, by the time that a major repair comes to be needed, they will have moved on and some successor will be left to foot the bill. In this way tenements come to deteriorate, and sometimes can be rescued only by the injection of public money. The position would be greatly improved if owners saved up as they went along so that, over a period of time, quite substantial sums became available for major repairs. The cost of such repairs would then no longer strike, randomly, at those who had the misfortune to be owners at the relevant time, but would be shared by all those who had ever owned a flat in the building. In Scheme B we make provision for a reserve (or sinking) fund to meet the cost of long-term repairs. The manager is empowered to include as part of his draft budget a contribution to a reserve fund. Any reserve fund would require to be held and invested separately from the general funds of the association. Over time it will build up. An owner leaves the fund behind when he sells, for to allow him to withdraw from it would defeat the whole purpose of the exercise. This need not be specially provided for. The reserve fund is the property of the association and not of its members. It will be returned to members only in the event of the association being wound up.[64]

6.37 We do not think that a reserve fund should be compulsory. Under Scheme B it is for the owners to manage their own affairs and, in deliberating on the draft budget, they must be free to accept or to reject the idea of a contribution for long-term repairs. But a flat in a tenement with a healthy reserve fund is likely to command a premium in the market place, and it is hoped that for this and for other reasons reserve funds will become a great deal more common than they are at present.

6.38 Contributions from members are levied by means of a service charge. The manager sends a notice of payment to the members. In the case of a flat owned in common, each *pro indiviso* owner must be sent a notice, and each is jointly and severally liable for the full amount attributable to that flat.[65] The notice must set out the amount due and the date or dates on which payment is required. These figures and dates will already have been approved at the annual general meeting, except where the amount claimed is an additional service charge. In practice we imagine that payment will often be by instalments spread throughout the year. The liability to pay crystallises on the date (or dates) stipulated in the notice.[66] If an owner pays more than 28 days late we think that the manager should have a discretion to require interest.

6.39 Scheme B provides that each flat contributes to the service charge in equal shares, but we expect this provision to be varied in cases where the flats are not of equal size. Unlike Scheme A, Scheme B does not usually differentiate between different items of expenditure. Instead all expenditure is combined into a single service charge. Thus the cost of repairing the roof is paid for in the same way and in the same proportions as the cost of employing a manager. Similarly, nothing rests on ownership or on use, so that a pipe on one side of the building falls to be maintained by all the owners and not merely by those whose flats it happens to service.[67] However, special provision is made in relation to common insurance. In a tenement with mixed commercial and residential use the cost of insuring the commercial units may exceed that of insuring the domestic units. The premium for a fish and chip shop, for example, is likely to be higher than the premium for a dwelling-house. In cases like this it would be unfair to expect the

---

63 See para 2.19.
64 For winding up, see paras 6.63 - 6.67.
65 Here we simply adopt the rule for Scheme A: see para 5.80.
66 This is important in cases where a flat changes hands: see paras 8.1 - 8.8.
67 However, a section of pipe which served one flat only would not be owned in common and hence would not be scheme property under Scheme B.

domestic units to subsidise the commercial units. Hence we suggest that the principle of equality of contribution be departed from, in relation to insurance costs, wherever it can be shown that the special characteristics of a particular unit have resulted in a higher premium.

6.40 An annual general meeting should look backwards as well as forwards. In addition to introducing his plans for the year ahead, the manager should be bound to account for the expenditure of the association during the year just ended. A manager must keep proper financial records and use them to prepare accounts for each financial year. In view of the relatively small sums involved we hesitate to require that the accounts should be audited, although it would be open to the members at a general meeting to require that an auditor be appointed. The accounts should be sent to members at the same time as the draft budget and at least 14 days before the annual general meeting. It is for the manager to fix the financial year of the association. Since accounts cannot be produced until the financial year is finished, it will often be sensible to hold the annual general meeting in the opening months of the new financial year. A suitable date would be one which is neither too early for the production of accounts for the financial year just ended nor too late for the approval of a draft budget for the current year.

6.41 We recommend that:

23(a) The manager should fix the financial year of the association.

(b) The manager should keep proper financial records of the association and prepare accounts for each financial year.

(c) Not later than 14 days before an annual general meeting the manager should send to each member -

(i) the accounts for the financial year just ended and

(ii) a draft budget for the new financial year.

(d) The draft budget should set out an estimate of the income and expenditure of the association, the total service charge for the year, and the date or dates on which the service charge will be due for payment.

(e) The draft budget may also make provision for contributions to a reserve fund.

(f) At the annual general meeting the association should be entitled either to approve the budget, whether in its original or in an amended form, or to reject it.

(g) If the budget is rejected, the manager should be bound to bring a revised draft budget to another general meeting within two months.

(h) If the budget is approved, the manager should be bound to levy the service charge accordingly and to implement the budget.

(i) The manager should be empowered without further approval to levy an additional service charge up to an amount not exceeding 25% of the total service charge for that year.

(j) The manager should not be entitled to levy further sums without first preparing a supplementary budget which is submitted to and approved by the association at a general meeting.

(k) A service charge should be levied by sending to each owner a notice setting out the amount due and the date or dates on which it is to be paid.

(l) If an owner is more than 28 days late in making payment of the service charge (or part of it) the manager should be able to charge interest on the amount outstanding at such rate (being a reasonable rate) and from such date as he may choose.

(m) The amount of service charge should be the same for each flat.

(n) **However, any additional premium on a common policy of insurance which is attributable to the special characteristics of a particular flat or the purposes for which it is used, should be payable by the owner of that flat.**

(o) **A reserve fund should be adequately invested and should be kept separately from the general funds of the association.**

(Scheme B, rules 7(d) and (e), 10 and 11)

Maintenance and improvements

6.42 Whereas under Scheme A each repair must be individually sanctioned by the owners,[68] in Scheme B most of the decision-making is delegated to the manager. As part of his duties a manager must carry out regular inspections of the property. Where maintenance is found to be required he is able to instruct it without the specific approval of the owners; and, provided that he has done his budgeting properly, the association should already be in funds to pay for the cost. The manager should monitor the work and not release the money until he is satisfied that it has been properly carried out.

6.43 The extent to which the owners play a part in the maintenance process is largely a matter for them. Often - perhaps very often - they will be content to pay their service charges and to allow the manager to make his own decisions, which can then be reported at the next annual general meeting. A more interventionist approach would be to require the manager to list in advance, as part of the annual budgeting process, the maintenance which is likely to be required over the next 12 months. The list could then be discussed and, if necessary, amended by the owners. Even if no detailed list is requested or produced, owners are always free at a general meeting to require of the manager that a particular repair be carried out or, as the case may be, not be carried out.[69] Owners may also have to make a decision as to whether payment should made from the general funds of the association or from the reserve fund.[70]

6.44 We do not think that the manager's discretionary powers should extend beyond maintenance so as to include alterations and improvements.[71] "Maintenance" here carries the same meaning as in Scheme A.[72] While the association has a general power to make alterations and improvements to scheme property,[73] such power should only be capable of being exercised by the owners at a general meeting. A similar restriction operates in a number of other countries.[74] We recommended earlier that alterations and improvements should require to be agreed by an absolute majority of owners and not merely by a majority of those who happen to be present at the meeting.[75] Even so, this remains a more lenient rule than at common law where improvements to common property require unanimity.

6.45 In some cases property which is scheme property under Scheme B may turn out to be individually owned.[76] That a sole owner should not have his property altered or improved against his will is a principle which hardly needs to be justified. Accordingly we suggest that, notwithstanding an appropriate vote at a general meeting, an act of alteration or improvement should not be allowed to go ahead unless the owner consents in writing at the time when the work is to be carried out.

---

68 Although there is power to delegate to a factor or manager: see para 5.73.

69 This is because the general meeting is empowered to give the manager instructions or to impose restrictions on his authority. See para 6.19 and recommendation 21(b).

70 A payment from the reserve fund requires to be authorised by an absolute majority of the total number of votes: see para 6.30 and recommendation 22(n)(ii).

71 "Alterations" and "improvements" are not synonyms. The replacement of a tennis court with a swimming pool is an alteration but not, or at least not necessarily, an improvement.

72 Paras 5.40 - 5.51 and recommendation 10(b).

73 Para 6.9 and recommendation 18(f)(i).

74 For a summary account, see van der Merwe, paras 348 and 374.

75 Para 6.30 and recommendation 22(n)(iii).

76 In other words, property falling within rule 16.1(b) of Scheme B.

6.46 We recommend that:

24(a) The manager should be under a duty to carry out regular inspections of the scheme property and to arrange for maintenance.

(b) No alteration or improvement should be carried out to scheme property which is individually owned unless the owner has given his consent in writing.

(Scheme B, rules 7(a) and (b) and 12.2)

Payment of debts

6.47 In most cases the only assets of an owners' association will be the contributions received from its members by way of service charge. The amount held at any one time will vary depending on the incidence of particular items of expenditure but, unless a reserve fund is in place, the total assets of the association are always likely to be small. This may cause difficulties in practice. A contractor will be reluctant to undertake expensive work on a tenement unless he has clear assurance of payment. As in the case of tenements governed by Management Scheme A, he may insist that he is put in funds first, or at least that earmarked funds are placed in trust for payment on completion of the contract. But arrangements of this kind may not always be possible or, even if possible, desirable. Further, any funds which are set aside might not in the end be sufficient to meet the full cost of the work. In those circumstances the contractor will not be content with a remedy against the association but will wish a right of direct recourse against the individual members.

6.48 A right of direct recourse against members is a standard feature of management schemes in other countries,[77] although precise techniques differ. We support its adoption for Scotland also. In practice it is not likely to be used very often. Faced with an unpaid bill, the association will simply levy an additional service charge on its members,[78] so that there will be direct recourse by the manager rather than by the creditor. A creditor will need to act only where the internal organisation of an association is so moribund that service charges are no longer being raised.

6.49 An important initial question is whether members should be liable *in solidum* for the whole unpaid debts of the association, or whether each member should be liable only for his own individual share.[79] Here the underlying issue is whether inconvenience should lie with the creditor or with the members. If a member is liable only for his own share of the debt, the creditor has the inconvenience of having to recover individually from each. Conversely, if members are liable *in solidum* any one member can be made to pay the whole debt of the association and will be left with the labour of recovery *pro rata* from his fellow members. In most other countries the liability of individual members is restricted to their own share, and we are persuaded that this is the correct approach. Joint and several liability seems too great a burden for the owner of an individual flat. Unlike the creditor, he has no commercial involvement in the contract. He may have no liquid assets and might have to sell the flat to pay the bill. He might even become bankrupt. By contrast, the creditor is much better able to protect himself. The contract was freely entered into and the terms of payment were a matter of negotiation. It was for him to assess the commercial risks.

6.50 One possible method of providing for direct recourse would be to allow diligence against members on the basis of an initial decree against the association. This solution is used in partnership law, where each partner is liable *in solidum* for the debts of the firm.[80] It would work less well where, as here, individual liability is to be restricted, for the decree would show only the total sum due and not the amounts due from each individual member. A further problem is the potentially large number of members of an owners' association and the difficulty, in some cases at least,[81] of establishing their identity. Where

77 See for example Sectional Titles Act No 95 of 1986 s 47 (South Africa).

78 Para 6.35.

79 The share would be calculated on the same basis as service charges. In the enacted version of Scheme B the basis of liability would be equality: see para 6.39.

80 Partnership Act 1890 s 4(2).

81 For example, where a flat has recently been sold.

there was a dispute, questions of identity would require to be resolved judicially. These considerations point to a requirement of separate decrees against individual members in respect of individual indebtedness. This would allow for the proper constitution of individual debts, and avoid the risk of the wrong debtor being pursued for the wrong amount. Of course in many cases the members will simply pay their share without the need for court process. There is no reason to suppose a greater reluctance to pay a share of a repair bill directly, to the creditor, than to pay the same share indirectly, to the manager.

6.51 We suggest that direct recourse is achieved most simply by allowing the creditor to levy an additional service charge as if he were the manager. This has the advantage of making the creditor subject to the ready-made procedural rules set out in Scheme B.[82] Thus no liability would arise until a written request for payment had been made. The proportion due from each flat would be determined by the appropriate rule. Where a flat had changed hands in the period between the work being carried out and payment being requested, liability would rest with the new owner and not with the old.[83] Finally, the creditor would be protected against the insolvency of an owner, because any payment which proved irrecoverable could be recovered *pro rata* from the other owners,[84] and so to this extent, at least, there is liability of the members *in solidum*.

6.52 Direct recourse should not be available unless the creditor has tried, and failed, to obtain payment from the association. In effect, the members are acting as cautioners for the debts of the association, but as cautioners they should not be denied the benefit of discussion. Hence as a condition of direct recourse, the creditor should be required to constitute the debt against the association, whether by decree or by registration for execution; and where the association appears to have assets he should first attempt to attach these assets by diligence. Only where he has sought recovery but failed should direct recourse be available.

6.53 A problem may arise if the association has been dissolved or is in the course of being wound up. There may then be no one for the creditor to sue. In that situation the creditor should be permitted to proceed directly against those who were owners of flats as at the date of commencement of the winding up as if Scheme B were, to that extent, still in force.

6.54 We recommend that

25 In Management Scheme B where either (i) the association is being or has been wound up or (ii) a debt due by the association has been constituted by decree or a document has been registered in the Books of Council and Session or the sheriff court books, and the creditor has executed diligence but not recovered the debt, then the creditor should be entitled to recover the debt from the members, as if he were the manager.

(Clause 10)

Transactions with third parties

6.55 We next consider whether special protection is needed for third parties who transact with the owners' association. The potential risks here are well-known. By contrast with a natural person, a body corporate does not have unlimited legal capacity. On the contrary, its capacity is limited by reference to the objects for which it was formed and any act which goes beyond those objects is, in principle, *ultra vires* and void. Furthermore, a body corporate cannot act directly for itself but depends on agents acting on its behalf. In the case of an owners' association, the normal agent will be the manager. But an agent's powers are not unlimited. How is a contractor to determine that the manager who offers an attractive contract for a major repair is acting within his powers? Thus third parties require a degree of protection. There is, however, a need for balance here. A provision which said that all contracts entered into by a manager bind the association regardless of *vires* or authority to act would be attractive to third parties

82 See paras 6.38 and 6.39.
83 See paras 8.1 - 8.8.
84 Para 6.6, and Scheme B, rule 11.6.

but unfair to the owners of flats in a tenement. It would mean that the association, and hence its members, would be bound by a contract entered into by the manager to buy an aeroplane or a shopping centre. The question to be decided is whether an appropriate balance is already struck by the general law, or whether there is a need for a special statutory rule.

6.56 Under the general law, a contract beyond the *vires* of a body corporate is void; and while in recent years this rule has been abolished in the case of most companies incorporated under the Companies Acts,[85] it remains in place for other bodies corporate. We are not persuaded that *ultra vires* should be abolished in the case of owners' associations. The objects and powers of such associations are narrowly defined. In essence an association has only such powers as are necessary for the management of the scheme property of the tenement. Furthermore, an association is not permitted to trade, or buy land.[86] The narrowness of the powers is intended as a protection to the members. That protection would be wholly defeated if the *ultra vires* rule ceased to operate. We do not think that the *ultra vires* rule is unfair to third parties. Owners' associations are not like ordinary companies. There is no significant diversity in their objects and powers. A third party will know that he is dealing with an association because "owners' association" will appear as part of its name,[87] and he will know, or ought to know, that an owners' association has only limited powers.

6.57 Under Scheme B a manager is an agent of the association and can exercise all of its powers.[88] Thus, provided that an act is *intra vires* of the association it can usually be performed by the manager. There is an identity between the powers of the association and the powers of the manager; and this simple principle disposes of most of the difficulties which arise in other bodies corporate where an agent exceeds his powers. From the point of view of a third party, three possible difficulties remain. First, the third party will wish to be sure that the person conducting the negotiations is truly the manager of the association. Secondly, special procedural rules apply in the case of improvements to scheme property (as opposed to ordinary acts of maintenance), which must be approved by the association by a special majority at a general meeting.[89] Finally, the members can vote at a general meeting for limits on the powers of the manager thus removing, in what is likely to be an unusual case, the identity between the powers of the association and the powers of the manager.[90]

6.58 There is no perfect solution to the first difficulty, which is a general problem in the law of agency. Scheme B goes perhaps as far as is useful by making provision for a written certificate of appointment executed on behalf of the association.[91] The possibility of procedural irregularity in relation to improvements seems covered by the rule in *Royal British Bank v Turquand*.[92] A person entering into a contract with an association in good faith to carry out improvements to scheme property would not be affected by a prior failure to put the matter to a vote at a general meeting. The most difficult issue is the final one. It would be possible to make express statutory provision that, in a question with a third party, a manager is deemed to exercise all the powers of the association.[93] But this seems neither desirable nor necessary. It is not desirable because it leans too far in the direction of the third party and leaves association members too vulnerable to unauthorised liabilities undertaken by the manager. And it is not necessary because the common law of agency already provides a more balanced solution.[94] At common law an agent binds his principal if he acts within his apparent authority even where the act is beyond his actual authority. To benefit from this rule a third party dealing with the agent must be in good faith in the sense that he must not know, or reasonably suspect, the absence of actual authority. Since, in the normal case,

---

85 Companies Act 1985 s 35 (inserted by Companies Act 1989 s 108(1)).
86 Para 6.9 and recommendation 18(g).
87 Scheme B, rule 1.2.
88 Paras 6.12 and 6.13.
89 Para 6.30 and recommendation 22(n)(iii).
90 Para 6.19 and recommendation 21(b).
91 Para 6.13 and recommendation 19(e).
92 (1855) 5 E & B 248.
93 This is close to the effect achieved by s 35A of the Companies Act 1985. But there are special reasons for this provision, including the need to be consistent with the abolition of *ultra vires* effected by s 35.
94 Of course it would be possible to re-state the common law, as has been done in the case of partnerships (by s 5 of the Partnership Act 1890), but perhaps not very useful.

a manager may exercise all the powers of the owners' association, it can hardly be doubted that such powers fall within his actual authority. Hence a third party could rely on the manager's power to bind in all matters concerning the management of the tenement unless he knew of a restriction on the manager's power or unless the proposed contract was so extravagant or unusual that the possibility of a restriction might reasonably be expected.

Names and addresses of members

6.59 Under our proposals an owners' association is largely unregulated. There is no register of owners' associations. There is no requirement to make public the name of the manager, or of the members. The association accounts need not be audited let alone be made available for public inspection. The only information that is publicly available, by means of the Sasine or Land Register, is the fact that the tenement is governed by Scheme B and hence that an owners' association is in existence. This lack of regulation is deliberate. Scheme B would be extremely unattractive if associations were regulated in the same manner as a company incorporated under the Companies Acts. No higher degree of formality should be required than is absolutely necessary for a body which has only modest administrative responsibilities coupled with a modest budget. One indispensable formality, however, is an accurate list of members. The manager must know who the members are and, if they are non-resident, where they live, for under the rules of the scheme he has to communicate with members quite frequently and to recover payment of service charges from them. The duty of maintaining an accurate list of names and addresses should fall on the manager, but to assist him an owner who is about to dispose of his flat should be obliged to provide a forwarding address as well as the name and address of the incoming owner and of his solicitor. The manager should also be told the date on which the new owner is to become entitled to take entry.[95] In practice, the rules about transmission of liability[96] are likely to encourage the purchaser's solicitor to make early contact with the manager to enquire about outstanding service charges, the state of any reserve fund, the projected budget for the year, and no doubt other matters also.

6.60 The register of names and addresses should be available for any member of the association to inspect, as should any other documentation held by the manager in relation to the tenement. However, in the interests of confidentiality there should be no obligation on the manager to disclose correspondence with individual members.

6.61 We recommend that:

26(a) The manager should be under a duty to keep a record of the name and address of each member of the association.

(b) On disposal of a flat an owner should be obliged to notify the manager of -

(i) his own forwarding address;

(ii) the name and address of the new owner;

(iii) the name and address of the solicitor or other agent acting for the new owner; and

(iv) the date on which the new owner will be entitled to take entry.

(c) Any member should be entitled to inspect any document relating to the management of the tenement which is in the possession of the manager or which it is reasonably practicable for the manager to obtain; but this entitlement should not extend to correspondence passing between the manager and individual members.

(Scheme B, rules 7(h) and 15.1 and 15.2)

---

95 In practice this is usually the date on which the acquirer is considered to become "owner": see paras 8.27 and 8.28 and recommendation 36(d).

96 For these rules see Part 8.

Execution of deeds

6.62 From time to time the association may have to sign contracts or execute deeds. We suggest that it be provided that an association signs through its manager or some other person nominated for this purpose at a general meeting.[97] Under the Requirements of Writing (Scotland) Act 1995 the addition of a witness's signature would make the document self-proving or "probative".[98] Thus we recommend that:

> **27 A document should be treated as signed by an owners' association if it is signed on its behalf by the manager or by a person nominated for the purpose by the association at a general meeting.**

(Scheme B, rule 4)

Winding up and dissolution of owners' association

6.63 An owners' association is required for as long as Scheme B is in operation; but if Scheme B ceases to govern there is no further role for such an association. We recommended earlier[99] that the association should come into existence on the date on which Scheme B first applies to a tenement. We now make the parallel recommendation that the winding up of the association should begin on the date on which Scheme B ceases to apply. There are only two occasions on which Scheme B might cease to apply. The first is where the owners decide to replace Scheme B with Scheme A or some other management scheme. The second is where the tenement is demolished or otherwise destroyed. In both cases disapplication is effected by deed of conditions,[100] following a vote by special majority at a general meeting.[101] The deed must be registered in the Land Register or Register of Sasines.

6.64 Who should conduct the winding up? In the case of a members' voluntary winding up of a company, a liquidator is appointed by the company at a general meeting.[102] However, by comparison with most companies an owners' association is likely to have few assets and the conduct of the winding up will be a simple affair. We see no reason why the winding up should not be carried out by the manager, although, as always under Scheme B, the members could if they wished appoint a new manager specially for the winding up.[103]

6.65 The winding up will begin on the day when Scheme B ceases to apply to the tenement. From that date the association will lose its power to manage the tenement, and the manager's role will be confined to paying the debts of the association and distributing any remaining assets to its members. Just as each owner of a flat has an equal liability for association costs,[104] so each owner should have an equal entitlement to association assets.[105] The manager must produce final accounts and send them to all members. In most cases winding up should take only a few weeks, but in any event the manager should be taken bound to complete the winding up, including the production of final accounts, within six months, except where the members decide otherwise. The association will dissolve automatically on completion of the time set for the winding up.

6.66 An association will not usually become insolvent. If it cannot meet its debts, the manager can raise money by means of an additional service charge[106] or, if he fails to do so, any creditor can act in

97 Under the Requirements of Writing (Scotland) Act 1995 the execution of documents by bodies corporate other than a company or local authority is regulated by para 5 of Schedule 2. Our proposal will replace the default rule set out in para 5(2).

98 1995 Act s 3(1) (as applied to bodies corporate by Schedule 2, para 5(5)).

99 Para 6.7 and recommendation 18(a).

100 Under clause 5(2) of the Bill.

101 Para 6.30 and recommendation 22(n)(i).

102 Insolvency Act 1986 s 91.

103 Members are always free to replace the manager at a general meeting: see paras 6.11 and 6.14 and recommendation 19(b) and (h).

104 Para 6.39 and recommendation 23(m).

105 However, this rule can be varied by the deed of conditions which brings Scheme B into operation.

106 Para 6.35 and recommendation 23(i).

his place.[107] Nonetheless, the theoretical possibility of insolvency remains. We do not think that insolvency should be a ground for the winding up of the association. Scheme B presupposes the continuing existence of the association, and the Scheme could no longer operate if the association came to be dissolved. Under the present law, bodies corporate which are not companies are subject to sequestration under the Bankruptcy (Scotland) Act 1985,[108] and not to liquidation, and we propose that an owners' association should likewise be subject to sequestration.

6.67 We recommend that

28(a) If Management Scheme B ceases to apply to a tenement, the winding up of the owners' association should begin on the day of such cessation.

(b) The winding up should end after a period of six months or on such other date as the members may decide, whereupon the association should be automatically dissolved.

(c) The winding up should be conducted by the manager, who should

(i) pay any debts of the association;

(ii) distribute any remaining funds of the association to those who owned flats at the date of the commencement of the winding up, an equal share being apportioned to each flat; and

(iii) prepare and send to each member final accounts of the association showing how the winding up was conducted and the funds of the association disposed of.

(d) Once Scheme B has been disapplied, and the winding up commenced, the owners' association should cease to manage the scheme property of the tenement.

(e) An insolvent association should be subject to sequestration proceedings under the Bankruptcy (Scotland) Act 1985.

(Scheme B, rules 5 and 15.4)

Taxation

6.68 In taxation terms our proposals[109] are thought to be neutral and do not give rise to liabilities which are not already encountered in the management of tenements. Nonetheless it may be helpful to review briefly the taxation position of an owners' association.

6.69 An owners' association is a body corporate and hence a separate legal person. For the purposes of income and corporation tax it is classified as a "company" - a classification which applies equally to unincorporated residents' associations under present law and practice.[110] The owners' association will be liable to corporation tax on such income as it has - in practice, usually only interest and other income from funds which have been invested. Corporation tax will be payable at the small companies rate, currently 21%, although in the calculation of taxable income no account can be taken of management expenses.[111] An association with five members or fewer would probably be classified as a close company,[112] and also as a close investment-holding company,[113] which would have the undesirable consequence of attracting the full rate of corporation tax, currently 31%. However, in practice we do not expect Scheme B to be used for small tenements,[114] and indeed the taxation position is a further reason for discouraging such use.

107 Paras 6.47 - 6.54 and recommendation 25.
108 Bankruptcy (Scotland) Act 1985 s 6(1)(c), (2).
109 Including our proposals for Scheme A.
110 Income and Corporation Taxes Act 1988 s 832(1).
111 See eg *Tintern Close Residents Society Ltd v Winter* [1995] STC 57.
112 Income and Corporation Taxes Act 1988 s 414.
113 Income and Corporation Taxes Act 1988 s 13A (inserted by Finance Act 1989 s 105).
114 Para 6.3.

6.70 The payments of service charge will not normally be subject to tax. Certainly they are not subject to corporation tax: the identity between those who contribute to the management fund and those entitled to participate in any surplus brings into play the mutuality principle and prevents the payments from being treated as income of the association.[115] Nor will VAT be payable except in highly unusual cases. Currently VAT is payable only where there is a taxable turnover of £48,000. In relation to an owners' association the only part of the turnover which is likely to count towards this figure is the fee paid to the manager.[116] It seems safe to assume that this figure will not be exceeded, but in any event service charges paid by the occupants of residential property are the subject of an extra-statutory concession by Customs and Excise.[117] However, while VAT will not be due on the service charge as such, it may need to be paid on specific services provided by third parties, such as builders or indeed professional managers.

115 *English and Scottish Joint Co-operative Wholesale Society Ltd v Commissioner of Agricultural Income Tax, Assam* [1948] AC 405; *Municipal Mutual Insurance Ltd v Hills* (1932) 16 TC 430; *Walter Fletcher v Income Tax Commissioner* [1972] AC 414.

116 *Trustees of the Nell Gwyn House Maintenance Fund v Customs & Excise Commissioners* [1996] STC 310. We understand that there may be an appeal from this decision to the House of Lords.

117 Extra-statutory concession on Service Charges on Dwellings, effective from 1 April 1994. This exempts various mandatory service charges paid by occupants for residential property from VAT.

Part 7 Common Interest

General doctrine or specific rules?

7.1 In a tenement there are separate flats but only one building. These physical facts have consequences. Each owner is unusually vulnerable to the behaviour of his neighbours; and at the same time each shares with the others an interest in the well-being of the building as a whole. This means that the normal rules of ownership cannot operate unchecked, and that each owner must accept restraints on the use made of his own property, in the interests of the tenement as a whole.

7.2 The restraining mechanism developed by the common law was common interest. At common law each person in a tenement owns his own flat, but in addition he has a right of common interest in those parts of the building which he does not own. Common interest comprises both a right and also an obligation. An owner is restrained in the use which he makes of his flat; but he has a right to insist that similar restraints apply to his neighbours. The early law was content to identify common interest and to name it, and it was then for the courts to develop its content on a case by case basis. By about the middle of the nineteenth century the content of common interest had become fixed in the form of a small number of specific rules. In summary these rules are:[1]

(i) that an owner must maintain his own property to the extent that it provides support and shelter for the rest of the building;

(ii) that an owner may not alter his property if to do so would imperil support or shelter;

(iii) that the owner of any land forming part of the tenement may not build on that land so as to interfere with the natural light enjoyed by any flat; and

(iv) that the owner of a wall must allow the use of any pre-existing chimney flues.

7.3 We are satisfied that these are useful rules which should be taken over into the new law. But a preliminary question is whether this is best done by preserving the general doctrine of common interest, or by re-stating the specific rules. We have come to the view that the latter would be the more sensible course. The general doctrine now serves no useful purpose. The law has long since ceased to develop. The general doctrine has been transformed into four rules, and this change should be acknowledged in any new legislation. Moreover common interest is in some respects an unsatisfactory doctrine, defying easy analysis.[2] It is not ownership, but neither is it servitude or real burden. It overlaps with nuisance and resembles it in arising by operation of law, but is nonetheless part of the law of property and not of the law of obligations. Common interest is persistently confused with common property, although the similarities are confined to a shared first word. We think that nothing would be lost, and something gained, by the express abolition of common interest in the context of tenements. However, common interest would continue to survive in a small number of other contexts, most notably boundary walls (including common gables between tenements) and non-tidal rivers and lochs. We therefore recommend that:

29 The common law doctrine of common interest should be abolished to the extent that it applies to tenements.

(Clause 11)

---

1 Reid paras 232-7; Gordon paras 15-31 - 15-45.
2 Reid, paras 354-74.

Support and shelter

7.4 In relation to support and shelter common interest imposes both a positive obligation (to maintain one's property) and also a negative one (to refrain from alterations).[3]

7.5 There are only two reported cases in which the positive obligation has been enforced, one from 1695 and the other from 1826.[4] This suggests that in practice the positive obligation is not very important. Under our proposals its role will be diminished still further. With the introduction of management schemes, repairs should be carried out more often and more readily than under the present law; and a repair which is genuinely necessary for support or shelter is likely to command majority support and hence to be undertaken promptly. At one stage, indeed, we were tending towards the view that the positive obligation could be dispensed with altogether. Nonetheless we are now persuaded that it should be retained. Everyone in a tenement has an interest in its structural integrity. The value of individual flats depends on the state of the building as a whole. A persistent failure to maintain the roof and the walls would, in the end, make the individual flats uninhabitable. We think that an owner who is unable to persuade a sufficient number of his neighbours to carry out a repair ought to have a second line of attack.[5] If the repair is essential for shelter or support he should be able to insist, if necessary by litigation, that it be carried out. In practice the prospect of litigation would often of itself persuade the majority to act. We do not imagine that attempts to enforce the positive obligation of support and shelter would be more common than they are at present.

7.6 There is also a second reason why the positive obligation should be retained. The management schemes do not apply to every part of the building which might conceivably be of structural significance. While scheme property, under both Schemes A and B, extends to external walls and to any internal walls which are load-bearing, other load-bearing parts - floors, joists, columns and the like - are not included.[6] Parts which are not scheme property are not maintained at common expense,[7] and without a positive obligation of support and shelter there would be nothing to stop the owners of those parts allowing them to fall into disrepair.

7.7 At common law the positive obligation of support and shelter is laid on the person who owns the part in question. Thus the owner of the roof must maintain the roof for shelter, while a corresponding obligation of maintenance for support is laid on the owners of walls and other structural parts. There is some tension between this rule and the manner in which the management schemes are likely to operate. Under the management schemes there is no necessary connection between ownership and maintenance. All property which is scheme property is commonly maintained, but not all scheme property is owned in common.[8] Hence, unless special provision is made, there is a danger that, in relation to any scheme property which is individually owned, a majority of owners might block a repair in the knowledge that the same repair could then be achieved, at the sole expense of the individual owner, by virtue of the positive obligation of support and shelter. For example, the roof is scheme property but it is not always common property. Under the background law it is regarded as a part of the top floor flat or flats. The person who is sole owner of a roof might find his neighbours unwilling to agree to a scheme repair, which would require to be paid for by everyone. He could then be forced to carry out the repair himself, at his own expense. The problem revealed by this example can be quite easily solved. We propose that the cost of a repair which is carried out to scheme property in implement of the positive obligation of support or shelter should be recoverable from the other proprietors *pro rata* as if the repair had taken place under the management scheme in force for the tenement. This rule would apply not merely where the positive obligation has been enforced against an owner but also where an owner decided, on his own initiative, that a repair necessary for support or shelter needs to be carried out. The owner of a roof who is unable to persuade his neighbours to replace some slates should be able to carry out the work himself and then

3 See para 7.2(i) and (ii).

4 *Lake v Dundass* (1695) 4 Brown's Supp 258; *McNair v McLauchlan and McKeand* (1826) 4 S 546.

5 Further lines of attack may also be available: see paras 5.45 - 5.50.

6 Para 5.7.

7 Except of course where the titles provide otherwise.

8 Para 5.6.

recover the cost. However, his right to do so would be subject to the reasonableness test described below. Where, conversely, the property being repaired is not scheme property, the owner would have to bear the full cost of maintenance himself, except in cases (which would be unusual in practice) where the cost was redistributed by a real burden in the title of the tenement.

7.8 At common law the obligation of support and shelter is not unlimited. In *Thomson v St Cuthbert's Co-operative Association Ltd,*[9] which is the leading modern case, Lord Justice-Clerk Thomson[10] doubted whether, in relation to the obligation of shelter laid on the owner of a roof

> ".. his obligation to maintain the roof is an absolute one which persists in perpetuity, whatever age the property has reached or into whatever condition it has fallen .. [N]o .. absolute obligation exists and .. the obligation to keep one's own part of the tenement in conformity with common interest is a relative one and falls to be measured by the standard of the prudent man of affairs."

The point may arrive at which a building has ceased to be worth repairing. Of course, in theory it is always possible to repair a building, even where it is in a dilapidated state, but the huge cost of doing so is likely to be out of all scale with any possible benefits which might result. Thus we accept the principle of the common law that an owner should not be forced to throw good money after bad. Under the management schemes contained in our proposals, owners are free to make their own decisions on repairs, without reference to the positive obligation of support and shelter. If a decision to carry out repairs is foolish, it can be challenged by application to the sheriff. The sheriff can annul a decision to carry out repairs where it is not in the best interests of the owners, having regard in particular to the age and condition of the building and the probable cost of carrying out the work.[11] In our view identical qualifications should apply to the positive obligation of support and shelter. An owner should not be bound to maintain where to do so would be unreasonable, having regard in particular to the age and condition of the tenement and the likely cost of any maintenance. One practical reason for using a uniform test is that it should not be easier to carry out an unwise repair under the positive obligation of support and shelter than under the rules of the management schemes.

7.9 Failure to comply with the positive obligation may result in consequential damage to a neighbour's property. For example, if the top floor owner neglects the roof, there may be rain penetration to the flat underneath. Under general principles of delict, liability for such damage would not be strict but would depend on a finding of fault. It would have to be shown, for example, that the owner had a duty of inspection which he had failed to discharge, or that he had known of the defect but had taken no steps to see to its repair. Common interest did not depart from this established principle[12] and there seems no reason why its statutory replacement should do so either. No express provision seems necessary on this subject.

7.10 We turn now to the negative obligation, which is an obligation to refrain from any alterations to or work on the building which might interfere with support or shelter.[13] That such an obligation is needed seems self-evident. Owners who are bent on a programme of renovation and improvement must have proper regard to the integrity of the building as a whole. Where there is a genuine risk to the building, the other owners should be able to prevent the works from taking place. The standard example is where an owner interferes with a wall or other part which is of structural significance. In a sequence of cases decided at the beginning of the nineteenth century, owners were interdicted from adding new doors and lengthening windows for fear that the gable wall would be materially weakened.[14] Today better building

---

9 1958 SC 380.

10 At p 390.

11 Para 5.22 and recommendation 7(f). The sheriff is also to have regard to the reasonableness of the cost. For example, he may decide that it is both possible and sensible that a particular repair be carried out more cheaply. But this is not relevant for common interest.

12 *Thomson v St Cuthbert's Co-operative Association Ltd* 1958 SC 380.

13 Para 7.2(ii).

14 *Fergusson v Marjoribanks* 12 Nov 1816 FC; *Pirnie v McRitchie* 5 June 1819 FC; *Dennistoun v Bell and Brown* (1824) 2 S 784; *Gray v Greig* (1825) 4 S 104.

techniques may have made alterations safer and hence less subject to challenge. The negative obligation applies to the whole building and not merely to those parts which currently provide support or shelter. For example, the owner of a top floor flat is disabled from installing a swimming pool, or adding an additional storey, because both would increase significantly the loading in the building.

7.11 Under the existing law it is uncertain whether the obligation of support and shelter extends to parts of the building which are owned in common, such as the common passage and stair.[15] But there seems no reason to make any distinction. The mere fact that a part is common property should not relieve its owners from the obligation to maintain it, or to refrain from acts tending to make it less serviceable. The obligations of support and shelter should apply to the entire building, regardless of ownership. A slightly different question is whether the obligation should be confined to the owner or owners or whether it should extend also to tenants and other occupiers. It seems fairly clear that the positive obligation, which involves the expenditure of money, should be confined to owners. But there seems no reason why the negative obligation should be so confined. If a tenant of commercial property, holding on a 99-year lease, proposes to demolish a load-bearing wall, it is unsatisfactory to say that the only remedy of his neighbours is against the landlord, and that the ability of the landlord to restrain his tenant will then depend on the terms of the lease. We propose therefore that the negative obligation should be enforceable against occupiers as well as against owners.

7.12 Currently the right to enforce rests with the owners of the flats in the tenement. However, we suggest that an owner should not be able to enforce where he is unable to show any interest to do so. Such cases will be rare. Later we recommend the introduction of a right of access in cases where this is needed to monitor compliance.[16]

7.13 We recommend that:

30(a) Any part of the tenement building which provides, or is designed to provide, support or shelter should be maintained by its owner to a standard sufficient to provide that support or shelter; but maintenance should not be required where it is not reasonable, having regard in particular to the age of the tenement, its condition and the likely cost of the maintenance.

(b) Where in implement of (a) an owner carries out maintenance to property which is scheme property under the management scheme applying to the tenement, he should be entitled to recover from any other owner any share of the cost for which that other owner would have been liable if the maintenance had been carried out under the scheme.

(c) An owner or occupier should not be entitled to carry out work on the tenement if it would or would be reasonably likely to impair support or shelter to a material extent.

(d) The obligations contained in this recommendation and in recommendation 31 should be enforceable by the owner of any flat in the tenement who has an interest to do so.

(Clauses 12 - 14)

Beyond support and shelter

7.14 Occasionally it is suggested that the common interest within a tenement building might extend beyond support and shelter. In particular it has been said that common interest protects any "danger or injury" to individual flats, or the "security or interest of the other proprietors".[17] In the case in which these remarks were made, an owner was prevented from opening doors in the common gable between that tenement and an adjoining building. Although the decision turned mainly on other matters, mention was made of the increased risk of the spread of fire. But this decision is hardly authority for an extension

15 Reid, para 232.
16 Paras 10.10 - 10.21 and recommendation 43.
17 *Gellatly v Arrol* (1863) 1 M 592 at 595 per Lord Kinloch and at 599 per Lord Justice-Clerk Inglis.

of common interest. The court seemed unclear whether the mutual gable was a matter of common property or of common interest, and the decision was distinguished in a later case[18] where the opening of a door in the common gable was allowed. The point is perhaps not very important, for it is difficult to think of an alteration which would pose a general danger to the building without at the same time imperilling either support or shelter.

7.15 A much more important issue in modern practice is dry rot and other forms of infestation. If an outbreak of dry rot occurs in one part of the building, it may spread rapidly unless preventive action is taken. Where dry rot originates in scheme property, eradication will be a scheme repair and there should be no real difficulty.[19] But if the rot occurs, and is known to have occurred, within an individual flat, it may not always be easy to persuade the owner to incur the expenditure necessary for proper eradication. We considered whether the positive obligation to maintain discussed earlier should be extended to include a positive obligation to eradicate dry rot and similar infestations, even where these do not directly interfere with support and shelter. However, we are satisfied that the situation is already sufficiently covered under the general law. The spread of dry rot has been recognised as constituting a nuisance, in the legal sense.[20] Hence if there are reasonable grounds for supposing that dry rot might spread from one flat to another, the owner of the flat at risk could seek an interdict, with the result that the owner of the affected flat would be bound to carry out a programme of eradication. Alternatively, there is some authority to suggest that the owner at risk could, with due notice, enter the affected flat and carry out the work himself.[21]

7.16 There may be other cases also where nuisance is an alternative, or supplement, to common interest (or its statutory replacement). Even the loss of support within a tenement has been held to be actionable in nuisance.[22] If the law of nuisance had existed at the time when the common law of the tenement was first developing, it might not have been necessary to invent common interest at all.[23]

7.17 So far we have considered only physical damage. But an owner may also suffer economic damage through the activities of his neighbours, for the market value of a flat is affected by the condition or use of the other flats in the building. In some cases where market value is reduced, the neighbour's activities might be perfectly reasonable in themselves, such as the conversion of a ground floor dwelling-house into a restaurant. At other times they might be harder to justify, as where an owner paints the glass in his windows pink, or sells the slates on the roof and replaces them with an inferior covering. We considered, but in the end rejected, a prohibition on activities which might tend to reduce the market value of other flats in the tenement. Such a prohibition would require to be qualified by reference to the reasonableness of the activity contemplated; but, as so qualified, it would apply so rarely as hardly to be worth introducing. Furthermore, and by contrast with loss of support or shelter, the loss of market value is not an issue which is confined to tenements, although it may arise there in a heightened form. Even where properties are physically separate, the value of one may often be affected by the use made of another. Hence, if a statutory solution is required, it should not be confined to tenements. Finally, the problem, such as it is, is dealt with at least to some extent by the existing law. Thus activities amounting to abuse of the right of ownership could be challenged under the law of nuisance or *aemulatio vicini*; and certain types of use, such as use for commercial purposes, are quite commonly prohibited by real burdens.

Right to light

7.18 Common interest also applies outside the tenement building. At common law the garden and other land must not be built upon in such a way as to interfere with the natural light reaching individual flats.[24]

---

18 *Todd v Wilson* (1894) 22 R 172.

19 The joists between flats will not usually be scheme property. See para 5.7. The cost of eradicating dry rot in the joists will therefore be a shared expense for the owners of the two flats concerned. See D J Cusine (ed), *The Conveyancing Opinions of J M Halliday* (1992) pp 207-10.

20 *Watt v Jamieson* 1954 SC 56.

21 *Stair Memorial Encyclopaedia* vol 14, para 2158.

22 *Macnab v McDevitt* 1971 SLT (Sh Ct) 41; *Kennedy v Glenbelle Ltd* 1996 SC 95.

23 *Stair Memorial Encyclopaedia* vol 14, para 2030.

24 Para 7.2(iii).

In effect there is right to light, analogous to a servitude of light.[25] The prohibition is confined to light, and does not prevent building which is injurious only to prospect[26] or to general amenity.[27] The common law here seems well-judged and it was not suggested to us that it ought to be changed. We therefore recommend that:

31. An owner or occupier should not be allowed to build on any land forming part of the tenement if this interferes with the natural light enjoyed by any part of the tenement building.

(Clause 13(1)(b))

In practice the right to light is important only where the land concerned is individually owned. In cases of common ownership - as, typically, with the back green - the rules of common property would prevent any new building from being erected without the consent of all of the owners.

Chimney flues

7.19 The common law position is probably that chimney flues or vents are part of the wall in which they are located, but subject to a common interest obligation to allow the discharge of smoke.[28] Thus, while a flue leading from a flat on the first floor will cease to belong to that flat once it reaches second floor level, the owner of the flat is entitled to make use of its full length to service his fire. A more logical rule, and one which sits neatly with our recommendations on pipes and other pertinents,[29] would be to allocate ownership of flues according to the flats which they serve. Accordingly, we recommend that:

32. There should attach to each flat as a pertinent ownership of any chimney flue which serves that flat.

(Clause 3(4))

---

25 *Heron v Gray* (1880) 8 R 155; *Boswell v Magistrates of Edinburgh* (1881) 8 R 986; *Arrol v Inches* (1887) 14 R 394.

26 *Birrell v Lumley* (1905) 12 SLT 719.

27 *Barclay v McEwen* (1880) 7 R 792; *Calder v Merchant Co of Edinburgh* (1886) 13 R 623.

28 *Gellatly v Arrol* (1863) 1 M 592. And see para 7.2(iv).

29 Paras 4.23 - 4.25, and recommendation 4(e)-(g).

Part 8 Liability on Disposal

Liability of outgoing owner

8.1 In this part of the report we are concerned with liability for maintenance and other costs in cases where a flat is sold or disposed of. A number of questions arise. Does a person remain liable for scheme costs once he has ceased to be owner? Does the incoming owner inherit the unpaid debts of his predecessor? If so, is there a right of relief against the previous owner, and to what extent? When does liability for a particular debt crystallise and - and a related question - when for the purposes of our proposals does a person become the "owner" of his flat?

8.2 We begin with the liability of the outgoing owner. Under the existing law liability for maintenance and other costs can arise in one of three ways. Either the titles may contain a real burden in appropriate terms; or expenditure may be required to satisfy the common interest obligations of support and shelter; or again liability may arise simply from the fact of common ownership.[1] Under our proposals, by contrast, liability will usually have as its single source the management scheme in force for the tenement, although there may occasionally be separate liability under the proposed replacement for common interest[2] or under other provisions of the legislation. The existing law seems to be that the outgoing owner is liable for all obligations which have become prestable during his period of ownership.[3] That at least is the settled rule in the case of liability founded on real burdens, and it may be hazarded that similar principles operate under the other two heads of liability also. It is not always clear when an obligation becomes prestable - or, in other words, when liability crystallises. An obligation to build a fence within two years becomes prestable, at the latest, on the expiry of the two years. But the position is less clear with general obligations of maintenance. Property is rarely so perfect that it could not benefit from maintenance. But if imperfection were enough to trigger an obligation to maintain, sellers would remain liable for routine repairs long after they had ceased to own. This suggests that a more marked degree of deterioration is probably required before a repair becomes "due". But it is not clear how much. Must all of the slates fall off a roof, or 50% of them, or only 5%? If the existing law is strong on principle it is weak on detail, and there seems no clear answer to this question.

8.3 While in some countries liability is lost automatically with ownership,[4] there seems much to be said for the principle of the existing law by which liability which has already crystallised is not avoided by the simple expedient of disposing of the property. Thus an owner who is faced with a bill for the cost of demolition of a tenement should not be able to avoid liability by transferring his stratum of airspace to a company with no assets,[5] or, more prosaically, an owner who has sale in contemplation should not be able to cast a careless vote for repairs without at the same time accepting financial responsibility for the decision.

8.4 The rules on crystallisation of liability will vary from management scheme to management scheme, but the most important thing is that they should be clear. Under Management Scheme B the position is straightforward. A service charge is collected by the manager on behalf of the owners' association, usually

1 We are concerned here only with the liability of one owner in the building to another or others. In addition there may also be liability to third parties. Thus an owner who instructs a builder to repair the roof is liable to the builder in contract. A local authority which carries out repairs in implement of a statutory notice has a right of recovery against the owners, a point pursued further at para 5.66.

2 Paras 7.4 - 7.9 and recommendation 30(a) and (b).

3 Reid, para 412.

4 For example France: see Code Civil, art 699.

5 *Marshall v Callander and Trossachs Hydropathic Co Ltd* (1895) 22 R 954.

in regular instalments. The date on which particular payments become due must be agreed at the annual general meeting and then notified to the owners in writing. It seems obvious that this should also be the date on which liability crystallises. Hence if the service charge is payable four times a year, on the last days of March, June, September and December, an owner who sells with effect from[6] 18 September will be liable for the June instalment of service charge but not for the September instalment. There is an element of rough justice here. A fastidious purchaser might take the view that the service charge should be treated as accruing evenly day by day throughout the year and ought to be apportioned accordingly. On this view the seller would have additional liability for the period from 1 July to 17 September. But such matters are best left for the parties to regulate by contract. In some cases the pattern of service charge may not be as even as in our example, and the position may be further complicated by the levying of an additional service charge to meet some unexpected expense.

8.5 Under Scheme A liability arises unpredictably and at irregular intervals, but in most cases at least it is triggered by a scheme decision. Thus we suggest that as a general rule an obligation to pay for maintenance or other scheme costs should crystallise on the date of the relevant scheme decision. A person who votes for expenditure should do so in the knowledge that immediate liability will result. Quite often projected expenditure will be discussed on more than one occasion. For example, owners having first met to decide on the principle of a repair may meet for a second or third time to consider estimates and to give the final go-ahead for the work. Here it is the final meeting which leads directly to the expenditure and hence which marks the crystallisation of liability. In cases of substantial expenditure it will be important for the owners to keep accurate records of what was decided and when.[7] If a decision is taken without a meeting, as is possible under Scheme A, the relevant date in relation to any person should be taken to be the date on which notification of the decision was sent to that person. A similar rule should also apply in relation to a person who was absent from the meeting at which a decision was taken.[8]

8.6 There are three types of cost under Scheme A for which separate provision is required. These are: the cost of emergency work; costs paid to a local authority for work carried out under a statutory notice and which the owners now wish to recover from one another; and recurrent and continuing costs such as insurance premiums and management fees. In the first two cases the expenditure is not preceded by a decision at all, while in the third the decision may be remote in time from the expenditure. Liability for emergency work should be fixed at the time when the work is ordered, and liability arising under a statutory notice from the date of the notice. The fairest way of treating costs falling into the third category is to regard them as accruing evenly day by day.

8.7 In a case where some other management scheme applies in place of Schemes A and B it is for the particular scheme to make provision for the crystallisation of liabilities.

8.8 We recommend that:

33(a) In Management Scheme A an owner should become liable for a scheme cost -

(i) on the day when the scheme decision to incur that cost was made, or

(ii) if the decision was made without a meeting or if the meeting was not attended by the owner, on the day when notification of the decision was sent to the owner.

(b) However, notwithstanding the rule set out at (a) -

(i) an owner should be liable for the cost of emergency work from the date on which the work is instructed;

6 See paras 8.28 - 8.29 for the rules on when ownership is considered to have changed.

7 See para 5.35.

8 The artificially extended meaning of date of decision suggested here follows the recommendation made earlier in the context of the running of the 21-day period for applications for judicial annulment. See para 5.23 and recommendation 7(b).

(ii) an owner should be liable (in a question with other owners) for the costs recovered by a local authority under a statutory notice from the date of the statutory notice; and

(iii) an owner should be liable for any recurrent and continuing costs on a day-to-day basis.

(c) In Management Scheme B an owner should become liable for payment of an instalment of service charge on the date specified for payment in the notice sent in terms of recommendation 23(k).

(d) An owner who has become liable for costs under the management scheme in force for the tenement or under any other of our recommendations should not cease to be liable merely because he has ceased to be owner.

(Clause 15(1); Scheme A, rules 5.9 and 5.10; Scheme B, rule 11.4)

Liability of incoming owner

8.9 The fact that the outgoing owner is liable for "prestable" obligations does not, under the existing law, exonerate the incoming owner. On the contrary, both are liable, jointly and severally, for implementation of the obligation. The position may be different where the seller has already carried out the maintenance or other work and has nothing further to do but contribute his share of the bill. In *David Watson Property Management v Woolwich Equitable Building Society*[9] the owner of a tenement flat fell into arrears of common charges. The charges comprised maintenance costs, insurance premiums and the factors' management charges. Since he was also in default in his mortgage the heritable creditors had entered into possession. The factors sought to recover from the heritable creditors the arrears of common charges. Section 20(5) of the Conveyancing and Feudal Reform (Scotland) Act 1970 assigns to a heritable creditor in possession "all rights and obligations of the proprietor relating to .. the management and maintenance of the subjects .." It was argued for the factors that the arrears of common charges were "obligations" within this provision. The House of Lords disagreed. In their Lordships' view the obligations which passed under s 20(5) were confined to those which were due *qua* proprietor; and the test for whether an obligation was due *qua* proprietor was whether, if the property came to be sold, the obligation would transmit against an incoming owner. The House of Lords considered that the obligation to pay arrears of common charges would not so transmit. There was a difference between an obligation to maintain and an obligation to pay for maintenance which had already been carried out. Only the former transmitted against successors:

> "[A]n obligation .. to maintain the subjects of the grant imposed as a condition of the title will be enforceable against singular successors. The practical carrying out of the obligation may involve payment of sums of money which can only be ascertained by reference to the nature of the required work as and when it becomes necessary. The obligation to maintain will carry with it the obligation to pay for this work, but when the obligation to pay for a particular sum thus arises that will be a debt due by the owner who was so at the time when the work was carried out. Therefore where an obligation to repair has been carried out and a debt is due in consequence by the owner who has by carrying out the work performed this obligation to repair, the obligation to pay the unpaid debt of that owner will not be transmissible. To hold the contrary would be inconsistent with the doctrine that an obligation to pay an indefinite sum of money cannot be constituted a real burden or condition of the title binding on singular successors".[10]

8.10 The decision in *David Watson* penalises the well-run tenement. If the repairs in that case had been postponed instead of being carried out expeditiously, an incoming owner - and hence presumably the heritable creditors - would have been liable for the cost. But because the repairs had already been carried out no liability transmitted. This seems wrong in principle. In any case it seems artificial and unhelpful

9 1992 SC (HL) 21.
10 1992 SC (HL) 21 at 36 *per* Lord Mackay of Clashfern.

to distinguish between the obligation to carry out repairs and the obligation to pay for repairs which have already been carried out. Both should be treated in the same way, and if the incoming owner is liable for the one he should be liable for the other also. On the more general question we have little doubt that an incoming owner ought to be liable. The rapid turnover of tenement flats is one of the main obstacles to a stable system of maintenance. The kind of problem which arises may easily be imagined. The owners agree to carry out a repair. They instruct the work. The work is duly carried out, but in the meantime one of the owners has sold his flat. The first the other owners know about this is when the removal van arrives. There is no forwarding address. Who is to pay the share of the repair costs attributable to that flat? If the outgoing owner cannot be made to pay, only two possibilities are left: either the remaining owners must pay, or the purchaser of the flat. In our view the purchaser should be liable. The purchaser at least knows about the change of ownership, he will probably know where to find the seller if a claim has to be made, and he is able to protect himself in advance by appropriate provisions in the missives. Later we consider whether some additional protection is required.[11] If the purchaser is not made liable in the manner suggested, then the fact that a flat is soon to go on the market is likely to freeze all repair proposals for the tenement. The repair may then never get done. On consultation very strong support was expressed for the view that an incoming owner should be liable for the costs left unpaid by his predecessor.[12]

8.11 The existing law is in any event far from certain. In the *David Watson* case the title obligation was in the form of a positive obligation of maintenance,[13] and the court was influenced by the fact that, in a narrow sense, this obligation had been fulfilled by the time that the heritable creditors took possession. It is not clear whether the result would have been the same or different if, as is very commonly the case, the obligation imposed by the title was to pay for maintenance rather than to carry maintenance out. For in that case the title obligation would not have been fulfilled. But even in cases where the existing law would make the purchaser liable there remain unanswered questions. The seller and purchaser are said to be liable jointly and severally, but it is not clear how liability divides *inter se*. If the purchaser is made to pay, can he recover the full cost from the seller, or part only, or none at all? Another uncertainty concerns the number of obligations in existence. Is there only a single obligation, for which seller and purchaser are liable jointly and severally? Or does the purchaser, on acquisition of ownership, become bound by a new and separate obligation? The answer may be important in relation to issues such as prescription and defences.

8.12 There are two ways in which an incoming owner might be made liable for the unpaid scheme costs of his predecessor. One is to impose real liability and the other is to impose personal liability. International comparisons yield examples of both models.[14] Real liability is achieved by securing the unpaid costs on the flat.[15] In most countries where this is done, the heritable security arises automatically and does not appear in any public register. Indeed it could hardly be otherwise: a system which required the other owners in the tenement to prepare and register an appropriate deed, rather in the manner of a local authority charging order, would not be workable in practice. Owners would only rarely get around to making the necessary arrangements, and quite often their efforts would be too late. As a result, any protection conferred would be largely illusory. Personal liability is achieved by making the incoming owner jointly and severally liable for the unpaid debts of his predecessor.[16] As we have seen, the existing law makes use of personal liability.

8.13 We are not attracted by real liability. The system of registration of title, which is expected to be extended to the whole country by 2003,[17] depends for its effectiveness on the thesis that all, or almost all, real rights affecting land can be determined from an inspection of the Land Register. We do not think

---

11 Para 8.18.

12 See para 2.18.

13 The relevant part of the deed of conditions is quoted in the report at 1989 SLT (Sh Ct) 4 at 5H.

14 Van der Merwe, paras 261-2, 268-70 and 274-5.

15 This is standard in the United States. See s 23 of the Federal Housing Administration's Model Statute 1962 for the Creation of Apartment Ownership, (the Model Statute) and art 3-116 of the Uniform Condominium Act of 1980.

16 See eg s 24 of the Model Statute where personal liability is used to supplement real liability.

17 See Registers of Scotland Executive Agency: Annual Report and Accounts 1996-97, published July 1997.

that the problem which we are trying to solve is so grave, and so intractable, that it requires an infringement of this fundamental principle. It is true that, in theory at least, real liability has the advantage that it prevails on the insolvency of the new owner, but in practice a personal liability which binds successors may achieve much the same result. Thus suppose that A sells a flat to B at a time when A owes £5000 of unpaid charges. B then becomes insolvent. A system of personal liability would mean that A and B were jointly and severally liable for the debt. Thus the other owners, or their factor, could sue A. But alternatively they could wait until B's trustee in sequestration (or heritable creditor) came to sell the flat. C, the purchaser from B's trustee, would also be jointly and severally liable for the debt and could be sued directly. In practice it is likely that C would make it a condition of the purchase that the debt was cleared by the trustee.

8.14 We suggest therefore that an incoming owner should be jointly and severally liable with his predecessor for any outstanding debts owed by that predecessor under the management scheme or under any other provision of the proposed legislation. The new owner should not be viewed as liable for a new debt. Rather he is acting as cautioner for a debt which already exists; and as with caution there should be a full right of relief. The underlying liability rests with the old owner and not with the new, and if the new owner is required by his fellow owners to pay, he should be able to make recovery from the old owner. Sometimes chains of liability may arise. Thus suppose that within a short period of time A sells a flat to B who then re-sells to C, and further suppose that A has incurred unpaid charges of £2000 and B further unpaid charges of £1000. In a question with the other owners in the tenement A would be liable for £2000 and B and C for £3000; but if C has to pay he could recover the full amount from B or alternatively £2000 from A and £1000 from B. If B has to pay he could recover £2000 from A.

8.15 Our proposals would not, of course, be retrospective. The choice seems to be to apply them either (i) to any liability incurred on or after the legislation comes into force or (ii) to any transmission of a flat on or after that date and without regard to the date of the liability. The former seems both simpler and fairer.

8.16 We recommend that:

34(a) An incoming owner of a flat should be jointly and severally liable with the former owner of that flat for any costs for which the former owner is liable under the management scheme applying to the tenement or under any other of our recommendations.

(b) Where the incoming owner pays the costs he should have a right of relief against the former owner.

(c) This rule should apply to costs for which an owner becomes liable on or after the date on which the legislation comes into force.

(Clause 15(2),(4) and (6))

8.17 Special mention may be made of statutory repairs notices.[18] Often a statutory notice does no more than act as a stimulus to have work carried out. The owners then meet and agree to have the work done. From the point of view of liability there is no difference between work commissioned in this way and work which is carried out without the prompt of a statutory notice. The position is different, however, if the owners are unable to agree on their response to the notice, so that the work comes to be carried out by the local authority. In that case the local authority will seek to recover the cost from the owners, and it is settled that, in cases where a flat has changed hands, recovery is to be made from the current owner and not from the person who was owner at the time when the original notice was served.[19] It is unclear under the present law whether the new owner has a right of relief against the old, although in practice the matter is usually regulated by the missives. Our proposals will clarify the position, at least where

18 See para 2.21.
19 *Purves v City of Edinburgh District Council* 1987 SLT 366.

Scheme A applies,[20] by fixing underlying liability at the date of the statutory notice and by providing the purchaser with a right of relief.[21]

Protection of incoming owner

8.18 If our proposals confer benefits on the owners of the remaining flats in the building, they also present risks to the new owner of the flat which is being sold. Under our proposals an incoming owner will be jointly and severally liable for the unpaid debts of his predecessor, and while a right of relief is available, he would doubtless much prefer not to have to exercise it. The key issue here is knowledge. If a purchaser knows in advance about outstanding liabilities, he can make the necessary financial adjustments before handing over the purchase price. What is to be avoided is the unpleasant surprise some weeks or months later that repairs to the tenement have been carried out but not yet paid for. It is much easier to make a retention from the purchase price than to raise an action against the seller in the exercise of a right of relief. The problem here is not, of course, a new one. It is perfectly possible under the existing law for a purchaser to become liable for the repair bills of his predecessor,[22] but under our proposals liability will transmit more frequently and so the risks to a purchaser are correspondingly increased.

8.19 There is no easy solution. A decision among the owners to carry out a particular repair is not a publicly verifiable act in the same way as a repairs notice issued by a local authority. The property enquiry certificates[23] will shed no light on private agreements made within a tenement. Moreover, in the large majority of cases where there are no repair proposals and no outstanding liabilities, there remains the familiar difficulty of proving a negative. Having considered the whole issue carefully, we doubt whether the present practice of conveyancers can be much improved upon. Enquiries must be made of the seller. If the tenement is factored, the factor or other manager can be asked to advise on repair proposals and on outstanding charges. The seller can be asked to give a warranty in missives that there are no outstanding liabilities. As a last resort the statutory right of relief will be available.

8.20 With Scheme B tenements it is possible to go further. Under Scheme B all repair and other scheme costs pass through the hands of the manager and there is little or no scope for private initiative on the part of the owners. In those circumstances, and adopting a model found in a number of other countries,[24] we suggest that the manager should be bound, on request, to issue a certificate giving details of any service charge which is outstanding in relation to the flat in question. If there are no sums outstanding the certificate should say so. So far as the purchaser is concerned, such a certificate should be treated as conclusive. In other words, a purchaser could not be asked to pay more than the figure stated in the certificate in respect of liabilities accrued up to that date. Hence if the manager were to make a mistake and under-estimate the amount outstanding, the additional amount would not be due by the purchaser and could be recovered only from the seller. No doubt in practice a purchaser would also wish to have other information, and documentation, from the manager. For example he might want details of the current service charge, the current budget, any reserve fund, and plans for future expenditure. He might also wish to see the latest accounts, and minutes of the last annual general meeting. But only the certificate in relation to service charge would carry the special status of being treated as conclusively correct.

8.21 At one time we were attracted by the idea of extending the statutory certificate to all tenements, or at least to all tenements where there was available a factor or other manager to sign it. However, in the end we concluded that this might make matters worse and not better. For on the one hand, conveyancers would feel bound to get hold of an appropriate piece of paper at all costs; and in cases where none could be obtained might insist on indemnity insurance. But on the other hand factors would often be unwilling to issue a certificate except perhaps in a form so heavily qualified that it would fail to attract the statutory

20 In practice it seems unlikely that the administration of a Scheme B tenement will be so chaotic that a local authority has to intervene to carry out repairs.

21 Recommendations 33(b)(ii) and 34(b).

22 Para 8.9.

23 Property Enquiry Certificates give details of any outstanding statutory notices for repair etc. They are issued by local authorities on request and usually at a cost.

24 Van der Merwe, paras 270 and 275; and see in particular s 24 of the Model Statute.

protection. For a factor has no control over the private initiatives of the owners. Not all repairs are routed though the factor. Thus the factor would be unable to guarantee that the liability for scheme costs affecting a particular flat does not exceed a particular figure. The most he could do would be to give details of the outstanding liabilities of which he is aware. But this he will do anyway, without the need for express statutory provision.

8.22 Where outstanding obligations are discovered to exist at the time of a sale, the general law will usually be supplemented by some private arrangement between the parties. This is familiar terrain for conveyancers,[25] and no doubt practice here will continue to evolve. The key question is who is to pay. If the seller is to pay, the purchaser will wish to make a retention from the price, while if the purchaser is to pay the price will usually be reduced. The risk of insolvency - whether of seller or of purchaser - is avoided if the sums concerned are placed on joint deposit receipt or otherwise put in trust. Where, as may commonly be the case, the outstanding obligation is in respect of a repair which has been agreed on but not yet carried out, the parties will need to have regard to the possibility of cost drift and may wish to err on the side of caution.

8.23 The potential liability of a purchaser under our proposals is limited by negative prescription. As the law currently stands an obligation to pay a scheme cost would prescribe only after 20 years. This is because the obligation does not seem to fit any of the categories listed for the quinquennial prescription in the Prescription and Limitation (Scotland) Act 1973;[26] and because even if a possible category could be identified, the obligation would probably be excluded by the exception which applies to obligations relating to land.[27] Twenty years seems too long for the cost of replacing slates on a roof or a missed premium on a contract of insurance. In a question with the contractor or insurance company the obligation would be at an end after only 5 years,[28] and we think that the same rule should apply in a question between the owners. The issue is of particular importance to purchasers. It is one thing to impose concurrent liability in relation to debts which are less than 5 years old. It is quite another to expose a purchaser to debts which may have lain unpaid for 18 or 19 years and been forgotten about by everyone. The starting point for prescription would be the time when the original owner became liable for the cost[29] and not the time when the new owner acquired the flat in question. Thus, except in the rare cases where prescription has been interrupted, an incoming purchaser would have to look back no more than 5 years.

8.24 We recommend that:

35(a) In Management Scheme B the manager should be bound, on request, to provide and sign a certificate setting out, as at the date of the certificate, that no service charge is outstanding or, as the case may be, that a specified amount of service charge is outstanding in respect of a flat.

(b) The liability of an incoming owner for service charges outstanding at the date of the certificate should not exceed the figure stated in the certificate.

(c) The obligation of an owner for costs under the management scheme applying to the tenement or under any other of our recommendations should be subject to negative prescription after 5 years.

(Clauses 15(3) and 16; Scheme B, rule 3.9)

---

25 D J Cusine and Robert Rennie, *Missives* (1993) paras 4.18, 4.19 and 4.58; G L Gretton and K G C Reid, *Conveyancing* (1993) pp 59-60.

26 Prescription and Limitation (Scotland) Act 1973, Sched 1, para 1.

27 Prescription and Limitation (Scotland) Act 1973, Sched 1, para 2(e). And see on this provision *Barratt Scotland Ltd v Keith* 1994 SLT 1337 and 1343, and *University of Strathclyde (Properties) Ltd v Fleeting Organisation Ltd* 1992 GWD 14-822.

28 Prescription and Limitation (Scotland) Act 1973, Sched 1, para 1(g).

29 As for when an owner becomes liable for scheme costs, see recommendation 33(a)-(c).

Meaning of "owner"

8.25 Under our proposals the "owner" of a flat has both rights and obligations. On the one hand he is entitled to participate in the management of the tenement; but on the other hand he is liable for the maintenance and other costs incurred as part of that management. There seems no reason why "owner" should not carry its normal meaning; and since almost all land is held on feudal tenure, the normal meaning in this context would be the person holding the feudal interest of *dominium utile*.

8.26 One exception seems necessary. A heritable creditor who enters into possession of the security subjects is usually regarded as standing in the place of the owner.[30] In particular, by s 20(5) of the Conveyancing and Feudal Reform (Scotland) Act 1970 there is assigned to such a creditor "all rights and obligations of the proprietor relating to .. the management and maintenance of the subjects". It may be that this provision is sufficient of itself to make a heritable creditor in possession the "owner" for the purposes of our proposals. Thus the management rights which the creditor is allowed to exercise would presumably include the right to participate in the management of the tenement as a whole and to cast the vote allocated to the flat. Similarly, the obligations which pass to the creditor would include the obligation to pay maintenance and other costs due under the management scheme. However, it would make matters clear beyond doubt if "owner" were to be defined as including a heritable creditor in possession. For the duration of the possession a creditor would then be owner for all the purposes of the law of the tenement and not merely for those which are thought to come within s 20(5) of the 1970 Act. This approach would also have the merit of removing any lingering doubt that, following the *David Watson* case,[31] a heritable creditor might not be liable for arrears of scheme costs due by the debtor.[32] A heritable creditor who sought to avoid this liability by not entering into possession would face the difficulty that a purchaser would be unlikely to accept the title unless the liability had been discharged.[33]

8.27 So far as crystallisation of liability is concerned, the most important question is the identification of the moment when ownership passes. The outgoing owner is liable only for those costs which became due during his period of ownership. If an obligation becomes due on the day after he ceased to be owner, sole liability rests with the incoming owner. Of course as a matter of strict law there is no doubt when ownership of a flat passes: ownership passes at the moment of registration in the Land or Sasine Register. Nor is this view disturbed by the recent decision of the House of Lords in *Sharp v Thomson*[34] that a purchaser holding on a delivered but unregistered conveyance is protected in the receivership of the seller. But there is an obvious difficulty in using registration as the test in the present case. Registration is a matter for the incoming and not for the outgoing owner; and an incoming owner may choose not to register. If he does not register, the outgoing owner would remain liable for new scheme costs into the indefinite future. Non-registration is of course extremely rare where property is transmitted by sale, but it is quite common in certain other cases, for example where an heir has acquired the property by succession. Similarly, the grantees of judicial conveyances - trustees in sequestration, executors and the like - very rarely make up title by registration.

8.28 We suggest, therefore, that for the limited purposes of our proposals a person should become an owner of a flat when he is entitled to take entry under a conveyance of the flat in question. This would apply both to voluntary and to judicial conveyances. In the case of voluntary conveyances the date of entry is usually the date on which the conveyance is delivered to the grantee.

---

30 Gloag and Irvine, *Law of Rights in Security* (1897) pp 100-101.

31 *David Watson Property Management v Woolwich Equitable Building Society* 1992 SC (HL) 21, discussed at paras 8.9-8.11 above.

32 In fact, since the liability for scheme costs is, under our proposals, a liability incurred *qua* owner, it is almost certain that this result would follow under s 20(5) of the 1970 Act and without the need for further provision.

33 See para 8.13.

34 1997 SC (HL) 66.

8.29 We recommend that:

36(a) "Owner" be defined to mean -

(i) Where a flat is held on feudal tenure, the person holding the interest of *dominium utile* in the flat;

(ii) Where a flat is not held on feudal tenure, the owner.

(iii) Where a heritable creditor has entered into lawful possession of a flat, the heritable creditor in possession of the flat.

(b) For the purposes of recommendation 36(a)(i) and (ii) a person becomes owner (and the last owner ceases to be owner) when that person is entitled to take entry under a conveyance of the flat in question.

(Clause 29)

Part 9 Insurance and Demolition

Compulsory insurance

9.1 Although the subject of insurance was not touched on in our discussion paper, a number of consultees emphasised its importance and suggested that in a tenement insurance ought to be compulsory. Among those expressing this view were the Law Society of Scotland, the Faculty of Advocates, the Property Managers Association Scotland Ltd, and a number of local authorities. The argument in favour of compulsory insurance is straightforward and powerful. Within a tenement each owner is uniquely vulnerable to the physical condition of the property of his neighbours. Since a flat is no more than a single unit in a larger building, an owner may often be affected by damage to parts of the building which are not his. Hence he has an interest not merely in the insurance of his own flat but in the insurance of the other flats in the building. In the most extreme case, where a tenement is badly damaged or destroyed, the fact that even one of the flats is uninsured, or underinsured, may be enough to prevent the building from being restored. In summary, in a tenement an owner is not adequately insured unless his neighbours are insured also.

9.2 We are persuaded by this argument. Compulsory insurance is already found in other fields of activity, for example for motor vehicles, and there can be no objection to the idea in principle. In other countries compulsory insurance is a normal part of strata or sectional ownership.[1] Even at the moment, of course, owners do usually insure their flats, either because they choose to do so or because they have a mortgage,[2] or sometimes because they are required to insure by a real burden in the titles. But in some cases there is either no insurance or under-insurance. A person who repays his mortgage may fail to renew his insurance policy. An owner who inherited his flat may never have troubled to take out insurance. In any event, not all insurance cover is adequate, whether in relation to extent,[3] to the value insured or to the risks covered.

9.3 We suggest that the owner of a tenement flat should be under a duty to insure both the flat and also any pertinents which attach to it - for example a cellar or a *pro indiviso* share in the close. This obligation would not apply to the Crown, which bears its own risk. Insurance should be for reinstatement value rather than for market value. In the case particularly of stone tenements the cost of reinstatement is likely greatly to exceed market value, and there would be no prospects of re-building if the cover were restricted to market value. The lending institutions, property managers and surveyors whom we consulted were in favour of insurance for reinstatement value.[4]

9.4 It would be too inflexible to specify, in primary legislation, the risks against which insurance cover should be taken. Insurance practice changes over time and any fixed list would inevitably become out of date. Instead we suggest that the Secretary of State should have power to prescribe a list of risks by statutory instrument, and that the list should be capable of being varied over time. No doubt the Secretary of State would wish to consult appropriate interests, such as the insurance industry, lending institutions,

---

1 We note that compulsory insurance is also a feature of the commonhold scheme proposed for England and Wales: see Commonhold Draft Bill (Lord Chancellor's Department, July 1996), Sched 5, para 7.

2 One of the standard conditions in a standard security is that the debtor must insure for market value against the risk of fire and such other risks as the creditor may reasonably require. See Conveyancing and Feudal Reform (Scotland) Act 1970, Sched 3, standard condition 5.

3 For example, the common parts of the building may not be included.

4 Where there is a loan over a flat, the Standard Conditions are almost always amended to provide that insurance shall be for reinstatement value rather than market value (see Sched 3, para 5 to the Conveyancing and Feudal Reform (Scotland) Act 1970). See D J Cusine, *Standard Securities*, (1991) para 5.18.

surveyors and the legal profession, prior to finalising the list. In our view the following standard risks ought to be covered by any scheme of compulsory insurance -

- fire, smoke, lightning, explosion, earthquake
- storm or flood
- theft or attempted theft
- riot, civil commotion, strike, labour or political disturbance
- subsidence, heave of the site beneath the tenement or landslip
- escape of water from water tanks, pipes, apparatus and domestic appliances
- frost damage to fixed water, drainage and heating installations
- falling trees
- malicious persons or vandals
- impact by aircraft or other aerial devices or articles falling from them
- impact by road vehicles or articles falling from them
- falling radio and television receiving aerials including satellite dishes, and
- leakage of oil from fixed heating installations

9.5 The statutory obligation to insure is intended to set a minimum standard for insurance. It should not be taken as an infallible guide to the amount or type of cover needed in particular cases, and there is of course nothing to stop owners from taking out additional cover. In some cases a lender might insist on further cover as a condition of advancing a loan. It will be seen that the statutory requirement is limited to damage to the property and does not touch on liability to third parties.

9.6 Occasionally it may turn out to be impossible or impractical to obtain cover in respect of one of the prescribed risks. A tenement in an area subject to flooding may not be easy to insure against flood damage, while a convicted arsonist may find that insurers are reluctant to offer cover against fire. In these unusual cases the statutory obligation should be modified. The obligation to insure should not apply to the extent that insurance cannot actually be obtained against a particular prescribed risk, or can only be obtained at a cost which is unreasonably high.

9.7 Enforcement of the statutory obligation is a difficult issue. A criminal sanction is obviously inappropriate. There is no suitable regulatory body which might be used to monitor compliance, and we have no proposals for creating one. In the end, enforcement must be a matter for the individual owners within the tenement. Insurance of the building is a private rather than a public interest. The obligation to insure should be enforceable by the owners among themselves; and in order to assist the enforcement process each owner should be bound, on request, to produce to any other owner the policy (or a copy of it) together with evidence of payment of the current premium.

9.8 We recommend that:

37(a) The owner of a flat should be under a duty to insure the flat and any pertinents attaching to the flat for reinstatement value and against such risks as may be prescribed by the Secretary of State.

(b) The duty to insure should not apply to a risk in respect of which the owner cannot obtain insurance or can obtain insurance only at a cost which is unreasonably high.

(c) The duty to insure should be enforceable by the owner of any flat in the tenement.

(d) On request an owner should be obliged to produce to any other owner

(i) the policy of insurance or a copy of the policy, and

(ii) evidence of payment of the current premium.

(e) The obligation to insure under recommendation 37(a) should not apply to the Crown.

(Clause 19(1), (3), (4), (5) and (6) and clause 32(3))

Insurance by common policy

9.9 There are two ways of arranging insurance for a tenement: either each flat can be insured separately, or a common policy can be obtained for the whole building. There are obvious advantages in using a common policy:

- It is likely to be cheaper.
- It guarantees that the whole building is properly insured, the common parts as well as the individual flats.
- It eliminates the duplication of cover which can occur with a series of individual policies.
- Finally, in the event of a claim being made, it means that only a single insurer need be dealt with and that there is no need to apportion repair costs among the different units in the building.

As well as being advantageous to owners, common policies are, we understand, usually acceptable to lenders.

9.10 Despite these advantages we do not suggest that the use of a common policy should be mandatory. Our policy objective is satisfied if insurance cover is obtained, and it is not for legislation to instruct proprietors as to how this is to be done. To this libertarian point may be added some practical considerations. In the case of many tenements a statutory rule requiring common insurance could not be complied with either easily or quickly. Existing individual policies would require to be discontinued. The consent of lenders would have to be obtained. In tenements without a factor someone would have to be found who was willing to take on the organisational role of arranging a new policy and co-ordinating the termination of existing policies. We suspect that a significant number of tenements would simply ignore the statutory requirement. Furthermore, there would be cases where a common policy was not appropriate. For example, in a tenement with shops on the bottom and houses above, it might be more sensible for the shops to be individually insured and for the common policy to be confined to the houses.

9.11 But while a common policy should not be mandatory, it ought to be encouraged. We have three proposals for its encouragement. In the first place, Scheme B should require the manager to take out a common policy for the tenement. This would be a mandatory provision of a non-mandatory, and freely variable, scheme. But for tenements to which Scheme B is applied in the form set out in Schedule 2 to the draft Bill,[5] a common policy would be compulsory. It is envisaged that the policy would be taken out in the name of the owners' association, and that the association should be deemed to have an insurable interest.

9.12 Secondly, in Scheme A tenements owners should be empowered to make a scheme decision to have a common policy. Hence if a majority of owners became convinced of the merits of common insurance an appropriate policy could be arranged, and the premiums paid for under the terms of the scheme. Both here and in Scheme B[6] the common policy obtained would have to cover all of the prescribed risks but could also cover such additional risks[7] as may be decided.

9.13 Thirdly, in cases where title provisions already require the use of a common policy, we suggest that the statutory obligation to insure should also require to be met by a common policy. Title provisions of this kind are not uncommon but, in the case of older titles, the level of cover and the risks to be insured against fall far short of the proposed new statutory requirement and in many cases the requirements of lenders. In such cases the title policy is often supplemented by individual policies for individual flats, so that there is an element of double insurance. The effect of our proposal would be to require the cover under the common policy to be increased in order to satisfy the statutory obligation. Individual policies would then cease to be required.

---

5 See Scheme B, rule 7(c).

6 So far as Scheme B is concerned, this is because (i) the owners' association has power to insure the tenement or any part of it (rule 2.2(b), and (ii) the manager can exercise the powers of the association (rule 3.6(a)).

7 For example, employers' liability insurance if there is a shop on the ground floor of the tenement.

9.14 We recommend that:

38(a) Where the title to the tenement requires the building to be insured by means of a common policy, the duty to insure mentioned in recommendation 37(a) should be complied with by means of a common policy.

(b) Under Management Scheme A the owners should be entitled to make a scheme decision to arrange a common policy of insurance against the statutory risks for reinstatement value and against such other risks as may be agreed.

(c) Under Management Scheme B the manager should be under a duty to ensure that there is in force for the tenement building a common policy of insurance against the statutory risks for reinstatement value and against such other risks as the owners may decide.

(d) The policy mentioned at (c) should be taken in the name of the owners' association which, for this purpose, should be deemed to have an insurable interest in the tenement.

(Clause 19(2); Scheme A, rule 2.2(d); Scheme B, rules 2.2(b) and 7(c))

Buildings in serious disrepair

9.15 A tenement may fall into serious disrepair either by gradual neglect or by some sudden disaster, such as a fire. Three outcomes are then possible. Either the building is repaired, or it is left alone and allowed to decay, or it is demolished.

9.16 Under our proposals, a majority of owners would usually be entitled to insist on repair, at least of the external structure of the building. External walls, load-bearing walls, and the roof are scheme property within both Scheme A and Scheme B, and a majority of owners can require that they be maintained. "Maintenance" is defined to include "the reinstatement of a part (but not most) of the tenement building".[8] So if the top floor of a building is gutted by fire, repairs can go ahead under the usual maintenance regime. In practice the cost would usually be borne by insurers. An improvident decision to repair might be successfully challenged before the sheriff under the annulment procedure.[9]

9.17 The position is different where the owners are unable to agree. In the absence of majority support for reinstatement, the Scheme maintenance regime cannot be used. Sometimes the titles contain a real burden requiring reinstatement, and this could be enforced. As a last resort an owner might invoke the residual statutory obligation placed on all owners to provide support and shelter, but that obligation is subject to a reasonableness test which has particular regard to the age of the tenement, its condition and the likely cost of the proposed repair.[10] A court might readily conclude that an expensive repair to a failing tenement was unreasonable, particularly if it was opposed by most of the other owners.

9.18 If a deteriorating tenement is left alone then, sooner or later, the question of demolition will arise. The building may no longer be capable of economic repair. It may have become dangerous. It may no longer be occupied. Some of the owners may wish to demolish and to sell the site for redevelopment. Under the general law an owner is always free to demolish his own property,[11] subject to the consent of any heritable creditor;[12] but within a tenement the integrity of one flat affects the integrity of the building as a whole and unilateral demolition is not usually possible. Even under the present law it would be possible for the owners of the flats at the highest level of the building to agree to demolition of their particular storey, and this could not be objected to by the other owners provided that, in implement of the common interest obligation of shelter, adequate arrangements were made for re-roofing. In theory the demolition of the top storey might then be followed by the demolition of the next storey down. Plainly, a lower proprietor could not demolish because this could not be done without bringing down the rest of the building, in breach of the common interest obligation of support. Thus, except in the case of the

8 Scheme A, rule 1.4; Scheme B, rule 16.3.

9 See paras 5.19-5.25 and recommendation 7.

10 See paras 7.4-7.13 and recommendation 30(a).

11 This is the *jus abutendi* which is traditionally seen as part of ownership.

12 Conveyancing and Feudal Reform (Scotland) Act 1970, Sched 3 standard condition 2(b).

creeping, storey-by-storey demolition mentioned earlier, demolition under the present law requires the consent of all of the owners in the tenement. We do not think that this rule should be altered.[13] An owner should not be deprived of his property merely by the action of his neighbours - even if those neighbours are in a majority. If a person chooses to continue living in a flat in a tenement which is in serious disrepair, then that is a matter for him. He should not be forced to give up occupation, and nor should he be forced to bear the cost of demolition.

9.19 However, a legitimate criticism of the present law is the danger of impasse.[14] A tenement may become semi-derelict. Most of the owners may then wish to demolish, but unanimity may be unattainable. Some of the owners may have abandoned the property many years ago and may now be impossible to trace. The property is then sterilised. In its present form it can barely be used; but, in the absence of unanimity, there cannot be demolition and redevelopment. There is no easy solution to this difficulty which does not intrude into the property rights of individual owners in a manner which we would not consider to be acceptable. Of course, if the building deteriorates to the point of becoming dangerous, the local authority must serve a notice under section 13 of the Building (Scotland) Act 1959 requiring its demolition.[15] Two recommendations which we make later are also of some assistance. First, we recommend a clear set of rules governing liability for the cost of demolition and entitlement to the proceeds of any subsequent disposal of the site.[16] We hope that the existence of such rules might help focus discussion amongst owners and encourage agreement in relation to demolition. Secondly, we recommend that where, due to physical deterioration, a tenement building is no longer occupied, the owner of any flat in the building should be entitled to have the site and building sold and the proceeds divided amongst all the owners.[17] The new, single owner would then be free to demolish or restore as he wished.

Cost of demolition

9.20 It is probably the present law that liability for the cost of demolition is tied to ownership.[18] But in a tenement the complex way in which ownership is intermingled makes for difficulties in practice. Indeed it is not clear what the rule really means in the context of tenements. Even in the simplest case, where all flats are of exactly the same size and each has identical common rights, it cannot be assumed that each owner pays an equal share. For it is likely to be more difficult, and more expensive, to demolish the upper storeys of the building than the lower storeys. Does this mean that the upper proprietors must bear a greater share of the cost of demolition, and, if so, how much greater? Of course, in many tenements, flats are not of equal size and the calculations are correspondingly more complex.

9.21 A simpler rule seems to be required. We suggest that, in general, liability for the cost of demolition should be borne equally by the owner of each flat. That will achieve rough justice in most cases, and has the advantages of certainty and simplicity. However, it would be unfair to apply this rule where there are substantial differences in the sizes of the flats. Adopting here the approach which we recommended earlier in relation to residual liability for repairs,[19] we suggest that where the floor area of any one flat exceeds by one and a half times that of any other flat in the building, the equality rule should give way to a rule based on the relative floor area of each flat.

9.22 Partial demolition is potentially more complex. Under the present law there is some authority to suggest that the owners of all flats must contribute to demolition costs, at least if it can be shown that the building as a whole was structurally unsound and that demolition of a part was employed simply as

13 Hence the definition of "maintenance" in the Schemes excludes demolition except where reasonably incidental to maintenance. See Scheme A, rule 1.4 and Scheme B, rule 16.3. And by recommendation 30(c) an owner is prohibited from interfering with support or shelter.

14 On consultation, this and a series of related points were made by Mr Lionel Most, solicitor.

15 Parallel provisions are contained in s 115 of the Housing (Scotland) Act 1987 in relation to buildings comprising flats which are not of a tolerable standard.

16 Paras 9.20 - 9.24 and Recommendation 39.

17 Paras 9.31 - 9.35 and Recommendation 40(b)(iv).

18 Reid, para 249.

19 Paras 5.63 - 5.65 and Recommendation 13(a) Rule 5.

a means of saving the rest.[20] But in the application of this rule the difficulties mentioned above are compounded. It is not clear how much the surviving flats should pay. Is the principle equality, or should the liability be reduced in acknowledgement of the fact that no actual demolition has taken place? Is liability affected by the degree to which the tenement was previously unstable? Once again we think that there is merit in a simple approach. We see no strong reason why the owners of flats which survive should share the cost of work carried out on those which do not survive. Any general rule fixing liability on such flats would be arbitrary and, in many cases, unfair. On the whole, we think it is a sounder principle that liability should fall only on those flats which are demolished. As before, liability should be equally shared except where flats are of substantially different sizes.

9.23 In a few cases the underlying problem which led to demolition may be actionable in delict. Here the owners would usually have a claim, not merely for the value of their flat, but also for the cost of demolition. Another possibility is that the titles might make provision for demolition costs, although this is very rare in practice. Our proposals as to allocation of liability are without prejudice to any right of recovery otherwise arising.

9.24 We recommend that:

39(a) Except where the title to the tenement provides otherwise, the cost of demolishing a tenement should be borne equally by all the flats in the tenement.

(b) In the event of partial demolition, the cost should be borne equally by the flats in the part which has been demolished.

(c) In a case where the floor area of the largest flat was more than one and a half times that of the smallest flat, the principle of equality of contribution should be replaced by the rule that each flat must contribute in proportion to respective floor areas.

(Clause 23)

Rebuilding, or disposal of the site

9.25 On demolition the question arises as to what is to happen to the vacant site. A preliminary issue is to determine ownership. While there may be merit in reaffirming the principle in statutory form, it seems reasonably clear that demolition does not of itself bring existing ownership to an end.[21] The person who, before demolition, owned a flat on the second floor of the building continues, after demolition, to own the airspace formerly occupied by that flat. Similarly, the owner of the solum - who under the general law is the owner of the lowest flat in the building - continues, as before, to own the airspace above the roof of the former tenement. The result is rather like common property. Each owner has a share (albeit a physical share, held in layers) in the ownership of the site; and, as with common property, it seems correct in principle that each owner should have an equal voice in its future.

9.26 Usually there is garden ground and other land which forms part of the tenement. Sometimes, as, typically, with a back green, the land is the common property of all the owners in the tenement. Less frequently some or all of the land is individually owned. We are not concerned with such land here. If the land is large enough and useful enough to be marketable, it can be sold; and if it is owned in common, the fact that the tenement has been demolished is probably sufficient to remove the usual bar on division and sale.[22] No change is required here to the existing law.

9.27 So far as the site of the former building is concerned, there are two effective choices. Either there can be rebuilding, whether of the tenement or of some other building, or the site can be sold, possibly along with the other land associated with the tenement.

---

20 *Smith v Giuliani* 1925 SC (HL) 45.
21 *Barr v Bass Ltd* 1972 SLT (Lands Tr) 5.
22 *McLean v City of Glasgow District Council* 1987 SLT (Lands Tr) 2.

9.28 Quite frequently titles contain a real burden requiring that the tenement be rebuilt. Usually such a burden would be enforceable by the owners among themselves and also, sometimes, by a third party, such as a feudal superior. Unless the burden is discharged, whether consensually or by order of the Lands Tribunal, it requires to be complied with, and would continue to affect the land in the hands of anyone who came to purchase the site. In practice, the existence of a real burden is likely to lead to the tenement being promptly rebuilt. Standard securities over individual flats may also contain an obligation to rebuild, as a variation of the standard conditions, but this does not affect the owners of other flats and so could not of itself bring about the reconstruction of the tenement.

9.29 In the absence of a real burden, rebuilding cannot proceed without the agreement of all of the owners. For each owns his own section of airspace and can prevent that airspace being built into by the others. In practice owners often do agree to rebuild and, with the introduction of compulsory insurance for reinstatement value,[23] such agreement is likely to become more common in the future. A technical problem with rebuilding is that, however carefully the new building is modelled on the old, it will not occupy precisely the same airspace. In all cases there will be some discrepancies, and in a few cases the discrepancies may be significant. Usually this will not matter. In the law of the tenement accession operates within the boundaries of individual flats, although not beyond them.[24] Accordingly, when a tenement is re-erected in a slightly different position from that which it formerly occupied, the owner of each flat will acquire some airspace by accession but at the same time lose a corresponding amount of airspace to his neighbour. Overall there will be little or no change. The position is less clear where there are very substantial discrepancies, and in such cases recourse may be required to remedial conveyancing.[25]

9.30 Difficulties arise where there is neither a real burden nor unanimous agreement to rebuild. In this situation the owner (or owners) of the lowest flat (or flats) in the former building is at a significant advantage. He has the airspace at the bottom of the building and he alone can build without waiting for others to build first. Alternatively he could sell to a developer who could build in his place. The reason for this privileged position is not, as is sometimes supposed, that the ground floor owner owns the solum (as he does at common law). The position would be exactly the same even if exclusive rights to the solum were vested in the top floor proprietor. The key to privilege is ownership not of the solum but of the lowest stratum of airspace in the former building. Only the lowest stratum is usable airspace. However, the advantage enjoyed here should not be exaggerated. The ground flat proprietor is limited in what he can do. He cannot build higher than the height formerly occupied by his flat. Nor can he build on the part of the site formerly occupied by the common passage and stair. Nonetheless we do not think that his advantage can be justified. When the tenement was still in existence, each proprietor had broadly equivalent rights, and that position of rough equality ought not to be disturbed by demolition. As was mentioned earlier, there is an obvious analogy with common property. The site of the former building is in multiple ownership. Under the rules of common property, no one *pro indiviso* owner can innovate on the property by carrying out building work. We consider that the part owners of the vacant site of a tenement should be subject to a similar disability. Unless all part owners give their consent, building should not be allowed to proceed.

9.31 If, as suggested above, building must proceed by agreement, and if agreement is not then forthcoming, the only alternative course of action is to dispose of the site. In our view disposal should not require agreement. Partly this is for practical reasons. If agreement could be obtained neither for rebuilding nor for disposal, the property would be sterilised. But there is also an important issue of policy. In common property a *pro indiviso* owner is always free to realise his share by division or by division and sale - a rule which recognises the fact that a *pro indiviso* share is not, in itself, a very marketable commodity.[26] Similar considerations apply to part ownership of a tenement site. Indeed they seem even stronger. In common property, division and sale sometimes operates unfairly against the other owners,

---

23 See paras 9.1-9.8 and recommendation 37.
24 Reid, para 585.
25 In other words, it might be necessary for all the owners to concur in new conveyances of the individual flats.
26 Reid, para 32.

who may have a strong interest in continuing to own, and to use, the property in question.[27] By contrast a part owner of a tenement site has little or no interest in continued ownership or use. We suggest therefore that, following the demolition of a tenement, any part owner of the site should be entitled to insist on its sale. As a matter of property law all part owners would require to sign the disposition. Unco-operative owners might have to be persuaded by litigation, and, as with common property, there would be power in the clerk of court, following decree, to sign the disposition on their behalf.[28] The only case in which the right to sale should not be available is where the owners are bound to rebuild, either because they have entered into an agreement to that effect or because of the existence of a real burden. In principle, of course, a real burden binds successors but, except where there was a third party interest, the acquisition of the site by a single owner would result in the extinction of the burden by confusion. Hence, without this limitation on sale, a sale by one part owner could be used to defeat a real burden to rebuild.

9.32 It seems self-evident that the sale proceeds should be allocated in the same manner as the demolition costs. There seems no reason to give special weighting to the person who happened to own the solum. In most cases the solum is commonly owned - the almost invariable position in modern tenements - and where it is not the position is historically determined and has nothing to do with the present owner. We propose, therefore, that as a general rule the sale proceeds should be divided equally among the owners. However, where the floor area of the largest flat in the tenement was more than one and a half times that of the smallest, the price should be allocated on the basis of floor area. Of course we appreciate that since, by definition, the tenement no longer exists, there may be difficulties in determining what the floor areas were. Sometimes there may be records, but not always. However this is an issue for the person seeking to disturb the general principle of equality. If the case is not made out, the general principle will apply.

9.33 Sometimes a tenement is only partly demolished, typically to ground floor level. It would be unfair in that case to prevent the ground floor proprietor from continuing to use and enjoy his property. The owners of the demolished storeys can collect their insurance money. They should have no right to insist on the sale of the site. The position is different if the ground proprietor (or his successor) later decides to demolish the property, perhaps with a view to redevelopment. At this point partial demolition becomes full demolition, albeit achieved in two stages. There seems no reason for failing to apply the principles suggested above. Thus redevelopment should not be possible without the consent of the part owners (or their successors as part owners); and any part owner should be able to require sale of the site. If many years elapse between partial demolition and full demolition there may be serious difficulties in identifying the part owners. The Sasine or Land Register will still disclose the fact that the land is, notionally, tenement land, but the information about the ownership of the shadow flats is likely to be out of date. The proper procedure in that case would be for the ground floor owner to raise an action of division and sale in order to cleanse the title of the part owners through the signature of the clerk of court on the disposition. The alternative strategy, of redeveloping without consent, would carry the risk that a part owner might appear later and insist on the sale of the site in its redeveloped form. Of course all difficulties would be avoided if, at the time of the partial demolition, the ground floor proprietor buys out the interests of the other owners, and this seems the path of prudence in cases where redevelopment is likely.

9.34 Sometimes a tenement is not demolished but has become derelict. The property is not usable in its existing form, but under the present law there is no method available for the part owners to realise their shares. We consider that a right of sale would be appropriate in this case also. If no one is using the building, there are no special interests which require to be protected. A share in the sale proceeds seems a reasonable exchange for a share in a derelict building. Once again the problem of untraceable owners, common in practice, can be managed by obtaining the signature of the clerk of court on the disposition.

---

27 See, for example, *Upper Crathes Fishings Ltd v Bailey's Executors* 1991 SLT 747.

28 Or on behalf of owners who cannot be traced. See *Whyte v Whyte* 1913 2 SLT 85, and Sheriff Courts (Scotland) Act 1907 s 5A.

9.35 When the site of a former tenement is sold, the shadow flats will cease to exist, and multiple ownership will be replaced by unitary ownership. What is the position of subordinate real rights which affected the former flats? Only two need be mentioned here. On demolition any lease would be extinguished by *rei interitus*. Heritable securities, however, would survive, although the shadow flats over which they are secured would have little or no value. Three options seem to be available here. One would be to provide that, on sale of the site, any heritable security was deemed to be discharged. The second would be to treat the security as a security over the whole site. The final option would be to treat the security as a security over a *pro indiviso* share in the whole site, the fractional size of the share corresponding to number of flats in the former tenement.[29] Of these three options, the first would be unjust to the heritable creditor while the second would give him too much. The final option seems the least unattractive. In practice a purchaser is likely to insist on the discharge of any outstanding securities before agreeing to buy the site.

9.36 We recommend that:

40(a) The demolition of a tenement should not of itself affect the ownership rights of any person.

(b) Where a tenement building has been wholly demolished (whether in a single act or in two or more stages) but the former flats (or some of them) continue to be separately owned, the following rules should apply in relation to the site of the former building:

(i) it should not be permissible to erect buildings or other structures on the site except with the consent of, or in implement of an obligation binding on, the owners of all of the former flats;

(ii) subject to (iii), any owner of a former flat should be entitled to have the site sold;

(iii) the entitlement to sell should not arise if there has been lawful rebuilding under (i) or if the owners of all the former flats are subject to an enforceable obligation to rebuild the tenement or some other building;

(iv) except where the title to the tenement provides otherwise, the free proceeds of sale should be divided equally among the owners of the former flats, except that in a case where the floor area of the largest flat was more than one and a half times that of the smallest flat the proceeds should be divided in proportion to respective floor areas; and

(v) on the registration of a conveyance in implement of the sale, any heritable security which burdened a former flat should be deemed to burden the site to the extent of a fractional *pro indiviso* share corresponding to the number of flats in the former tenement.

(c) Where (i) due to its physical condition, a tenement building has been wholly unoccupied for more than 6 months and (ii) it is unlikely that any owner or other person will return to occupy any part of the tenement building, the owner of any flat should be entitled to have the tenement building sold and the proceeds divided.

(Clauses 22, and 24 - 26)

29 In other words, if there were eight flats in the former tenement, the security would be deemed to burden a one eighth *pro indiviso* share of the site.

Part 10 Miscellaneous topics

Television aerials and satellite dishes

10.1 It comes as no surprise that a law of the tenement which developed in the seventeenth century fails to deal adequately with the requirements of radio and television. Indeed on a strict view of that law, most television and radio aerials are placed unlawfully and ought to be removed. At common law the roof of a tenement belongs to the proprietor of the highest flat while the airspace above belongs to proprietor of the lowest flat - a division which prevents either proprietor from putting a television aerial on the roof without encroaching to some degree on the property of the other. The proprietor of one of the intermediate flats is in a still worse position, being owner neither of the roof nor of the airspace. Nor are matters much improved if, as often happens, the roof and airspace are made common property in the titles, for the rules of common property prevent any one owner from making exclusive and permanent use of any part of the property which is owned together.[1] Of course it may be that, with a little ingenuity, a court could explain away the forests of television aerials which are found on many tenement roofs. Common interest is one possible justification.[2] A second is servitude. After twenty years a servitude might possibly be constituted by positive prescription.[3] But in recent years the courts have rejected the idea of a servitude for electricity,[4] and it seems open to doubt whether they would extend the concept of servitude to include television aerials and the related wiring.

10.2 The issue can be dealt with simply by legislation. We suggest that each owner in a tenement should be entitled to fix to the roof or chimney stack a television or radio aerial, and to lead the wires necessary for its operation from the aerial to his own flat. Except where there is a communal aerial installed at the time the building was constructed, wiring is usually led down the outside of a building.

10.3 Satellite dishes are more commonly placed on the walls than on the roof. Under our proposals, as at common law, each proprietor will own the walls of his own flat and hence be at liberty to fix a satellite dish. While some sections of wall will no doubt be more favourable for reception of the signal than others, it would be unduly intrusive to allow owners to use a part of the wall which does not belong to them. However, there seems no objection to satellite dishes on the roof, or attached to a chimney stack and we suggest that owners should be entitled to place them there regardless of ownership.

10.4 It seems scarcely necessary to add that the rights which we wish to confer would be without prejudice to any requirement to obtain planning permission or building consent from the relevant authorities.[5]

10.5 We recommend that:

41(a) The owner of a flat in a tenement should be entitled -

(i) to fix to the outside surface of any roof or to any chimney stack a television or radio aerial, satellite dish, or other equipment relating to television or radio broadcasting, and

(ii) to lead wires or cables from the aerial, dish or other equipment to his flat.

---

1 *Bailey v Scott* (1860) 22 D 1105 at 1109 per Lord Benholme.
2 Reid, para 238.
3 Prescription and Limitation (Scotland) Act 1973 s 3.
4 *Neill v Scobie* 1993 GWD 13-887.
5 See the Scottish Office leaflet : Householder's Planning Guide on the Installation of Satellite Television Dishes.

(b) This right should be without prejudice to any requirement on an owner under any enactment relating to planning or building.

(Clause 20)

Gas and other services

10.6 In a tenement it is often not possible for a flat to receive basic services such as electricity, gas, and water without encroaching to some degree on common property or on a part of the building which belongs to another flat. Usually this does not matter. Existing tenements will almost always have the basic services already, and no new tenement is likely to be built without such services. In cases where a new service is required - cable television, for example - matters normally proceed by agreement among the owners and there is no difficulty. Where for any reason agreement cannot be obtained, there is usually an alternative method of proceeding provided by statute. For example, s 88 of the Civic Government (Scotland) Act 1982 allows an owner who has been refused consent by his neighbours for the installation of pipes and drains required in connection with water supply or with soil, waste or rainwater drainage to apply to the sheriff for a warrant authorising such installation. The sheriff may grant the warrant if it is reasonable that the installation be carried out. A similar provision exists for the installation of telecommunication apparatus,[6] and in disposing of the application the sheriff is directed to have regard to "the principle that no person should unreasonably be denied access to a telecommunication system".[7] "Telecommunication apparatus" is defined very broadly,[8] and would include for example cables for cable television.[9] Electricity is treated more favourably still, with special provision being made for tenements. There is an absolute right to lay and maintain electric lines and plant in through or across any stair passage or court forming a common access to a tenement, and only the person receiving the supply need consent.[10] The right is exercisable by Scottish Power plc or by Scottish Hydro-Electric plc. The supplier is under a duty to cause as little damage as possible and to make good any damage that is caused.

10.7 The one notable omission from the statute book is gas. This point was drawn to our attention, on consultation, by British Gas plc:

> "[N]ot infrequently the expressed wish of the majority of owners of a tenement to have a gas supply is thwarted because one of the owners in common refuses to consent to the gas supply pipe being laid through the common property - sometimes this is simply the building itself where it adjoins the pavement, but where the tenement is surrounded by ground held in common with the other proprietors it would also involve the laying of the pipe through that common ground ... [I]n the case of a public gas supplier, no pipe may be laid in ground which has not been dedicated to the public use without the consent of the owners.[11] A public gas supplier does have powers of compulsory purchase[12] but for various reasons it is neither practical nor sensible to invoke these powers in the situation .. described."

British Gas concluded that:

> "Whilst the rights of the individual must be protected, this must be kept in balance with the rights of the majority and some consideration has to be given to the common good."

Historically, the inferior position of gas may be connected with worries about safety standards; but if that is correct, such worries do not seem justified today. We understand that modern practice is to introduce gas by means of a pipe running up the outside of the tenement, a practice which is both less intrusive

---

6 Telecommunications Act 1984 Sched 2 (the Telecommunications Code), para 5. By contrast with the Civic Government (Scotland) Act provisions, the application is to be made by the operator and not by the person who hopes to benefit from the installation.

7 Telecommunications Code, para 5(3).

8 Telecommunications Act 1984, s 4(3) and Sched 2, para1.1.

9 Cable and Broadcasting Act 1984 s 2(1).

10 South of Scotland Electricity Order Confirmation Act 1956 s 33 (as amended by The Electricity Act 1989 (Modification of Local Enactments) (Scotland) Order 1990, SI 1990/393, Sched, Pt I, paras 3 and 11); North of Scotland Electricity Order Confirmation Act 1958 s 26 (as amended by the 1990 Order, Sched, Pt II, paras 6 and 12).

11 Gas Act 1986 Sched 4, para 3(1).

12 Gas Act 1986 Sched 3.

than an internal pipe and also safer in the event of a leak. In our view there is no good reason why the supply of gas should not now be put in the same position as the supply of electricity. Hence we suggest that the owner of a flat should be entitled to install in the tenement (including the garden ground) pipes and other apparatus necessary for the supply of gas. However, there should be no right of installation in or through individual flats. The access provisions discussed below[13] would apply insofar as access is needed for the work to be carried out.

10.8 There may be a case for extending the same rule to other services, and in any event new technology will no doubt produce new services in the future. We have no firm proposals on this subject, but we think that in the interests of flexibility the Secretary of State should be entitled by statutory instrument to extend the rule to such other service or services as he may choose to prescribe.

10.9 We recommend that:

42(a) The owner of a flat should be entitled to lead through the tenement such pipes, cables and other apparatus as are required for the provision to his flat of -

(i) gas, and

(ii) such other services as the Secretary of State may by regulations prescribe.

(b) However, there should be no right of installation within an individual flat (other than the flat which is to receive the service).

(c) This right should be without prejudice to any requirement on an owner under any enactment relating to planning or building or to the provision of the service in question.

(Clause 21)

Rights of access

10.10 Sometimes common repairs cannot be done exclusively from common property and it becomes necessary to intrude on parts of the tenement which are individually owned. A roof repair, for example, might require access to be taken from or through the roof space. Repairs to the outside walls will often involve scaffolding being erected in the garden. Although the titles may provide otherwise, the rule under the general law is that the roof space is owned by the proprietor of the highest flat in the building and the garden by the proprietor of the lowest; and indeed outside walls, although the subject of common maintenance under both Schemes A and B, are themselves owned in individual sections corresponding to the location of the individual flats. We asked in our discussion paper[14] whether statutory powers of entry might be needed to enable repairs which had been agreed by a majority to be carried out. Under the present law repairs usually require unanimity, and access is not a live issue, but the position might change under a system where a bare majority can decide. A person who voted against a particular repair might refuse access and so prevent it from taking place. A difficulty of a different kind arises where property is tenanted. Here the landlord might vote in favour of a repair only to find that the tenant, who has an exclusive (if temporary) right of possession, refuses access. Sometimes, of course, a right of access for repairs is conferred, or may be implied, as a servitude in the titles of a tenement, but this is uncommon at least in older properties.

10.11 On consultation the idea of a statutory right of access was warmly supported. It was suggested that without such a right there was a serious risk that repairs which had won majority approval might nonetheless fail to take place. The argument seems unanswerable. Access should be available in respect of all maintenance which has been duly authorised under the management scheme in force for the tenement in question. For Scheme A tenements this would mean maintenance to scheme property which had been approved by a majority of owners.[15] In Scheme B the manager has a general authority to instruct

13 See paras 10.10 - 10.21.

14 Discussion Paper No 91, Para 5.10.

15 Scheme A, rules 2 and 3. Emergency work would also be covered: see rule 7.

maintenance to scheme property,[16] although subject to the possibility of checks imposed by the owners at a general meeting.[17] Other management schemes are likely to have equivalent rules.

10.12 A related but separate problem is access for repairs to individual flats. An owner might not be able to carry out work on his own flat without taking access through another flat or through a part of the building which is in common ownership. The law here is obscure. It is arguable, although not certain, that common property could be used, on the basis that repair of adjoining property is a permitted "ordinary" use of the common property.[18] The access position for property in individual ownership seems never to have been judicially tested, at least in a reported case, and the only authority on the subject is the following passage from the *Lectures* of Baron Hume:[19]

> "I think it may be maintained with respect to conterminous proprietors in a Burgh, which in many instances, owing to the crowded situation of the building, cannot be repaired without some temporary interference, as by resting ladders on the next area, or suspending a scaffold over the next area, that this slight and temporary inconvenience must be put up with, from the necessity of the case."

It may be noted that both of Hume's examples concern use external to the building and it is not clear that this passage would support access over individual flats. We think that it should be made clear that access over individual flats is permissible. Of course, as Hume's account shows, the question of access for repairs is not confined to relations within tenements. In England and Wales general provision for access was made by the Access to Neighbouring Land Act 1992, which implemented a Law Commission Report.[20] This Act empowers courts to order access in cases where a repair cannot be carried out or would be substantially more difficult to carry out without entry upon neighbouring property. It may be that more general legislation ought to be considered for Scotland also, although for present purposes our recommendations are confined to tenements.

10.13 We recommended earlier[21] that owners should be able to fix television aerials and other telecommunications equipment to the roof or chimney stacks. If the hatchway to the roof is situated within an individual flat, appropriate access rights will be required. Similarly, access rights may be required for the installation of gas and other prescribed services.[22]

10.14 A repair will usually be preceded by a preliminary inspection. Furthermore, prudent proprietors may wish to carry out a regular programme of inspections, especially in relation to property which is commonly maintained. By their very nature such inspections will not always lead to work being carried out. Hence access rights are required not merely for repairs but also for inspections.

10.15 Another case where inspection may be required is to monitor the obligations placed on the owners of individual flats in relation to support and shelter.[23]

10.16 Finally, if unusually, access may be required to measure floor area. Under Scheme A, liability for maintenance and running costs is residually determined by reference to the floor areas of individual flats.[24] We expect that the floor area for the whole tenement would normally be measured either by a person appointed for that purpose by the owners, or by the manager if there is one. Occasionally there may be access difficulties which would be solved by the existence of a formal right.

---

16 The manager can exercise the powers of the association (rule 3.6) which, by rule 2.2(a), include the carrying out of maintenance, alterations or improvements to scheme property. Improvements, however, require the prior approval of a special majority under rule 12.

17 The checks can either be direct, under rule 3.8, or indirect, by amending or rejecting the draft budget under rule 10.3.

18 Reid, para 24.

19 Hume, *Lectures* III, 207.

20 Rights of Access to Neighbouring Land (Law Com No 151, 1985).

21 Paras 10.1 - 10.5.

22 See paras 10.6 - 10.9.

23 Paras 7.4 - 7.13 and recommendation 30.

24 Scheme A, rule 5.5(b).

10.17 We are conscious that rights of access are potentially open to abuse. Inspection could be used as a pretext for gaining entry to a neighbour's flat. A neighbour who is officious, or merely curious, might seek access more often than is really necessary. It is not clear that an obsessive repairer should be allowed access over his neighbour's flat whenever he feels the urge to take up tools. Nor is it clear that access should be allowed merely on the ground that it is more convenient to work from a neighbour's flat if the repair could in fact be carried out from one's own property. Some of the difficulties here are illustrated in a recent case[25] where the pursuer, who owned a first floor flat, wished to replace the wiring and needed access to the void above his ceiling. Rather than break through the plaster he sought an order ordaining the owner of the flat above to allow access by lifting his floorboards. The case collapsed on a point of pleading, but the issues raised are of considerable interest. Some sort of reasonableness test seems required if owners are to be prevented from making repeated and unjustified demands for access. Further, even if the demand is reasonable in itself an owner should be entitled to refuse access when the timing is inconvenient or inappropriate.

10.18 Access rights are most appropriately conferred on the owners of flats and, in the case of Scheme B tenements, on the manager of the owners' association also. But it should be possible for the owners and the manager to authorise others - typically tradesmen - to exercise the right on their behalf. Except where the work is urgent access should be preceded by reasonable notice. In an emergency, immediate access should be permitted, as it is at common law.[26] Both Scheme A and Scheme B authorise owners to carry out emergency repairs to scheme property.[27]

10.19 Like a servitude right of access, the statutory right should be exercised in a manner which causes the least possible disruption to the owner of the property. Of course a degree of interference with that property will often be unavoidable. Floor boards may have to be lifted, holes bored in walls, and so forth. In some cases the property to which access is sought may itself be the property which is being maintained.[28] On general principles of law the person causing the damage will be liable for the cost of reinstatement. When that person is a tradesman we think that the owner on whose behalf the access is exercised should share the liability jointly and severally. The person suffering the loss would then have a choice of debtors. The owner would in turn have a right of recovery against the tradesman, or alternatively, in the case of a common repair, against the other owners.[29]

10.20 The existence of a statutory right does not guarantee that the owner or occupier will let his neighbour over the threshold. If he does not, the right will require to be judicially enforced. We considered but rejected the establishment of a special procedure whereby the neighbour could apply to a sheriff or justice of the peace for an entry warrant.[30] Procedures of this kind seem better suited to public officials than to private individuals. Often they are accompanied by a right to force entry which could not appropriately be granted to neighbours in a tenement.[31] We are content to allow enforcement to rest on the general powers of the sheriff, described elsewhere in this report, to give effect to the provisions of our proposed legislation.[32]

---

25 *Taylor v Irvine* 1996 SCLR 937.

26 For example, to put out a fire. See Reid, para 181(5).

27 Scheme A, rule 7; Scheme B, rule 13.

28 This will occur in common repairs if the scheme property which is being repaired is not common property but is in individual ownership, such as the external walls.

29 The cost of reinstatement would normally be a "cost arising from a scheme decision to carry out maintenance" within rule 5.1(a) of Scheme A.

30 A standard example is s 102 of the Civic Government (Scotland) Act 1982 which provides for entry warrants for council officials in connection with statutory repairs and other notices.

31 However, where a flat is unoccupied some provision is required to allow forcible entry to be taken. See para 10.24 below.

32 See paras 10.22-10.27. For the Court of Session, power is conferred by the Court of Session Act 1988 s 45(b).

10.21 We recommend that:

43(a) The owner or occupier of part of a tenement should be bound, on being given reasonable notice, to allow access to or through that part to the owner of any flat and (in a case where the tenement is governed by Management Scheme B) to the manager of the owners' association for any of the following purposes:

(i) to carry out any maintenance or other works duly authorised under the management scheme applying to that tenement;

(ii) to carry out any maintenance or other works to a part of the tenement owned (whether solely or in common) by the person seeking access;

(iii) to fix a television aerial or other telecommunications equipment to the outside surface of the roof or a chimney stack;

(iv) to install gas or other prescribed services;

(v) to carry out an inspection to determine whether maintenance or works of the kind mentioned at (i) and (ii) above are necessary;

(vi) to determine whether the obligations of an owner or occupier relating to support and shelter have been complied with; and

(vii) in a case where liability for costs is calculated by reference to floor area, to measure the floor area of the part.

(b) Notice under (a) above should not be needed where access is required for the purpose of carrying out urgent maintenance.

(c) An owner or occupier should be entitled to refuse access, or access at a particular time, if it would be reasonable to do so having regard to the circumstances including whether the request for access is reasonble.

(d) An owner or manager who has a right of access under this recommendation should be able to authorise in writing any other person to exercise the right on his behalf.

(e) Where a person authorised under (d) causes damage to any part of the tenement, the owner who authorised him (or the association, where he was authorised by a manager) should be jointly and severally liable with the authorised person for the cost of making good the damage.

(f) An owner or association which makes payment under (e) should be entitled to recover the cost from the authorised person.

(Clause 18)

General power of sheriff to make orders

10.22 Occasionally the management schemes may require further support from the courts. The same may be true of other parts of the proposed legislation.[33] No management scheme can provide for every contingency. Inevitably situations will arise which are not directly covered by the scheme but yet which require to be resolved in the interests of the scheme as a whole. We have three examples particularly in mind, although no doubt there are others.

10.23 The first concerns common repairs. For reasons of health and safety it may be impossible to carry out a particular repair unless one of the flats is vacated for a period. Nonetheless the owner or occupier may refuse to leave, or he may only be willing to leave if he is paid relocation expenses which the other owners consider excessive. Unless the impasse is broken the repair cannot go ahead.

33 See para 10.20.

10.24 The second concerns rights of access. Earlier we recommended that an owner or occupier should be bound to allow access to his flat for certain purposes, including the carrying out of maintenance.[34] But occasionally a flat is unoccupied and the owner cannot be traced, or refuses to respond to letters. A point may be reached where forcible access may be required, in the interests of the other owners in the tenement.

10.25 The final example concerns common insurance. Under Scheme A a majority of owners can require that the tenement be made subject to a policy of common insurance. Under Scheme B common insurance is compulsory. But a recalcitrant owner might refuse to co-operate in the completion of the proposal form, which might in turn prevent a policy from being issued.

10.26 We believe that the best way of dealing with difficulties of the kind just described is to give to the sheriff a general discretion, on application by the owner of any flat, to make such orders as may be necessary to ensure the proper working of the management scheme which is in force for the tenement in question. Application to the sheriff would be by way of summary application. Any order could be made subject to such conditions as the sheriff saw fit.

10.27 We recommend that:

44(a) In relation to a tenement the sheriff should be empowered, on summary application, to grant such orders, and on such conditions, as he sees fit, being orders relating to any matter concerning the operation of the management scheme which applies to the tenement or any provision of the legislation as it applies to the tenement.

(b) An application under (a) should be capable of being brought by the owner of any flat in a tenement and, in the case of a tenement governed by Management Scheme B, by the manager of the owners' association.

(Clause 9)

Common property

10.28 Under our proposals common ownership is allocated by reference to use rather than to maintenance.[35] Those parts of a tenement which are used in common - for example the common close, or the entryphone system, or a system of pipes - are owned in common. But the mere fact that a part is to be maintained in common has not been considered sufficient reason for it to be common property.[36] The external walls, for example, although maintained in common, are owned in sections by the owners of the individual flats which they serve. The overall result of this approach is that common property is used less often under our proposals than would be typical in a modern deed of conditions. Nonetheless, important parts of a tenement, such as the close, are common property, and in many cases the list of parts in common ownership will be added to by the title deeds.

10.29 In a tenement the normal rules of common property cannot apply without some degree of modification. This was already recognised by the common law. In the authoritative account of common property which appears in his *Principles*, Bell noted that the rule entitling co-owners to the remedy of division and sale did not apply "where it is a thing of common and indispensable use, as a staircase or vestibule".[37] A recent decision by the Second Division[38] confirms that Bell's qualification applies to the common parts of a tenement:

> "We agree that the remedy of division and sale would not be available in the present case, and that Professor Bell's reference to 'a thing of common and indispensable use, as a staircase or vestibule'

---

34 Para 10.21 and recommendation 43(a)(i).

35 See paras 3.1-3.12 and recommendation 1(a).

36 See para 3.5.

37 Bell, *Principles* s 1082.

38 *Rafique v Amin* 1997 SLT 1385 per Lord Justice-Clerk Ross at p 1388B.

is apt to include all the common parts of a building such as the roof, the passage and stair, and the solum of the tenement."

There seems no reason for re-stating in our proposed legislation a rule which is now well-established and which applies more widely than in the law of the tenement.

10.30 A second modification is required as a direct result of our proposals. At common law any *pro indiviso* owner is entitled on his own initiative to carry out acts of necessary maintenance and to recover the cost *pro rata* from the other owners.[39] We would not wish to disturb the right to carry out maintenance: an owner should be able to repair his property if he chooses. But the right to recover the cost is inconsistent with the decision-making regime provided by our two management schemes, and with any other management scheme by which they might be replaced.[40] Common property is automatically scheme property under both Scheme A and Scheme B.[41] As scheme property its maintenance is subject to the decision-making regime of the schemes. Under Scheme A, for example, a majority must agree before a repair can be carried out at joint expense. It would defeat the operation of the schemes if a single owner could effect maintenance at joint expense simply by invoking the common law rules of common property. Hence we recommend that:

45 Any rule of common law which allows an owner of common property to recover the cost of necessary maintenance from the other owners of that property should not apply to any common property the maintenance of which is provided for in the management scheme which applies as respects the tenement.

(Clause 17)

Duty of care to contributors to maintenance

10.31 There is no precise relationship, in Schemes A and B, between the ownership of property and liability to contribute to its maintenance. Of course much of scheme property, under both schemes, is common property, and in such a case ownership and liability for maintenance go together. But sometimes scheme property, though individually owned, requires to be collectively maintained. For example, and subject to possible variation in the titles, the external walls of a tenement are treated, section by section, as a part of the individual flats which they bound, but under our proposals their maintenance is a matter for everybody.[42] The same might be true under a management scheme which is introduced in place of Schemes A and B. In cases where liability for maintenance is severed from ownership, a technical difficulty arises in relation to duty of care. If scheme property is damaged through the fault of another owner or of a third party, those who are liable to pay for its maintenance suffer loss. But, except where liability coincides with ownership, this is pure economic loss and so not recoverable under the general law.[43] In our view such loss ought to be recoverable. In the case of certain key parts of a tenement a person is made liable for maintenance, not because he owns the part (although he may own it), but because he owns a flat in the tenement and hence takes benefit from the part which is to be maintained.[44] Since ownership is not here the cause of the liability, there seems no reason for treating owners differently from non-owners. All must contribute to the maintenance of the part, and all should have the same right of recovery from a person who has caused the damage.

---

39 Reid, para 25.

40 In fact it is inconsistent with the decision-making procedures provided by many current deeds of conditions. So the problem already occurs under the present law.

41 See para 5.5 and recommendation 5(a).

42 Scheme A, rule 5.5(b) and Scheme B, rule 11.1.

43 In *Esso Petroleum Co Ltd v Hall Russell & Co Ltd* 1988 SLT 874, 886 the view was expressed by Lord Jauncey of Tullichettle, *obiter*, that sums which are paid out under an absolute statutory liability are a good head of damage in delict. But even if such a rule were more clearly established, it would not cover liability under a voluntary management scheme introduced in place of Scheme A; and it might also not apply in cases where the statutory schemes (Schemes A and B) had been altered.

44 See para 5.6.

10.32 We suggest therefore that where scheme property is damaged as a result of the fault of any person, an owner of a flat, who is bound under the management scheme in force for the tenement to pay for the resulting maintenance but who is not an owner of the property in question, should be treated as an owner of the property for the purpose of determining the existence of any liability by that person. The rule preventing recovery for pure economic loss would thus be avoided. The fiction of deemed ownership should apply only for the recovery of maintenance costs and not for the recovery of other losses or for any other purpose. "Fault" in the sense intended here means a wrongful act, breach of a statutory duty, or a negligent act or omission.[45]

10.33 We recommend that:

46(a) Where -

(i) any part of a tenement is damaged as a result of the fault of any person, and

(ii) under the management scheme which applies as respects the tenement the owner of a flat is required to pay, in whatever proportion, for the maintenance of that part

then, for the purpose of determining the existence of any liability on the part of the person causing the damage for the cost of any maintenance attributable to the damage, the owner of a flat (if he was not an owner of the part) should be treated as having been an owner of the part at the time of the damage.

(b) "Fault" should mean any wrongful act, breach of statutory duty, or negligent act or omission which gives rise to liability in damages.

(Clause 27)

45 This is based on the definition of "fault" in s 5(a) of the Law Reform (Contributory Negligence) Act 1945.

Part 11 List of Recommendations

General recommendations

1(a) The rules of ownership laid down by the common law of the tenement should be clarified and substantially re-stated.
(b) The new law of the tenement should be freely variable.

(Paragraph 3.12)

2(a) As a general rule Management Scheme A should apply to all tenements.
(b) However, the owners should be able to provide, by deed of conditions, that the tenement is instead to be governed by

(i) Management Scheme A as varied by the deed, or

(ii) Management Scheme B, or

(iii) Management Scheme B as varied by the deed, or

(iv) some other management scheme specified in the deed.

(c) A deed of conditions should take effect on registration in the Land Register or Register of Sasines or on such later date as the deed may specify, provided that no deed should take effect before the tenement comes into existence.
(d) In the case of a tenement which is governed by Management Scheme A or Management Scheme B, a decision to change management schemes should be capable of being taken by the owners of a majority of flats.
(e) A deed of conditions in implement of a decision under (d) which is executed by the owners of a majority of flats or, in a case where Management Scheme B applies, by the manager of the owners' association should, once it has taken effect, bind all the owners and any other person who has a real right in the tenement.

(Paragraph 3.21)

3(a) "Tenement" be defined to mean a building which comprises two or more flats in separate ownership and divided from each other horizontally, together with the solum and any other land pertaining to that building.
(b) "Flat" be defined to mean a dwelling-house or any business or other premises in a tenement.

(Paragraph 4.10)

4(a) The boundary between a flat or other unit and any contiguous flat or unit should be the mid-point of the structure which separates them; but any door or other item which wholly or mainly serves a particular flat or unit should be wholly part of that flat or unit.
(b) Where the boundary of a flat or other unit is an external surface of the building, the flat or unit should be taken to include the full thickness of that boundary.
(c) A top flat should extend to and include the roof over that flat.
(d) A bottom flat should extend to and include the solum under that flat.
(e) Ownership of a sloping roof (or part of the roof) should carry with it ownership of the triangle of airspace lying between the roof (or part) and the highest point of the building.
(f) Ownership of the solum (or part of the solum) should carry with it ownership of the airspace directly over the solum (or part) and above the tenement building.

(g) Except where (j) or (k) apply there should attach to each flat as a pertinent a right of property in any part of the tenement which serves that flat.
(h) To the extent that a part serves one flat only, the right of property mentioned at (g) should be a right of sole property.
(i) To the extent that a part serves two or more flats, the right of property mentioned at (g) should be a right of common property held in equal shares; except that where the part is a chimney stack the share allocated to each flat should be proportional to the number of flues.
(j) Any land pertaining to the tenement should attach as a pertinent to the bottom flat most nearly adjacent to the land.
(k) Any close or lift should attach as common property, in equal shares, to any flat to which it gives access.
(l) The rules given above should be subject to the title to the tenement and to the effect of any enactment.

(Paragraph 4.32)

Management Scheme A

5(a) Scheme property should include any part of a tenement, including any garden or other ground, which is the common property of some or all of the owners.
(b) Scheme property should also include the following parts of a tenement -

(i) the solum;

(ii) the foundations;

(iii) the external walls;

(iv) the roof;

(v) if the tenement is separated from another building by a gable wall, the part of the gable wall that is part of the tenement building; and

(vi) any other wall that is load-bearing.

(c) However there should be excluded from (b) -

(i) any offshoot which forms part of one flat only;

(ii) any door, window, skylight, vent or other opening; and

(iii) any chimney stack or chimney flue.

(Paragraph 5.11)

6(a) Decisions under Management Scheme A should be taken by a simple majority, one vote being allocated to each flat.
(b) However, where the decision relates to the maintenance of scheme property, no vote should be allocated to a flat the owner of which is not liable for the cost of such maintenance.
(c) An owner should be able to authorise a person to vote on his behalf.
(d) Where two or more persons own a flat, any one owner should be able to vote, but if the owners disagree as to how the vote is to be cast the vote should not be counted.
(e) Where the title to a tenement provides its own procedures for the making of decisions, those procedures should apply in place of the rules given above and in recommendations 8 and 9.

(Paragraph 5.18)

7(a) Where any vote allocated as respects a flat is not cast in favour of a scheme decision, the owner of that flat should be able, by summary application, to apply to the sheriff for an order annulling that decision.
(b) An application should be made no later than 21 days after (i) the date of the meeting at which the decision was made or (ii) where no meeting was held or where the applicant did not attend the meeting, the date on which notification of the decision was sent to him.

(c) During the appeal period mentioned at (b) it should not be competent to incur any expenditure in implementation of a scheme decision except in a case where work requires to be carried out urgently.

(d) If during the appeal period the owners receive notice of an application, the bar on expenditure should continue until the application has been disposed of or abandoned.

(e) The sheriff should be empowered to annul a scheme decision in whole or in part if he is satisfied that (i) it is not in the best interests of all the owners or (ii) it is unfairly prejudicial to one or more of the owners.

(f) In determining whether he is satisfied under (e) in relation to a decision to carry out maintenance, improvements or alterations, the sheriff should have regard to -

(i) the age and condition of the tenement;

(ii) the likely cost of carrying out the work; and

(iii) whether the cost of the work is reasonable.

(Paragraph 5.25)

8(a) If in relation to a particular decision the number of votes allocated does not exceed three, that decision should require to be reached unanimously.

(b) Where a decision which requires the expenditure of money is duly made but is not supported by those owners who are liable for 75% of the cost of such expenditure, those owners should be able to annul the decision by sending a notice to that effect to the other owners not later than the period for appeal mentioned in recommendation 7(b).

(Paragraph 5.32)

9(a) It should be possible to make a scheme decision without a meeting being held.

(b) If an owner wants to call a meeting, he should have to give 48 hours notice of its date, time, location and purpose.

(c) Where a meeting is not held, the person proposing the decision should consult all the owners (or representatives of the owners) except where it is impracticable to do so.

(d) A decision should be notified to all the owners as soon as practicable.

(e) Any notice which requires to be given to an owner under the Scheme may be given in writing by-

(i) delivering the notice to his flat;

(ii) posting it to that address or such other address as he is known to have; or

(iii) transmitting it to him by electronic means.

(f) An irregularity in procedure should not of itself invalidate a decision; but an owner who is directly affected by the irregularity should be relieved by the others of liability for any costs relating to that decision unless he was aware that they were being incurred and did not immediately object.

(Paragraph 5.39)

10(a) The owners should be entitled to make a scheme decision to carry out maintenance to scheme property.

(b) "Maintenance" should include repairs and replacement, cleaning, painting, and other routine works, gardening, the day-to-day running of a tenement and the reinstatement of a part (but not most) of a tenement; but it should not include demolition, alteration or improvement unless reasonably incidental to the maintenance.

(Paragraph 5.51)

11 If the owners decide under recommendation 10 to carry out maintenance to scheme property, they should thereafter be able to make a scheme decision to -

(i) appoint a person to manage the work;

(ii) instruct or arrange for the carrying out of the work;

(iii) require each owner to deposit an amount of money representing a reasonable estimate of that owner's share of the cost of the work; and

(iv) take such further steps as are necessary to ensure that the work is carried out to a satisfactory standard and completed in good time.

(Paragraph 5.53)

12(a) Any owner should be entitled to instruct or carry out emergency work to scheme property.

(b) The owners should be liable for the cost of any emergency work as if it had been authorised by a scheme decision.

(c) "Emergency work" should mean work which requires to be carried out at once and before a scheme decision can be taken in order (i) to prevent damage to any part of the tenement or (ii) in the interests of health or safety.

(d) The owners should be entitled to make a scheme decision to adopt and pay for maintenance which has already been carried out.

(Paragraph 5.57)

13(a) Maintenance costs of scheme property should be apportioned amongst the owners in accordance with the following rules (the first applicable rule being the relevant one and excluding any later rule):

Rule 1. Costs are apportioned according to any express provision made in the title to the tenement; but this rule does not apply where part only of a particular cost is provided for.

Rule 2. If the property being maintained is common property, costs are apportioned according to the respective sizes of the shares held by the owners.

Rule 3. If (i) the express provision made in the title to the tenement deals with part only of a particular cost and (ii) the property being maintained is common property, the title provision is followed as far as possible and the balance of the cost is apportioned according to the respective sizes of the shares held by the owners.

Rule 4. Except where the floor area of the largest flat is more than one and a half times that of the smallest flat, costs are apportioned equally among the flats.

Rule 5. Costs are apportioned in accordance with the respective floor areas of each flat.

(b) "Maintenance costs" should mean (i) the cost of such maintenance as has been authorised under Scheme A and (ii) any cost due to or recovered by a local authority following the service of a statutory repairs notice.

(c) "Floor area" should mean the total floor area measured within the boundary walls, including the area occupied by internal walls and partitions, but excluding (i) any balcony or other pertinent and (ii) any basement or loft which is used only for storage.

(Paragraph 5.67)

14 The owners should be entitled to make a scheme decision to-

(i) appoint a person including a firm to manage the tenement, and, if desired, to delegate to that person the right to carry out or instruct maintenance of scheme property up to a stipulated amount;

(ii) arrange for the tenement a policy of common insurance in accordance with recommendation 37 and against such other risks as the owners may decide, and to determine on an equitable basis the liability of each owner to contribute to the premium;

(iii) determine that an owner is not required to pay all or part of scheme costs for which he would otherwise be liable;

(iv) determine that Management Scheme A should be varied, or disapplied and replaced with some other management scheme, but subject to the consent of any owner whose liability for costs would be thereby increased; and

(v) modify or revoke any scheme decision.

(Paragraph 5.78)

15(a) Scheme costs (other than maintenance costs) should be apportioned amongst the owners in accordance with the following rules:

(i) Scheme costs are apportioned in accordance with any express provision made in the title to the tenement, except that this rule does not apply where part only of a particular cost is provided for; and

(ii) where no express provision is made in the title to the tenement, scheme costs are apportioned equally among the flats, except that the premium on a policy of common insurance is apportioned by scheme decision under recommendation 14(ii).

(b) Co-owners of a flat should be jointly and severally liable for scheme costs (including maintenance costs), but as between themselves they should be liable in the proportions in which they own the flat.

(c) Where any share of a scheme cost (including the cost of maintenance) is irrecoverable or where a scheme decision is taken under recommendation 14(iii) to exempt an owner, whether in whole or in part, from liability for his share, that share should be paid by the other owners in the same proportions as the remainder of the cost; but in the case of an irrecoverable share there should be a right of relief against the defaulting owner.

(Paragraph 5.83)

16(a) Management Scheme A should bind the owners for the time being of flats.

(b) A scheme decision should be binding on the owners and their successors as owners.

(c) Any obligation imposed by Management Scheme A or arising from a scheme decision should be enforceable by any owner or by a person authorised by an owner in writing to act on his behalf.

(Paragraph 5.86)

Management Scheme B

17(a) The Secretary of State should have the power to alter Scheme B by statutory instrument, but such alterations should not apply to applications of Scheme B by a deed of conditions executed before the coming into force of the instrument.

(b) In varying Management Scheme B in terms of recommendation 2(b)(iii) it should not be possible to vary Part I of the scheme.

(Paragraph 6.2)

18(a) An owners' association should come into existence on the day on which Scheme B takes effect.

(b) The association should be a body corporate but not a company.

(c) The members of the association should be the owners for the time being of the flats in the tenement.

(d) Where two or more persons own a flat both (or all) of them should be members.

(e) The function of the association should be to manage the scheme property for the benefit of the owners of the flats in the tenement.

(f) The association should have power to do anything necessary for the carrying out of its function and in particular should be able to -

(i) carry out maintenance, improvements or alterations to scheme property;

(ii) enter into a contract of insurance in respect of the tenement or any part of it (and for that purpose the association should have an insurable interest);

(iii) purchase or otherwise acquire moveable property;

(iv) require owners to contribute by way of a service charge to association funds;

(v) open and maintain in the name of the association an account with any bank or building society;

(vi) invest in the name of the association any money held on its behalf;

(vii) borrow money;

(viii) engage employees or appoint agents;

(ix) act in accordance with any other powers conferred under the scheme.

(g) In varying Management Scheme B in terms of recommendation 2(b)(iii) it should not be possible to confer on the association the power to acquire land or the power to carry on any trade.

(Paragraph 6.10)

19(a) In an owners' association executive responsibility should be vested in a manager, who may but need not be a member of the association.

(b) A person including a firm should be appointed as manager by the association at a general meeting, and on such terms and conditions as the association may decide.

(c) However, it should be possible to nominate in the deed of conditions the person who is to act as the first manager of the association, and such person should serve until the first annual general meeting, be entitled to reasonable remuneration, and be eligible for reappointment.

(d) The actings of a manager should be valid even if there is an irregularity in the way he was appointed.

(e) Not later than a month after a manager's appointment a certificate should be prepared recording the making of the appointment and its duration, and the certificate should be signed by the manager and, on behalf of the association, by a member.

(f) The manager should have the duty to manage the scheme property for the benefit of the members.

(g) The manager should be an agent of the association.

(h) The association should be empowered to dismiss the manager at a general meeting before his term of office has expired.

(Paragraph 6.15)

20(a) At a general meeting the association should be entitled to elect an advisory committee of members to provide advice to the manager.

(b) If an advisory committee is appointed, the manager should be bound to consult it from time to time, but should not be bound to follow its advice.

(c) Any member of the advisory committee should be entitled to requisition a general meeting.

(Paragraph 6.18)

21(a) The powers of the association should be exercisable by the association in general meeting or by the manager, but subject in both cases to the other rules of the scheme.

(b) In the exercise of these powers the manager should be subject to any directions given by the association at a general meeting.

(c) Recommendation 7 (which confers on an owner a right to apply to the sheriff for annulment of a decision on certain grounds) should apply to decisions made by the association at a general meeting.

(d) The rules of Management Scheme B should be binding on the association, its members and on the manager.

(e) The association should be entitled to enforce any provision of the scheme and any obligation owed by any person to the association; and the manager should be under a duty to carry out such enforcement on behalf of the association.

(f) The duties imposed on the manager by the scheme should be owed to the association and to its members.

(Paragraph 6.24)

22(a) An annual general meeting of the association should be held every year, and not more than 15 months should elapse between the date of each successive meeting.

(b) The first annual general meeting should take place not later than 12 months after the establishment of the association.

(c) Members holding not less than 25% of the votes for the tenement should be entitled to requisition an additional general meeting at any time.

(d) The manager should be under a duty to call the annual general meeting and any other meeting which is requisitioned by a member or members. In addition, he should be able to call a general meeting at any time.

(e) Where the manager fails to call a general meeting, or where there is no manager, any member can call the meeting.

(f) A meeting should be called by sending to each member, at least 14 days in advance, an agenda and a notice of the date, time and place of the meeting.

(g) However, any inadvertent failure to send the required documentation should not affect the validity of proceedings at the meeting.

(h) At the meeting a quorum should be the members holding not less than 50% of the votes for the tenement; but where the tenement has more than 30 flats the figure should be reduced to 35%.

(i) A member should be able to be represented at the meeting by a person (other than the manager) duly nominated in writing.

(j) A quorum should be necessary for a general meeting to begin, but once the meeting has begun it should be able to continue thereafter even if a quorum has ceased to attend.

(k) If there is still no quorum 20 minutes after the time fixed for a general meeting, the meeting should be postponed until another day not less than 14 and not more than 28 days later. The postponed meeting should then be able to proceed even in the absence of a quorum.

(l) The meeting should be presided over by a chairman elected by the members.

(m) Decisions should be taken by a simple majority of the votes cast, one vote being allocated to each flat.

(n) However, an absolute majority of the votes for the tenement should be required for any decision to-

(i) vary, disapply or replace the scheme in terms of recommendation 2;

(ii) make payments from a reserve fund; or

(iii) carry out improvements or alterations to scheme property.

(o) Where two or more persons own a flat, any one owner should be able to vote, but if the owners disagree as to how the vote is to be cast the vote should not be counted.

(p) Voting should be taken by show of hands unless the chairman decides it should be by ballot.

(q) The manager should be under a duty to-

(i) attend all general meetings (except where he is unable to because of illness or some other good reason);

(ii) take minutes;

(iii) send a copy of the minutes to all members within 21 days; and

(iv) give effect to the decisions taken.

(Paragraph 6.32)

23(a) The manager should fix the financial year of the association.

(b) The manager should keep proper financial records of the association and prepare accounts for each financial year.

(c) Not later than 14 days before an annual general meeting the manager should send to each member -

   (i) the accounts for the financial year just ended: and

   (ii) a draft budget for the new financial year.

(d) The draft budget should set out an estimate of the income and expenditure of the association, the total service charge for the year, and the date or dates on which the service charge will be due for payment.
(e) The draft budget may also make provision for contributions to a reserve fund.
(f) At the annual general meeting the association should be entitled either to approve the budget, whether in its original or in an amended form, or to reject it.
(g) If the budget is rejected, the manager should be bound to bring a revised draft budget to another general meeting within two months.
(h) If the budget is approved, the manager should be bound to levy the service charge accordingly and to implement the budget.
(i) The manager should be empowered without further approval to levy an additional service charge up to an amount not exceeding 25% of the total service charge for that year.
(j) The manager should not be entitled to levy further sums without first preparing a supplementary budget which is submitted to and approved by the association at a general meeting.
(k) A service charge should be levied by sending to each owner a notice setting out the amount due and the date or dates on which it is to be paid.
(l) If an owner is more than 28 days late in making payment of the service charge (or part of it) the manager should be able to charge interest on the amount outstanding at such rate (being a reasonable rate) and from such date as he may choose.
(m) The amount of service charge should be the same for each flat.
(n) However, any additional premium on a common policy of insurance which is attributable to the special characteristics of a particular flat or the purposes for which it is used, should be payable by the owner of that flat.
(o) A reserve fund should be adequately invested and should be kept separately from the general funds of the association.

(Paragraph 6.41)

24(a) The manager should be under a duty to carry out regular inspections of the scheme property and to arrange for maintenance.
(b) No alteration or improvement should be carried out to scheme property which is individually owned unless the owner has given his consent in writing.

(Paragraph 6.46)

25 In Management Scheme B where either (i) the association is being or has been wound up or (ii) a debt due by the association has been constituted by decree or a document has been registered in the Books of Council and Session or the sheriff court books, and the creditor has executed diligence but not recovered the debt, then the creditor should be entitled to recover the debt from the members, as if he were the manager.

(Paragraph 6.54)

26(a) The manager should be under a duty to keep a record of the name and address of each member of the association.
(b) On disposal of a flat an owner should be obliged to notify the manager of -

   (i) his own forwarding address;

   (ii) the name and address of the new owner;

   (iii) the name and address of the solicitor or other agent acting for the new owner; and

(iv) the date on which the new owner will be entitled to take entry.

(c) Any member should be entitled to inspect any document relating to the management of the tenement which is in the possession of the manager or which it is reasonably practicable for the manager to obtain; but this entitlement should not extend to correspondence passing between the manager and individual members.

(Paragraph 6.61)

27 A document should be treated as signed by an owners' association if it is signed on its behalf by the manager or by a person nominated for the purpose by the association at a general meeting.

(Paragraph 6.62)

28(a) If Management Scheme B ceases to apply to a tenement, the winding up of the owners' association should begin on the day of such cessation.

(b) The winding up should end after a period of six months or on such other date as the members may decide, whereupon the association should be automatically dissolved.

(c) The winding up should be conducted by the manager, who should

(i) pay any debts of the association;

(ii) distribute any remaining funds of the association to those who owned flats at the date of the commencement of the winding up, an equal share being apportioned to each flat; and

(iii) prepare and send to each member final accounts of the association showing how the winding up was conducted and the funds of the association disposed of.

(d) Once Scheme B has been disapplied, and the winding up commenced, the owners' association should cease to manage the scheme property of the tenement.

(e) An insolvent association should be subject to sequestration proceedings under the Bankruptcy (Scotland) Act 1985.

(Paragraph 6.67)

Other recommendations

29 The common law doctrine of common interest should be abolished to the extent that it applies to tenements.

(Paragraph 7.3)

30(a) Any part of the tenement building which provides, or is designed to provide, support or shelter should be maintained by its owner to a standard sufficient to provide that support or shelter; but maintenance should not be required where it is not reasonable, having regard in particular to the age of the tenement, its condition and the likely cost of the maintenance.

(b) Where in implement of (a) an owner carries out maintenance to property which is scheme property under the management scheme applying to the tenement, he should be entitled to recover from any other owner any share of the cost for which that other owner would have been liable if the maintenance had been carried out under the scheme.

(c) An owner or occupier should not be entitled to carry out work on the tenement if it would or would be reasonably likely to impair support or shelter to a material extent.

(d) The obligations contained in this recommendation and in recommendation 31 should be enforceable by the owner of any flat in the tenement who has an interest to do so.

(Paragraph 7.13)

31. An owner or occupier should not be allowed to build on any land forming part of the tenement if this interferes with the natural light enjoyed by any part of the tenement building.

(Paragraph 7.18)

32. There should attach to each flat as a pertinent ownership of any chimney flue which serves that flat.

(Paragraph 7.19)

33(a) In Management Scheme A an owner should become liable for a scheme cost -

(i) on the day when the scheme decision to incur that cost was made, or

(ii) if the decision was made without a meeting or if the meeting was not attended by the owner, on the day when notification of the decision was sent to the owner.

(b) However, notwithstanding the rule set out at (a) -

(i) an owner should be liable for the cost of emergency work from the date on which the work is instructed;

(ii) an owner should be liable (in a question with other owners) for the costs recovered by a local authority under a statutory notice from the date of the statutory notice; and

(iii) an owner should be liable for any recurrent and continuing costs on a day-to-day basis.

(c) In Management Scheme B an owner should become liable for payment of an instalment of service charge on the date specified for payment in the notice sent in terms of recommendation 23(k).

(d) An owner who has become liable for costs under the management scheme in force for the tenement or under any other of our recommendations should not cease to be liable merely because he has ceased to be owner.

(Paragraph 8.8)

34(a) An incoming owner of a flat should be jointly and severally liable with the former owner of that flat for any costs for which the former owner is liable under the management scheme applying to the tenement or under any other of our recommendations.

(b) Where the incoming owner pays the costs he should have a right of relief against the former owner.

(c) This rule should apply to costs for which an owner becomes liable on or after the date on which the legislation comes into force.

(Paragraph 8.16)

35(a) In Management Scheme B the manager should be bound, on request, to provide and sign a certificate setting out, as at the date of the certificate, that no service charge is outstanding or, as the case may be, that a specified amount of service charge is outstanding in respect of a flat.

(b) The liability of an incoming owner for service charges outstanding at the date of the certificate should not exceed the figure stated in the certificate.

(c) The obligation of an owner for costs under the management scheme applying to the tenement or under any other of our recommendations should be subject to negative prescription after 5 years.

(Paragraph 8.24)

36(a) "Owner" be defined to mean -

(i) Where a flat is held on feudal tenure, the person holding the interest of *dominium utile* in the flat;

(ii) Where a flat is not held on feudal tenure, the owner.

(iii) Where a heritable creditor has entered into lawful possession of a flat, the heritable creditor in possession of the flat.

(b) For the purposes of recommendation 36(a)(i) and (ii) a person becomes owner (and the last owner ceases to be owner) when that person is entitled to take entry under a conveyance of the flat in question.

(Paragraph 8.29)

37(a) The owner of a flat should be under a duty to insure the flat and any pertinents attaching to the flat for reinstatement value and against such risks as may be prescribed by the Secretary of State.

(b) The duty to insure should not apply to a risk in respect of which the owner cannot obtain insurance or can obtain insurance only at a cost which is unreasonably high.

(c) The duty to insure should be enforceble by the owner of any flat in the tenement.

(d) On request an owner should be obliged to produce to any other owner

(i) the policy of insurance or a copy of the policy, and

(ii) evidence of payment of the current premium.

(e) The obligation to insure under recommendation 37(a) should not apply to the Crown.

(Paragraph 9.8)

38(a) Where the title to the tenement requires the building to be insured by means of a common policy, the duty to insure mentioned in recommendation 37(a) should be complied with by means of a common policy.

(b) Under Management Scheme A the owners should be entitled to make a scheme decision to arrange a common policy of insurance against the statutory risks for reinstatement value and against such other risks as may be agreed.

(c) In Management Scheme B the manager should be under a duty to ensure that there is in force for the tenement building a common policy of insurance against the statutory risks for reinstatement value and against such other risks as the owners may decide.

(d) The policy mentioned at (c) should be taken in the name of the owners' association which, for this purpose, should be deemed to have an insurable interest in the tenement.

(Paragraph 9.14)

39(a) Except where the title to the tenement provides otherwise, the cost of demolishing a tenement should be borne equally by all the flats in the tenement.

(b) In the event of partial demolition, the cost should be borne equally by the flats in the part which has been demolished.

(c) In a case where the floor area of the largest flat was more than one and a half times that of the smallest flat, the principle of equality of contribution should be replaced by the rule that each flat must contribute in proportion to respective floor areas.

(Paragraph 9.24)

40(a) The demolition of a tenement should not of itself affect the ownership rights of any person.

(b) Where a tenement building has been wholly demolished (whether in a single act or in two or more stages) but the former flats (or some of them) continue to be separately owned, the following rules should apply in relation to the site of the former building:

(i) it should not be permissible to erect buildings or other structures on the site except with the consent of, or in implement of an obligation binding on, the owners of all of the former flats;

(ii) subject to (iii), any owner of a former flat should be entitled to have the site sold;

(iii) the entitlement to sell should not arise if there has been lawful rebuilding under (i) or if the owners of all the former flats are subject to an enforceable obligation to rebuild the tenement or some other building;

(iv) except where the title to the tenement provides otherwise, the free proceeds of sale should be divided equally among the owners of the former flats, except that in a case where the floor area of the largest flat was more than one and a half times that of the smallest flat the proceeds should be divided in proportion to respective floor areas; and

(v) on the registration of a conveyance in implement of the sale, any heritable security which burdened a former flat should be deemed to burden the site to the extent of a fractional *pro indiviso* share corresponding to the number of flats in the former tenement.

(c) Where (i) due to its physical condition, a tenement building is wholly unoccupied for more than 6 months and (ii) it is unlikely that any owner or other person will return to occupy any part of the tenement building, the owner of any flat should be entitled to have the tenement building sold and the proceeds divided.

(Paragraph 9.36)

41(a) The owner of a flat should be entitled -

(i) to fix to the outside surface of any roof or to any chimney stack a television or radio aerial, satellite dish, or other equipment relating to television or radio broadcasting, and

(ii) to lead wires or cables from the aerial, dish or other equipment to his flat.

(b) This right should be without prejudice to any requirement on an owner under any enactment relating to planning or building.

(Paragraph 10.5)

42(a) The owner of a flat should be entitled to lead through the tenement such pipes, cables and other apparatus as are required for the provision to his flat of -

(i) gas, and

(ii) such other services as the Secretary of State may by regulations prescribe.

(b) However, there should be no right of installation within an individual flat (other than the flat which is to receive the service).

(c) This right should be without prejudice to any requirement on an owner under any enactment relating to planning or building or to the provision of the service in question.

(Paragraph 10.9)

43(a) The owner or occupier of part of a tenement should be bound, on being given reasonable notice, to allow access to or through that part to the owner of any flat and (in a case where the tenement is governed by Management Scheme B) to the manager of the owners' association for any of the following purposes:

(i) to carry out any maintenance or other works duly authorised under the management scheme applying to that tenement;

(ii) to carry out any maintenance or other works to a part of the tenement owned (whether solely or in common) by the person seeking access;

(iii) to fix a television aerial or other telecommunications equipment to the outside surface of the roof or a chimney stack;

(iv) to install gas or other prescribed services;

(v) to carry out an inspection to determine whether maintenance or works of the kind mentioned at (i) and (ii) above are necessary;

(vi) to determine whether the obligations of an owner or occupier relating to support and shelter have been complied with; and

(vii) in a case where liability for costs is calculated by reference to floor area, to measure the floor area of the part.

(b) Notice under (a) above should not be needed where access is required for the purpose of carrying out urgent maintenance.

(c) An owner or occupier should be entitled to refuse access, or access at a particular time, if it would be reasonable to do so having regard to the circumstances including whether the request for access is reasonable.

(d) An owner or manager who has a right of access under this recommendation should be able to authorise in writing any other person to exercise the right on his behalf.

(e) Where a person authorised under (d) causes damage to any part of the tenement, the owner who authorised him (or the association, where he was authorised by a manager) should be jointly and severally liable with the authorised person for the cost of making good the damage.

(f) An owner or association which makes payment under (e) should be entitled to recover the cost from the authorised person.

(Paragraph 10.21)

44(a) In relation to a tenement the sheriff should be empowered, on application, to grant such orders, and on such conditions, as he sees fit, being orders relating to any matter concerning the operation of the management scheme which applies to the tenement or any provision of the legislation as it applies to the tenement.

(b) An application under (a) should be capable of being brought by the owner of any flat in a tenement and, in the case of a tenement governed by Management Scheme B, by the manager of the owners' association.

(Paragraph 10.27)

45 Any rule of common law which allows an owner of common property to recover the cost of necessary maintenance from the other owners should not apply to any common property the maintenance of which is provided for in the management scheme which applies as respects the tenement.

(Paragraph 10.30)

46(a) Where -

(i) any part of a tenement is damaged as a result of the fault of any person, and

(ii) under the management scheme which applies as respects the tenement the owner of a flat is required to pay, in whatever proportion, for the maintenance of that part

then, for the purpose of determining the existence of any liability on the part of the person causing the damage for the cost of any maintenance attributable to the damage, the owner of a flat (if he was not an owner of the part) should be treated as having been an owner of the part at the time of the damage.

(b) "Fault" should mean wrongful act, breach of statutory duty, or negligent act or omission which gives rise to liability in damages.

(Paragraph 10.33)

Appendix A

Tenements (Scotland) Bill

ARRANGEMENT OF CLAUSES

Demolition and abandonment of tenement building

DRAFT

OF A

BILL

TO

Make provision as respects Scotland for the boundaries of tenements; for the management of tenements etc.; for the abolition of the common law of common interest in its application as respects tenements; for access to tenements for the purposes of effecting repairs and installing certain services and for costs arising from such repairs and installations; for insuring tenements; for rights of owners in relation to the use and disposal of demolished or abandoned tenements; and for connected purposes.

BE IT ENACTED by the Queen's most Excellent Majesty, by and with the advice and consent of the Lords Spiritual and Temporal, and Commons, in this present Parliament assembled, and by the authority of the same, as follows:

Boundaries and pertinents

1. Except in so far as any different boundaries or pertinents are constituted under or by virtue of the title to the tenement, or any enactment, the boundaries and pertinents of units of a tenement shall be determined in accordance with sections 2 and 3 of this Act.

Determination of boundaries and pertinents.

EXPLANATORY NOTES

Note:

These notes refer to the provisions of the Bill as if they had been enacted.

Clauses 1 to 3

These clauses implement recommendation 4. See paragraphs 4.15 to 4.32 of the report.

Clauses 2 and 3 taken together restate the common law rules of ownership within a tenement. These provisions apply to all tenements, whether existing or new, except to the extent that the title to the tenement or any enactment makes different provision. This is how the common law works at present. Thus clauses 2 and 3 provide the background law as to ownership of parts of a tenement. They will come into play only if the titles or any enactment does not make provision. For example, if the title to the tenement is silent about who owns the roof, clause 2(3) applies, with the effect that the roof is part of the top flat.

Clause 1

"Title to the tenement" and "enactment" are defined in clause 30(1). The enactment which is most likely to be relevant here is the Prescription and Limitation (Scotland) Act 1973.

2.—(1) Subject to subsections (3) to (7) below, the boundary between any two contiguous units is the median of the structure that separates them; and a unit- Tenement boundaries.

(a) extends in any direction to such a boundary; or

(b) if it does not first meet such a boundary-

(i) extends to and includes the solum or any structure which is an outer surface of the tenement building; or

(ii) extends to the boundary that separates the unit from a contiguous building which is not part of the tenement building.

(2) For the purposes of subsection (1) above, where the structure separating two contiguous units is or includes something (as for example, but without prejudice to the generality of this subsection, a door or window) which wholly or mainly serves only one of those units, the thing is in its entire thickness part of that unit.

(3) A top flat extends to and includes the roof over that flat.

(4) A bottom flat extends to and includes the solum under that flat.

(5) A close extends to and includes the roof over, and the solum under, the close.

(6) Where a unit includes the solum (or any part of it) the unit shall also include, subject to subsection (7) below, the airspace above the tenement building and directly over the solum (or part).

(7) Where the roof of the tenement building slopes, a unit which includes the roof (or any part of it) shall also include the airspace above the slope of the roof (or part) up to the level of the highest point of the roof.

Clause 2

This clause implements recommendations 4(a) - (f) and (l). See paragraphs 4.17 to 4.23 of the report.

This clause restates the common law rules of ownership of parts within a tenement. "Unit", "flat" and "tenement" are defined in clause 30(1). A unit can be a flat or some other separate part of a tenement such as the close or the roofspace. The use of "unit" is a convenient way of describing the parts which go to make up a tenement building.

Subsection (1)

This subsection sets out the boundaries of units in a tenement. "Solum" is defined in clause 30(1).

Subsection (2)

This subsection means that, for example, the front door of a flat leading to the close is part of the flat and not of the close.

Subsections (3) and (4)

These subsections restate the special rules of the common law in relation to the top and bottom flats of a tenement. In these provisions we are concerned with the boundaries of flats and not with the boundaries of units.

Subsection (3) provides that a top flat extends to include the roof over that flat. This means that the intermediate roofspace in so far as over the flat is also part of the top flat.

Subsection (4) provides that a bottom flat (which might be a ground or basement flat, depending on the tenement) extends to include the solum under that flat.

Subsection (5)

The "close" is the passage and stairs in the tenement (see clause 30(1)).

Subsection (6)

This subsection restates the common law rule that ownership of the airspace goes with ownership of the solum. "Solum" means the ground on which the tenement building is erected (clause 30(1)). Where under the titles the solum is common property of all the owners in the tenement, the airspace is likewise common property.

Subsection (7)

This qualifies subsection (6). Ownership of the triangle of airspace, lying between the surface of a sloping roof and an imaginary horizontal plane passing through the highest point of the roof, goes with ownership of the roof and not with ownership of the solum. This is important in cases where the owner of the top floor flat builds a dormer window into the airspace. See paragraph 4.22 of the report. Where under the titles the roof is common property of all the owners in the tenement, the triangle of airspace is likewise common property.

3.—(1) Subject to subsection (2) below, there shall attach to each of the flats, as a pertinent, a right of common property in (and in the whole of) the following parts of a tenement-

Pertinents.

(a) a close;

(b) a lift by means of which access can be obtained to more than one of the flats.

(2) If a close or lift does not afford a means of access to a flat then there shall not attach to that flat, as a pertinent, a right of common property in the close or, as the case may be, lift.

(3) Any land (other than the solum of the tenement building) pertaining to a tenement shall attach as a pertinent to the bottom flat most nearly adjacent to the land (or part of the land); but this subsection shall not apply to any part which constitutes a path, outside stair or other way affording access to any unit other than that flat.

(4) If a tenement includes any part (as for example, but without prejudice to the generality of this subsection, a path, outside stair, fire escape, rhone, pipe, flue, conduit, cable, tank or chimney stack) that does not fall within subsection (1) or (3) above and that part to any extent-

(a) wholly serves one flat, then it shall to that extent attach as a pertinent to that flat;

(b) serves two or more flats, then there shall attach to each of the flats, as a pertinent, to the extent that it serves the flats, a right of common property in the part.

(5) For the purposes of this section, references to rights of common property being attached to flats as pertinents are references to there attaching to each flat equal rights of common property; except that where the common property is a chimney stack the share allocated to a flat shall be determined in direct accordance with the ratio which the number of flues serving it in the stack bears to the total number of flues in the stack.

Management schemes

4. Except where any provision is made by virtue of section 5(1) of this Act, Management Scheme A, which is set out in Schedule 1 to this Act, shall apply in the form in which it is set out in that Schedule as respects the management of all tenements.

Automatic application of Management Scheme A.

Clause 3

This clause implements recommendations 4(g) - (l). See paragraphs 4.23 to 4.32 and paragraphs 4.33 to 4.34 of the report. Clause 3 applies only in so far as provision is not made in the titles (see clause 1).

Subsection (1)

The owners of all the flats have a right of common property in the close and in any lift. "Close" and "lift" are defined in clause 30(1). Subsection (5) regulates the size of *pro indiviso* shares.

Subsection (2)

There is no ownership of a close or lift which does not allow access to a particular flat.

Subsection (3)

This provides for ownership of land (for example, garden ground). The ground underneath the tenement building is already dealt with in clause 2(4) and (5) and so is excluded. A path, outside stair or any other means of access, which are covered by subsection (4) below, are also excluded.

Subsection (4)

This important subsection deals with those residual parts of a tenement which are not covered by clause 2 or by subsections (1) or (3) of clause 3. The subsection allocates ownership in accordance with a service test. Under the present law the ownership of these parts is often unclear.

Subsection (5)

This subsection provides that, except in the case of a chimney stack, rights of common property are to be held in equal shares. "Chimney stack" is defined in clause 30(1).

Clause 4

This clause implements recommendation 2(a). See paragraphs 3.16 and 5.1.

The effect of this clause is that, with certain exceptions, Management Scheme A as set out in Schedule 1 applies to regulate the management of all tenements. New tenements not yet built will also become subject to Scheme A unless the developer elects under clause 5(1) to use a different management scheme.

5.—(1) By deed of conditions it may be provided as respects the management of any tenement- Power to override section 4.

(a) that Management Scheme A shall apply subject to variations specified in the deed of conditions; or

(b) that Management Scheme B, which is set out in Schedule 2 to this Act-

(i) shall apply in the form in which it is set out in that Schedule; or

(ii) shall apply subject to any variations of Part II or III of it specified in the deed of conditions,

(and, in either case, the deed of conditions may state the name of any person nominated as the first manager of the owners' association); or

(c) that such other management scheme as may be specified in the deed of conditions shall apply.

(2) Where provision has been made under subsection (1) above, it may subsequently be provided by deed of conditions under that subsection that-

(a) the scheme applied shall cease to apply; and

(b) if it is intended that some management scheme other than Management Scheme A as set out in Schedule 1 to this Act should apply, such different provision as is mentioned in any of paragraphs (a) to (c) of that subsection shall instead be made.

(3) Where any development includes a tenement but also includes some other building then any deed of conditions relating to that other building may provide that the management scheme which applies as respects the tenement shall apply as respects the management of that building subject to any variations specified in the deed of conditions.

(4) A deed of conditions under this section shall not take effect before the date on which the tenement to which it relates comes into existence (the "relevant date"); but thereafter such a deed shall take effect-

(a) where on or after the relevant date the deed is recorded in the Register of Sasines or, as the case may be, the terms of the deed are registered in the Land Register of Scotland-

(i) on the date of such recording or registration; or

(ii) on such later date as the deed may specify; or

(b) where such recording or registration occurs before the relevant date-

(i) on the relevant date; or

(ii) on such later date as the deed may specify.

(5) Sections 3(4) (date of registration to be date of creation of a real right etc.) and 17 (effect of recording or registering deeds of conditions) of the Land Registration (Scotland) Act 1979 shall not apply as respects any provision made by deed of conditions under this section. 1979 c. 33.

(6) In this section (other than subsection (4) above)-

(a) any reference to a building includes a reference to the solum and any other land pertaining to the building;

(b) any reference to a tenement or to a building includes a reference to a tenement, or as the case may be building, not yet in existence; and

(c) "variations"-

(i) means variations referable to the purposes of the scheme in question and includes additions and deletions; and

(ii) includes, where the scheme in question is Management Scheme B, the granting of additional powers to the owners' association (other than the power to acquire land or carry on any trade the object of which is to make a profit).

Clause 5

This clause implements recommendation 2(b) and (c). See paragraphs 3.16 to 3.21 of the report.

Management Scheme A applies automatically to a tenement (see clause 4). But clause 5 enables the owners (in practice often a developer) to vary Scheme A or to choose a different management scheme altogether.

Subsection (1)

This subsection sets out 4 options, which may be selected by deed of conditions (as defined in clause 30(1)). The deed may be executed and registered before the tenement is actually built (see subsection (6)(b)).

Subsection (2)

This subsection allows owners, who have already made an election under subsection (1), to change their minds by means of a second deed of conditions. There are two options available. Either the owners can disapply the current management scheme, in which case Scheme A will automatically apply (except where the tenement has been demolished); or the owners can disapply the current management scheme and select a new one.

Subsection (3)

It is quite common for mixed developments (ie those comprising both blocks of flats and also villas or terraced houses) to be regulated by a single deed of conditions. This subsection provides that such a deed of conditions can extend the management scheme which is to apply to the blocks of flats to the other buildings in the development even although they are not tenements.

Subsection (4)

This subsection explains when a deed of conditions takes effect. It cannot take effect until the tenement concerned comes into existence. A tenement comes into existence when there are two flats in separate ownership in the building (see the definition of "tenement" in clause 30(1)). Thus in practice a tenement will usually come into existence when the purchaser of the first flat to be sold registers his disposition. Paragraph (b) covers the common case of where a developer executes and registers a deed of conditions before he has sold any of the flats.

Subsection (5)

This subsection is for the avoidance of doubt. A deed of conditions under clause 5 is to take effect only in accordance with the rules set out in subsection (4).

Subsection (6)

This subsection contains some definitions. The definition of "variations" acts as a control on otherwise wide powers of variation conferred by subsection (1).

6.—(1) Notwithstanding section 32 of the Conveyancing (Scotland) Act 1874 (method of importing conditions etc. by reference), if a decision that a deed of conditions under section 5 of this Act should be executed has been made-

Special provision as respects execution of certain deeds of conditions.
38 & 38 Vict. c. 94.

(a) where Management Scheme A applies as respects a tenement, in accordance with that scheme; or

(b) where Management Scheme B so applies, in accordance with that scheme,

then the deed may, in so far as it relates to the tenement, be executed in accordance with subsection (2) below.

(2) A deed of conditions is executed in accordance with this subsection-

(a) where Management Scheme A applies as respects the tenement, by being subscribed by the owners of the majority of the flats in the tenement; or

(b) where Management Scheme B so applies, by being subscribed on behalf of the owners' association of that tenement in accordance with rule 4 of Management Scheme B.

(3) A deed of conditions executed in accordance with subsection (2) above shall, if it has taken effect in accordance with section 5(4) of this Act, be binding on all the owners and any other person who has a real right in relation to the tenement.

7.—(1) The Secretary of State may by regulations vary Schedule 2 to this Act.

Secretary of State's power to vary Management Scheme B.

(2) Any variations of Schedule 2 contained in regulations made under subsection (1) above shall not apply as respects any application of that Schedule (or that Schedule subject to variation) by virtue of a deed of conditions under section 5 of this Act where that deed was executed before the coming into force of the regulations.

Clause 6

This clause implements recommendations 2(d) and (e). See paragraphs 3.16 to 3.21 of the report.

Section 32 of the Conveyancing (Scotland) Act 1874 provides that deeds of conditions are to be executed by (all of) the owners. This clause provides a simpler alternative in some cases falling under clause 5.

Subsection (1)

Clause 6 applies only where the tenement is already in existence and Management Scheme A or B is already in force. If the owners then decide to change management schemes, the simplified method of execution set out in subsection (2) is available. The clause should be read together with rules 2.2(g) and 2.4 of Scheme A and with rule 12.1(a) of Scheme B.

The reference to "in so far as" is intended to cover cases where a deed of conditions relates to a mixed development (and see also clause 5(3)). In such cases the deed may be executed in accordance with subsection (2) only in relation to the tenement.

Subsection (2)

This subsection sets out a simplified method of execution of deeds of conditions for the purposes of clause 5(1).

Subsection (3)

Although not signed by all of the owners, a deed of conditions executed under clause 6 binds all owners and all others holding real rights (such as heritable creditors or lessees).

Clause 7

This clause implements recommendation 17(a). See paragraphs 6.1 and 6.2 of the report.

Subsection (1)

This gives the Secretary of State power to make regulations to amend Management Scheme B as set out in Schedule 2 to the draft Bill. (See clause 31 for how regulations are to be made.) The reason for this is that over time the model scheme set out in the Schedule may become out of date and need to be amended to reflect current conveyancing and management practice.

Subsection (2)

The amendments are not to be retrospective. For example, if a deed of conditions applying Scheme B to a tenement is executed on 1 January and amending regulations come into force on 2 January, the tenement will be subject to the unamended version of Scheme B.

Application to sheriff for annulment of certain decisions made under Scheme A or B.

8.—(1) Where-

(a) Management Scheme A or Management Scheme B applies as respects the management of a tenement; and

(b) any vote allocated as respects a flat is not cast in favour of a relevant decision,

the owner of that flat may by summary application apply to the sheriff for an order annulling the decision.

(2) An application by an owner under subsection (1) above shall be made-

(a) in a case where the relevant decision was made at a meeting attended by the owner, not later than 21 days after the date of that meeting; or

(b) in any other case, not later than 21 days after the date on which notification of the making of the relevant decision was sent to the owner.

(3) The sheriff may-

(a) if satisfied that the relevant decision with which the application is concerned-

(i) is not in the best interests of all (or both) the owners; or

(ii) is unfairly prejudicial to one or more of the owners;

make an order annulling the relevant decision (in whole or in part); or

(b) if not so satisfied, dismiss the application.

(4) Where an application is made under subsection (1) above as respects a relevant decision to carry out maintenance, improvements or alterations, the sheriff shall, in determining whether he is satisfied as to the matters mentioned in subsection (3)(a) above, have regard to-

(a) the age of the tenement;

(b) its condition;

(c) the likely cost of any such maintenance, improvements or alterations; and

(d) the reasonableness of that cost.

(5) Where the sheriff makes an order under subsection (3)(a) above annulling a relevant decision (in whole or in part), he may make such order as he thinks fit as respects the liability of owners for any costs incurred before the date of his order under that subsection in relation to the implementation of that decision.

(6) Any party may not later than 14 days after the date of a decision of the sheriff under subsection (3) above appeal to the Court of Session on a point of law from that decision.

(7) A decision of the Court of Session on an appeal under subsection (6) above shall be final.

(8) In this section "relevant decision" means-

(a) if Management Scheme A applies as respects a tenement, a decision made by the owners in accordance with that scheme; or

(b) if Management Scheme B so applies, a decision made by the owners' association at a general meeting in accordance with that scheme.

(9) For the purposes of any application under subsection (1) above the defender shall be-

(a) if Management Scheme A applies, all the other owners;

(b) if Management Scheme B applies, the owners' association.

Clause 8

This clause implements recommendation 7. See paragraphs 5.19 to 5.25 of the report.

In cases where one of the statutory management schemes applies, an owner can apply for the annulment of a decision made under that scheme. This is intended as a form of protection of the minority.

Subsection (1)

Subsection (1) sets out the entitlement and the basic procedure. "Relevant decision" is defined in subsection (8) and Management Schemes A and B in clause 30(2). Where a flat is owned in common, any of the *pro indiviso* owners may apply (see clause 29(5)).

Subsection (2)

This sets out the time limit for making an application. The reference to "sent to" in paragraph (6) should be read in the light of clause 30(4). Where the decision concerned was made under Scheme A, this subsection needs to be read with rule 4 of that scheme, which provides that decisions must not be implemented until it is known whether an application is to be made, and, if made, until the application has been disposed of or abandoned.

Subsection (3)

This subsection deals with the powers of the sheriff. He may annul the decision in whole or in part or he may dismiss the application.

Subsection (4)

This subsection only applies in cases where the decision concerned relates to maintenance, improvements or alterations. It sets out the circumstances which the sheriff must take into account in deciding whether he is satisfied on the matters mentioned in subsection (3). These circumstances (other than (d)) are also of relevance for the statutory obligation of support and shelter (see clause 12(2)).

Not all the circumstances will be relevant in every case. Circumstances (a) to (c) will be important when it is argued that the building has deteriorated too far to make repair worthwhile. Circumstance (d) will be important when it is argued that the repair, while justifiable, could be carried out more cheaply.

Subsection (5)

In some cases, and despite rule 4 of Scheme A, costs might have been incurred before the application was disposed of by the sheriff. This subsection is intended to deal with such cases. It enables the sheriff, where he has annulled a decision (whether in whole or in part), to deal with the question of liability of the owners for costs already incurred in relation to that decision.

Subsection (6)

This subsection is based on section 106(5) of the Civic Government (Scotland) Act 1982

Subsection (7)

This subsection has similar effect to section 106(6) of the Civic Government (Scotland) Act 1982, on which it is based.

Subsection (8)

This defines "relevant decision" for the purposes of the clause.

Subsection (9)

This subsection explains who the defender is in relation to an application to the sheriff for an order annulling a decision.

Power of sheriff to resolve matters concerning operation of management scheme etc.

9.—(1) Any owner may by summary application apply to the sheriff for an order relating to any matter concerning the operation of-

(a) the management scheme which applies as respects the tenement; or

(b) any provision of this Act in its application as respects the tenement.

(2) Without prejudice to subsection (1) above, where Management Scheme B applies, an application under that subsection may be made by the manager of the owners' association.

(3) Where an application is made under subsection (1) above the sheriff may-

(a) subject to such conditions (if any) as he thinks fit-

(i) grant the order craved; or

(ii) make such other order under this section as he considers necessary or expedient; or

(b) dismiss the application.

(4) Any party may not later than 14 days after the date of a decision of the sheriff under subsection (3) above appeal to the Court of Session on a point of law from that decision.

(5) A decision of the Court of Session on an appeal under subsection (4) above shall be final.

Scheme B: rights of creditors of association.

10.—(1) Where Management Scheme B applies or, as the case may be, applied as respects a tenement, and-

(a) the owners' association established under that scheme is being, or has been, wound up; or

(b) a debt due by the association satisfies the conditions mentioned in subsection (2) below,

any creditor of the association shall be entitled to recover the debt from the members of the association (or, as the case may be, those who were at the commencement of the winding up such members) as if he were the manager of the association recovering, in accordance with the provisions of Management Scheme B, a service charge from the members (or those who were members).

(2) The conditions are that-

(a) the debt is constituted by-

(i) decree; or

(ii) a document which has been registered for execution in the Books of Council and Session or, as the case may be, in the appropriate sheriff court books kept for any sheriffdom; and

(b) the creditor has executed diligence but has not recovered the debt in full.

Clause 9

This implements recommendation 44. See paragraphs 10.22 to 10.27 of the report.

It gives the sheriff wide powers to make orders necessary for the proper operation of the management schemes and of the Bill.

Subsection (1)

Where a flat is owned in common, any of the *pro indiviso* owners may apply (see clause 29(5)).

Subsection (2)

In tenements governed by Management Scheme B, an application may be made either by one of the owners or by the manager of the owners' association.

Subsection (3)

This subsection sets out the powers of the sheriff.

Clause 10

This clause implements recommendation 25. See paragraphs 6.47 to 6.54 of the report.

In the case of Scheme B tenements this allows a creditor, in certain circumstances, to go behind the owners' association and make direct recovery from individual owners.

Subsection (1)

A creditor may make direct recovery only where the owners' association is being or has been wound up, or where the debt cannot be recovered from the association. The creditor is put in the same position as the manager and can recover from the members by means of a service charge under rule 11 of Scheme B. The liability of individual owners is regulated by rule 11.1. In a case where winding up has occurred, Scheme B is nevertheless treated as if still in force for this limited purpose.

Subsection (2)

This sets out the conditions referred to in subsection (1)(b). In effect the creditor must have tried but failed to recover the debt from the owners' association.

Support and shelter

Abolition as respects tenements of common law rules of common interest.

11.—Any rule of law relating to common interest shall, to the extent that it applies as respects a tenement, cease to have effect; but nothing in this section shall affect the operation of any such rule of law in its application to a question affecting both a tenement and-

(a) some other building or former building (whether or not a tenement); or

(b) any land not pertaining to the tenement.

Duty to maintain tenement building so as to provide support and shelter etc.

12.—(1) Subject to subsection (2) below, the owner of any part of a tenement building, being a part that provides, or is intended to provide, support or shelter to any other part, shall maintain the supporting or sheltering part so as to ensure that it provides support or shelter.

(2) An owner shall not by virtue of subsection (1) above be obliged to maintain any part of a tenement building if it would not be reasonable to do so, having regard to all the circumstances (and including, in particular, the age of the tenement building, its condition and the likely cost of any maintenance).

(3) The duty imposed by subsection (1) above on an owner of a part of a tenement building may be enforced by any other such owner who is, or would be, directly affected by any breach of the duty.

Prohibition on interference with support or shelter etc.

13.—(1) No owner or occupier of any part of a tenement shall be entitled to do anything in relation to that part which would, or would be reasonably likely to, impair to a material extent-

(a) the support or shelter provided to any part of the tenement building; or

(b) the natural light enjoyed by any part of the tenement building.

(2) The prohibition imposed by subsection (1) above on an owner or occupier of a part of a tenement may be enforced by any other such owner who is, or would be, directly affected by any breach of the prohibition.

Clause 11

This clause implements recommendation 29. See paragraphs 7.1 to 7.3 of the report.

It abolishes the common law rules of common interest as they apply to tenements. This clause should be read with clauses 12 and 13 which restate the common law rules in statutory form.

Clause 12

This implements recommendation 30(a) and (d). See paragraphs 7.4 to 7.13 of the report.

Along with clause 13 it restates in statutory form the common law doctrine of common interest in relation to support and shelter.

Subsection (1)

This imposes a positive obligation on the owner of any part of a tenement building to maintain that part so as to ensure that it provides support and shelter. The positive obligation is confined to the "tenement building" itself (defined in clause 30(1)), and does not extend to the solum or to any land which forms part of the tenement. When the part is owned in common, the obligation binds all of the *pro indiviso* owners (see clause 29(4) and (6)).

Subsection (2)

This subsection removes the obligation in cases where the building has ceased to be worth repairing. The particular circumstances listed here are also to be found in clause 8(4).

Subsection (3)

This subsection deals with enforcement. An owner can enforce provided he has interest to do so. Where a flat is owned in common, any of the *pro indiviso* owners may enforce (see clause 29(5)).

Clause 13

This implements recommendation 30(c) and (d) and recommendation 31. See paragraphs 7.4 to 7.18.

Along with clause 12 it restates in statutory form the common law doctrine of common interest in relation to support and shelter. The clause also covers the rule of common interest relating to the right to light. Unlike clause 12, this clause applies to occupiers of flats as well as to owners.

Subsection (1)

By contrast with clause 12, the prohibition applies to the whole tenement, including surrounding land (see the definition of "tenement" in clause 30(1)), and not merely to the tenement building.

Subsection (2)

An owner can enforce provided he has interest to do so. A mere occupier, though bound by the prohibition, has no right to enforce. Where a flat is owned in common, any of the *pro indiviso* owners may enforce (see clause 29(5)).

14. Where-

Recovery of share of cost of maintenance of certain property carried out by virtue of section 12.

(a) by virtue of section 12 of this Act an owner carries out maintenance to any part of a tenement; and

(b) the management scheme which applies as respects the tenement provides for the maintenance of that part,

the owner shall be entitled to recover from any other owner any share of the cost of the maintenance for which that other owner would have been liable had the maintenance been carried out under or by virtue of the management scheme in question.

Repairs: costs and access

Liability of owner and successors for certain costs.

15.—(1) Any owner who is liable for any relevant costs shall not, by virtue only of ceasing to be such an owner, cease to be liable for those costs.

(2) Where a person becomes an owner (any such person being referred to in this section as a "new owner") he shall, subject to subsection (3) below, be jointly and severally liable with any former owner of the flat for any relevant costs for which the former owner is liable.

(3) Where-

(a) Management Scheme B applies as respects a tenement; and

(b) a new owner (or a person who is to become a new owner) obtains a certificate signed by the manager of the owners' association stating that as at the date on which it is signed no service charge is outstanding as respects the flat or, as the case may be, that any service charge due does not exceed an amount specified in the certificate,

then, apart from service charge of an amount so specified, the new owner shall not be liable for any service charge which was outstanding on that date.

(4) Where a new owner pays any relevant costs for which a former owner of the flat is liable he may recover the amount so paid from the former owner.

(5) For the purposes of this section "relevant costs" means, as respects a flat-

(a) the share of any costs for which the owner is liable under or by virtue of the management scheme which applies as respects the tenement; and

(b) any other costs for which he is liable under or by virtue of this Act.

(6) This section applies as respects any relevant costs for which an owner becomes liable on or after the day on which this Act comes into force.

Clause 14

This implements recommendation 30(b). See paragraphs 7.7 and 7.13 of the report.

This is primarily an anti-avoidance provision, designed to discourage owners from preventing a repair being carried out, at joint expense, under the management scheme, in the knowledge that the same repair could be insisted on under clause 12. Clause 14 removes any advantage in preventing such a repair. If the cost of the repair would have been a scheme cost under the management scheme, an owner carrying out the repair under clause 12 can treat it as if it were a scheme cost and recover appropriately.

It may be noted that clause 14 also applies to cases where an owner carries out repairs entirely on his own initiative and without being pressed to do so by his neighbours.

Clause 15

This clause implements recommendations 33(d), 34 and 35(b) and (c). See paragraphs 2.18 and 8.1 to 8.24 of the report.

It deals with transmission of liability for repair and other costs when a flat changes hands.

Subsection (1)

This deals with the liability of the outgoing owner of a flat for "relevant costs", as defined in subsection (5), making it clear that he does not cease to be liable when he ceases to own the flat. This restates in statutory form the principle of the existing law by which liability which has already crystallised cannot be avoided by disposing of the property.

The rules as to crystallisation of liability under the management schemes are given in rules 5.9 and 5.10 of Scheme A and in rule 11.4 of Scheme B.

By clause 29(3) a person ceases to be owner on the date of entry stipulated in a conveyance granted by him, and without regard to when (or whether) the grantee registered the conveyance.

Subsection (2)

This deals with liability of an incoming or "new" owner of a flat for "relevant costs". A new owner of a flat is jointly and severally liable with the outgoing owner. If there are two (or more) new owners holding *pro indiviso*, both (or all) are bound (see clause 29(4) and (6)).

Subsection (3)

This subsection qualifies subsection (2) in cases where Management Scheme B applies. In effect the subsection limits the liability of the new owner to any amounts of service charge specified in a certificate issued by the manager of the owners' association.

Subsection (4)

This gives the new owner a right of relief against the former owners.

Subsection (5)

This defines "relevant costs" for the purpose of the clause.

Subsection (6)

This is a transitional provision.

16.—In Schedule 1 to the Prescription and Limitation (Scotland) Act 1973 (obligations affected by prescriptive periods of five years to which section 6 of that Act applies)-

Prescriptive period for costs to which section 15 relates.
1973 c. 52.

(a) after paragraph 1(a) there shall be inserted-

"(aa) to any obligation to pay a sum of money by way of costs to which section 15 of the Tenements (Scotland) Act 1997 applies;"; and

(b) in paragraph 2(e), after the words "paragraph 1(a)" there shall be inserted "or (aa)".

General right to recover cost of necessary maintenance of common property not to apply where provision made by scheme.

17.—Any rule of law which enables an owner of common property to recover the cost of necessary maintenance from the other owners of the property shall not apply in relation to any common property in a tenement where the maintenance of that property is provided for in the management scheme which applies as respects the tenement.

Clause 16

This clause implements recommendation 35(c). See paragraphs 8.23 and 8.24 of the report.

It applies the 5-year negative prescription to liability to pay the costs mentioned in clause 15(5).

Clause 17

This clause implements recommendation 45. See paragraphs 10.28 to 10.30 of the report.

This is primarily an anti-avoidance provision. Without it a *pro indiviso* owner of scheme property could carry out necessary acts of maintenance unilaterally and then recover the cost from his fellow owners - thus avoiding altogether the decision-making procedures in the management schemes. The effect of clause 17 is that shared costs cannot be achieved without shared decision-making.

Owner's right of access to or through other flat to carry out maintenance etc.

18.—(1) Where an owner gives reasonable notice to the owner or occupier of any other part of the tenement that he requires access to, or through, that part for any of the purposes mentioned in subsection (3) below, the person given notice shall, subject to subsection (5) below, allow access for that purpose.

(2) Without prejudice to subsection (1) above, where Management Scheme B applies, notice under that subsection may be given by the manager of the owners' association to the owner or occupier of any part of the tenement.

(3) The purposes are-

(a) carrying out, under or by virtue of the management scheme which applies as respects the tenement, maintenance or other works;

(b) carrying out maintenance or other works to any part of the tenement owned (whether solely or in common) by the person requiring access;

(c) carrying out an inspection to determine whether it is necessary to carry out maintenance or other works;

(d) determining whether the owner of the part is fulfilling the duty imposed on him by section 12(1) of this Act;

(e) determining whether the owner or occupier of the part is complying with the prohibition imposed on him by section 13(1) of this Act;

(f) carrying out any of the works mentioned in section 20(1) of this Act;

(g) carrying out any installation by virtue of section 21(1) of this Act; and

(h) where floor area is relevant for the purposes of determining any liability of owners, measuring floor area.

(4) Reasonable notice need not be given as mentioned in subsection (1) above where access is required for the purpose specified in subsection (3)(a) above and the works require to be carried out urgently.

(5) An owner or occupier may refuse to allow-

(a) access under subsection (1) above; or

(b) such access at a particular time,

if, having regard to all the circumstances (and, in particular, whether the requirement for access is reasonable), it is reasonable to refuse access.

(6) Where access is allowed under subsection (1) above for any purpose, such right of access may be exercised by-

(a) the owner or manager who gave notice that access was required; or

(b) such person as the owner or, as the case may be, manager may specify in writing for the purpose (any such person being referred to in this section as a "specified person").

(7) Where a specified person acting in accordance with subsection (6) above is liable under or by virtue of any enactment or rule of law for damage caused to any part of a tenement-

(a) the owner who specified him; or

(b) if he was specified by a manager, the owners' association concerned,

shall be jointly and severally liable with the specified person for the cost of remedying the damage; but an owner or, as the case may be, owners' association making any payment as respects that cost shall have a right of relief against the specified person.

Clause 18

This clause implements recommendation 43. See paragraphs 10.10 to 10.21 of the report.

It confers mutual rights of access for repairs and for certain other purposes.

Subsection (1)

The meaning of "owner" is given in clause 29. Where a flat is owned in common, any of the *pro indiviso* owners may exercise the right of access (clause 29(5)). If necessary the right can be enforced judicially under clause 9.

Subsection (2)

In tenements governed by Management Scheme B the right of access may also be exercised by the manager of the owners' association.

Subsection (3)

This subsection lists the purposes for which access is an entitlement. The list is exhaustive.

Subsection (4)

Urgent work includes, but is not confined to, emergency work. Emergency work, being an example of work carried out under or by virtue of a management scheme, falls within subsection (3)(a). See rule 7 of Management Scheme A and rule 13 of Management Scheme B.

Subsection (5)

This qualifies the right of access by reference to a reasonableness test.

Subsection (6)

This allows the right of access to be delegated, for example to a tradesman.

Subsection (7)

A person exercising a right of access indirectly, through someone else (such as a tradesman), shares in any liability incurred by that person in respect of damage caused, but has a right of relief. Hence the person whose property is damaged has a choice of defenders.

Insurance

Obligation of owner to insure.

19.—(1) It shall be the duty of each owner to effect and keep in force a contract of insurance against the prescribed risks for the reinstatement value of his flat and any part of the tenement building attaching to that flat as a pertinent.

(2) Where the title to the tenement requires each flat to be insured by way of a common policy of insurance as respects the entire tenement building, then for the purposes of satisfying the duty imposed on an owner by subsection (1) above, the contract of insurance mentioned in that subsection shall be a common policy of insurance.

(3) The Secretary of State may by regulations prescribe risks against which an owner shall require to insure (in this section referred to as the "prescribed risks").

(4) Where, whether because of the location of the tenement or otherwise, an owner-

(a) having made reasonable efforts to do so, is unable to obtain insurance against a particular prescribed risk; or

(b) would be able to obtain such insurance but only at a cost which is unreasonably high,

the duty imposed by subsection (1) above shall not require an owner to insure against that particular risk.

(5) Any owner may by notice in writing request the owner of any other flat in the tenement to produce to him-

(a) the policy in respect of any contract of insurance which the owner of that other flat is required to have or to effect; and

(b) evidence of payment of the premium for any such policy;

and not later than 14 days after that notice is given the recipient shall produce the policy (or a copy of it) and the evidence of payment.

(6) The duty imposed by subsection (1) above on an owner may be enforced by any other owner.

Television aerials etc.

Television aerials, satellite dishes etc.

20.—(1) Subject to section 18 of this Act, any owner shall be entitled to-

(a) fix to the outside surface of any roof of the tenement or to any chimney stack, and to keep there, any television aerial or radio aerial, satellite dish or other equipment relating to television or radio broadcasting services; and

(b) lead any wires or cables necessary for connection to any such aerial, dish or other equipment from it to his flat.

(2) This section is without prejudice to any requirement for an owner to obtain approval or consent under any enactment relating to planning or building.

Clause 19

This clause implements recommendations 37 and 38(a). See paragraphs 9.1 to 9.14 of the report.

It imposes an obligation on the owners of all flats in a tenement to insure the building, but there is an exception for the Crown (see clause 32(3)).

Subsection (1)

This subsection imposes the basic obligation to insure. "Owner" means owner of a flat or heritable creditor in possession (clause 29(1), (2)). Where a flat is owned in common, all the *pro indiviso* owners are bound (clause 29(4) and (6)).

Subsection (2)

If a common policy of insurance is required by the titles, then the obligation to insure imposed by subsection (1) must be met by use of such a common policy.

Subsection (3)

This subsection should be read with clause 31.

Subsection (4)

This modifies the obligation to insure in certain circumstances.

Subsection (5)

Where a flat is owned in common, any of the *pro indiviso* owners may exercise the right conferred by this provision (clause 29(5)).

Subsection (6)

This subsection deals with enforcement. The owner of any flat (or, if the flat is owned in common, any *pro indiviso* owner) may enforce the obligation to insure. For the meaning of "owner" see clause 29.

Clause 20

This clause implements recommendation 41. See paragraphs 10.1 to 10.5 of the report.

It confers rights in relation to the placing of television aerials and certain other equipment.

Subsection (1)

For the meaning of "owner", see clause 29. Where a flat is owned in common, any *pro indiviso* owner can exercise the right (clause 29(5)). The question of access is dealt with in clause 18.

Subsection (2)

This subsection makes it clear that the right conferred is a matter of the private law of the tenement only. Public law consents may still be required.

21.—(1) Subject to subsection (2) below and to section 18 of this Act, any owner shall be entitled to lead through any part of the tenement such pipe, cable or other equipment as is necessary for the provision to his flat of gas or such other service as the Secretary of State may by regulations prescribe; but nothing in this subsection authorises an owner to make any connections to a gas supply.

Installation of gas and other services through tenement.

(2) An owner may not by virtue of subsection (1) above lead any such pipe, cable or other equipment through any part which is wholly within another owner's flat.

(3) This section is without prejudice to any obligation imposed under or by virtue of any enactment relating to planning, building or gas or to any service prescribed under subsection (1) above.

Demolition and abandonment of tenement building

22. The demolition of a tenement building shall not alone-

Demolition of tenement building not to affect ownership or power to disapply management scheme.

(a) effect any change as respects any right of ownership; or

(b) make it incompetent for provision such as is mentioned in subsection (2)(a) of section 5 of this Act to be made in a deed of conditions under subsection (1) of that section.

Clause 21

This clause implements recommendation 42. See paragraphs 10.6 to 10.9 of the report.

It confers rights to lead gas pipes through the tenement.

Subsection (1)

For the meaning of "owner", see clause 29. Where a flat is owned in common, any *pro indiviso* owner can exercise the right (clause 29(5)). For the making of regulations by the Secretary of State, see clause 31. The question of access is dealt with in clause 18. The subsection makes it clear that the provision does not of itself entitle an owner to make a connection to a gas supply.

Subsection (2)

This subsection qualifies the right in subsection (1) by prohibiting an owner from leading pipes through another owner's flat. It does not prevent attachment to the outside wall of a flat, and in practice gas pipes are usually led up the outside wall of the building.

Subsection (3)

This subsection makes it clear that the right conferred is a matter of the private law of the tenement only. Public law consents may still be required.

Clause 22

This clause implements recommendation 40(a). See paragraph 9.25 and 9.36 of the report.

It is concerned with demolition of the tenement building. "Demolition" is defined in clause 30(1) to include destruction.

Paragraph (a)

Under this paragraph an owner continues to own the airspace formerly occupied by his flat.

Paragraph (b)

On demolition of a tenement which is subject to Management Scheme B, and in a case where the tenement is not to be rebuilt, the owners will wish to wind up the owners' association. By rule 5.1 of Scheme B this requires the execution and registration of a deed of conditions under clause 5(2)(a) disapplying the scheme. Without paragraph (b), a deed of conditions could not be executed in respect of a tenement which had ceased to exist (see clause 5(6)(b)).

23.—(1) Except where the title to the tenement otherwise provides, the cost of demolishing a tenement building shall, subject to subsection (2) below, be shared equally among all (or both) the flats in the tenement.

Cost of demolishing tenement building.

(2) Where the floor area of the largest (or larger) flat in the tenement is more than one and a half times that of the smallest (or smaller) flat the owner of each flat shall be liable to contribute towards the cost of demolition of the tenement building in the proportion which the floor area of his flat bears to the total floor area of all (or both) the flats.

(3) An owner is liable under this section for the cost of demolishing a tenement building-

(a) in the case where he agrees to the proposal that the tenement building be demolished, from the date of that agreement; or

(b) in any other case, from the date on which the carrying out of the demolition is instructed.

(4) This section applies as respects the demolition of part of a tenement building as it applies as respects the demolition of an entire tenement building but with any reference to a flat in the tenement being construed as a reference to a flat in the part.

(5) In this section references to flats in a tenement include references to flats which were comprehended by the tenement before its demolition.

(6) This section is subject to section 123 of the Housing (Scotland) Act 1987 (which makes provision as respects demolition of buildings in pursuance of local authority demolition orders and recovery of expenses by local authorities etc.).

1987 c. 26.

Clause 23

This clause implements recommendation 39. See paragraphs 9.20 to 9.24 of the report.

It apportions liability among the owners for the cost of demolition of a tenement building.

Subsection (1)

This provides a general rule of equality of contribution. The rule is concerned with the liability of owners among themselves and does not import liability in questions with third parties.

Subsection (2)

This qualifies the provisions of subsection (1) in certain circumstances. The method of calculating floor area is set out in clause 30(3).

Subsection (3)

This subsection states when an owner becomes liable for his share of the cost of demolition. This is particularly important in a case where a flat changes hands while the work is in progress (see clause 15(1)).

Subsection (4)

This subsection adapts the rule for cases of partial demolition.

Subsection (6)

Clause 23 is concerned with the liability of owners among themselves. It does nothing to disturb the rule, under section 123 of the Housing (Scotland) Act 1987, that a local authority which has carried out the demolition may recover the cost from the owners in such proportions as the owners may agree or, failing agreement, as is determined by arbitration.

24.—(1) This section applies where a tenement building is demolished and after the demolition two or more flats which were comprehended by the tenement building before its demolition (any such flat being referred to in this section as a "former flat") are owned by different persons.

Use and disposal of site where tenement building demolished.

(2) Except in so far as-

(a) the owners of all (or both) the former flats otherwise agree; or

(b) those owners are subject to a requirement (whether imposed by the title to the tenement or otherwise) to erect a building on the site or to rebuild the tenement,

no owner may build on, or otherwise develop, the site.

(3) Except where the owners have agreed, or are required, to build on or develop the site as mentioned in paragraphs (a) and (b) of subsection (2) above, any owner of a former flat shall be entitled to require that the entire site be sold.

(4) Except where the title to the tenement otherwise provides, the proceeds of any sale in pursuance of subsection (3) above shall, subject to subsection (5) below, be shared equally among all (or both) the former flats.

(5) Where the floor area of the largest (or larger) former flat was more than one and a half times that of the smallest (or smaller) former flat the proceeds of any sale shall be shared among (or between) the flats in the proportion which the floor area of each flat bore to the total floor area of all (or both) the flats.

(6) The prohibition imposed by subsection (2) above on an owner of a former flat may be enforced by any other such owner.

(7) In this section references to the site are references to the solum of the tenement building that occupied the site and to the airspace that is directly above the solum.

25.—(1) Where-

Effect of demolition of tenement and sale of site on certain undischarged securities over flats.

(a) a tenement building is demolished and the site is sold; but

(b) a heritable security over any flat formerly comprehended by the tenement has not, on or before such sale, been discharged,

the heritable security shall, by virtue of this subsection, be varied so as to secure instead a *pro indiviso* interest over the site fixed having regard to the total number of flats which were formerly comprehended by the tenement.

(2) A variation such as is mentioned in subsection (1) above shall take effect as from the date on which the deed conveying the site is recorded in the Register of Sasines or, as the case may be, the terms of the deed are registered in the Land Register of Scotland.

(3) In this section "site" shall be construed in accordance with section 24(7) of this Act.

Clause 24

This clause implements recommendation 40(b)(i) - (iv). See paragraphs 9.25 to 9.36 of the report.

It controls the use and disposal of the site in certain cases where a tenement building has been completely demolished.

Subsection (1)

This gives the two pre-conditions for application of the clause.

By clause 30(1) "demolition" includes destruction, and may occur on one occasion or over a period of time.

Subsection (2)

This subsection restricts the use of the "site" (defined in subsection (7)). Subsection (6) makes provision for enforcement.

Subsection (3)

In general, and subject to exceptions, any owner may require that the site be sold. Where a former flat is owned in common, any *pro indiviso* owner has this right (clause 29(5)).

Subsection (4)

This subsection apportions the proceeds of sale of the site.

Subsection (5)

This qualifies subsection (4). The method of calculating floor area is set out in clause 30(3).

Clause 25

This clause implements recommendation 40(b)(v). See paragraphs 9.35 and 9.36 of the report.

It deals with cases where a tenement building has been demolished and the site has been sold, and there remains an outstanding heritable security over one of the former flats.

"Demolition" is defined in clause 30(1) to include destruction.

Subsection (1)

On sale the heritable security is deemed to be varied so as to secure a proportionate *pro indiviso* share of the site (instead of the flat which it formerly secured). Thus if there were 8 flats in the former tenement, the heritable security would secure a one-eighth *pro indiviso* share of the site.

Subsection (2)

The deemed variation takes effect on registration of the conveyance.

26.—(1) Where- Sale of abandoned tenement building.

(a) because of its poor condition a tenement building has been entirely unoccupied by any owner or person authorised by an owner for a period of more than six months; and

(b) it is unlikely that any such owner or other person will return to occupy any part of the tenement building,

any owner shall be entitled to require that the tenement building be sold.

(2) Subsections (4) and (5) of section 24 of this Act shall apply as respects a sale in pursuance of subsection (1) above as those subsections apply as respects a sale in pursuance of subsection (3) of that section.

(3) In this section any reference to a tenement building includes a reference to its solum.

Miscellaneous and general

27.—(1) Where- Liability to non-owner of part of tenement for damage costs towards which he is required to contribute.

(a) any part of a tenement is damaged as the result of the fault of any person (that person being in this subsection referred to as "A"); and

(b) the management scheme which applies as respects the tenement makes provision for the maintenance of that part,

any owner of a flat in the tenement (that owner being in this subsection referred to as "B") who is required under or by virtue of that provision to contribute to any extent to the cost of maintenance of the damaged part but who at the time when the damage was done was not an owner of the part shall be treated, for the purpose of determining whether A is liable to B as respects the cost of maintenance arising from the damage, as if he were such an owner at that time.

(2) In this section "fault" means any wrongful act, breach of statutory duty or negligent act or omission which gives rise to liability in damages.

28.—(1) The Land Registration (Scotland) Act 1979 shall be amended in accordance with this section. Consequential amendments.

(2) In section 3 (effect of registration), at the end there shall be added- 1979 c. 33.

"(8) Subsection (4) above is subject to section 5(5) of the Tenements (Scotland) Act 1997.".

(3) In section 17 (deeds of declaration of conditions), at the end there shall be added-

"(3) This section is subject to section 5(5) of the Tenements (Scotland) Act 1997.".

Clause 26

This clause implements recommendation 40(c). See paragraphs 9.25 to 9.36 of the report.

It provides for the sale of derelict tenement buildings and the division of the proceeds.

Subsection (1)

This subsection gives any owner of a flat in a tenement the right, in certain circumstances, to require that the tenement building be sold. "Owner" is defined in clause 29. Where a flat is owned in common, any *pro indiviso* owner can exercise the right (clause 29(5)).

Subsection (2)

The sale proceeds are divided in the same way as when a vacant site is sold, following demolition.

Subsection (3)

This subsection makes it clear that the right to sell includes the solum (ie the ground on which the building is erected).

Clause 27

This implements recommendation 46. See paragraphs 10.31 to 10.33 of the report.

Subsection (1)

A person may have to maintain parts of the tenement which he does not own. The rule against pure economic loss would then exclude a remedy against a wrong-doer whose acts or omissions had made such maintenance necessary. This provision removes this technical difficulty by treating the person as if he were owner for the purposes of founding a claim.

Clause 28

This clause makes two minor consequential amendments to the Land Registration (Scotland) Act 1979, following on clause 5(5).

Meaning of "owner", determination of liability etc.

29.—(1) Subject to subsection (2) below, in this Act "owner" means-

(a) where a flat is held on feudal tenure, the person who holds the interest of *dominium utile* in the flat; or

(b) where a flat is not so held, the person who has the ownership of the flat.

(2) Where a heritable security has been granted over a flat and the heritable creditor has entered into lawful possession, "owner" means the heritable creditor in possession of the flat.

(3) For the purposes of subsection (1) above, a person becomes an owner (and the last owner ceases to be an owner) when he acquires a right to take entry under a conveyance of the flat concerned (or any document having effect as a conveyance).

(4) Subject to subsection (5) below, if more than one person owns a flat, any reference in this Act to an owner is a reference to both or, as the case may be, all of them.

(5) Any reference to an owner in sections 8(1) and (2), 9(1), 12(3), 13, 14, 18(1), (6) and (7), 19(5) and (6), 20, 21, 24, 26 and 27 of this Act shall be construed as a reference to any person who owns a flat either solely or in common with another.

(6) Where two or more persons own a flat-

(a) they are jointly and severally liable for the performance of any obligation imposed under or by virtue of this Act on the owner of that flat; and

(b) as between (or among) themselves they are liable in the proportions in which they own the flat.

Clause 29

This clause implements recommendation 36. See paragraphs 8.24 to 8.28 of the report.

It defines the meaning of "owner" for the purposes of the Bill.

Subsection (1)

This subsection explains the meaning of "owner" both in cases where a flat is held on feudal tenure and in cases where a flat is not held on feudal tenure (ie it is allodial).

Subsection (2)

This subsection extends the meaning of "owner" to include heritable creditors who have entered into lawful possession of a flat.

Subsection (3)

This subsection explains when a person becomes an owner for the purposes of subsection (1). It does not apply to the special meaning of "owner" in subsection (2). This subsection has particular importance for the provisions dealing with transmission of liability between an outgoing and an incoming owner (see clause 15).

Subsection (4)

In the case of a flat owned in common, "owner" usually means all of the owners. Hence, where an obligation is imposed by the Bill or the statutory management schemes on an "owner", the obligation is shared by all the *pro indiviso* owners. Subsection (6) provides that the liability of *pro indiviso* owners is joint and several.

Subsection (5)

This qualifies subsection (4). The provisions listed confer rights on the "owner" (as opposed to imposing obligations), and the effect of the subsection is that any pro indiviso owner is able to exercise the rights in question without reference to his fellow co-owners.

Subsection (6)

Obligations shared by co-owners (see subsection (4)) are due jointly and severally. The same principle operates in the statutory management schemes: see Scheme A, rule 6.1 and Scheme B rule, rule 11.5.

30.—(1) In this Act, unless the context otherwise requires- Interpretation.

"chimney stack" does not include flue or chimney pot;

"close" means a connected passage, stairs and landings within a tenement building which together constitute a common access to two or more of the flats;

"deed of conditions" means a deed mentioned in section 32 of the Conveyancing (Scotland) Act 1874 and executed in accordance with that section or section 6(2) of this Act; 37 & 38 Vict. c. 94.

"demolition" includes destruction and cognate expressions shall be construed accordingly; and demolition may occur on one occasion or over any period of time;

"door" includes its frame;

"enactment" includes an enactment contained in subordinate legislation;

"flat" means a dwelling-house, or any business or other premises, in a tenement building;

"lift" includes its shaft and operating machinery;

"solum" means the ground on which a building is erected;

"tenement"-

(a) means a building which comprises two or more flats which are in separate ownership and are divided from each other horizontally; and

(b) except where the context otherwise requires, includes the solum and any other land pertaining to that building;

and the expression "tenement building" shall be construed accordingly;

"title to the tenement" includes the title to any unit in the tenement;

"unit" means-

(a) a flat;

(b) any close or lift; or

(c) any other three-dimensional space not comprehended by a flat, close or lift;

and the tenement building shall be taken to be entirely divided into units; and

"window" includes its frame.

(2) In this Act, unless the context otherwise requires, any reference to-

(a) Management Scheme A is a reference to the scheme as set out in Schedule 1 to this Act or subject to variations specified in a deed of conditions under section 5 of this Act;

(b) Management Scheme B is a reference to the scheme as set out in Schedule 2 to this Act or subject to variations specified in a deed of conditions under section 5 of this Act.

(3) The floor area of a flat is calculated for the purposes of this Act by measuring the total floor area within its boundaries; but no account shall be taken of any pertinents or any of the following parts of a flat-

(a) a balcony; and

(b) except where it is used for any purpose other than storage, a loft or basement.

(4) For the purposes of any provision of this Act, a document sent shall be taken to be sent on the day on which it is despatched (by whatever means).

Clause 30

This clause defines some of the terms used in the Bill.

Subsection (1)

The definition of "flat" implements recommendation 3(b). See paragraphs 4.1 to 4.10 of the report.

The definition of "tenement" implements recommendation 3(a). See paragraphs 4.1 to 4.10 of the report. The definition makes a careful distinction between "tenement" and "tenement building".

"Unit" is used only in clause 2, in the context of boundaries. In the definition of "unit" the reference to "any three-dimensional space not comprehended by a flat, close or lift" is intended to make clear that boundaries are in issue only where units are in separate ownership. A broom cupboard within a flat, for example, would not be a unit for the purposes of the Bill.

Subsection (3)

In this subsection the explanation as to how " floor area" is to be calculated implements recommendation 13(c). See paragraph 5.65 of the report.

Subsection (4)

The date on which a document is sent is important in relation to the time limits in clause 8(2)(b) and in various parts of Management Schemes A and B. This provision should be read along with rule 8.6 of Scheme A and rule 15.3 of Scheme B.

31. Any power conferred by this Act to make regulations shall be exercisable by statutory instrument subject to annulment in pursuance of a resolution of either House of Parliament. Regulations.

32.—(1) This Act may be cited as the Tenements (Scotland) Act 1997. Short title, commencement, Crown application and extent.

(2) This Act shall come into force at the end of the period of 12 months beginning with the day on which it is passed.

(3) This Act, except section 19, binds the Crown.

(4) This Act extends to Scotland only.

Clause 31

This clause deals with the Parliamentary procedure relating to regulations made by the Secretary of State under Clauses 7, 19(3) and 21(1).

Clause 32

These are provisions in the usual form concerning the short title, commencement, application to the Crown and the extent to which the Act applies.

The reason for delaying the coming into force of the Act for 12 months after it is passed is to allow time for the Act to be publicised and leaflets prepared for owners (see paragraph 1.4 of the report).

With the exception of clause 19, the Act is to apply to the Crown. The exception is necessary because in practice the Crown carries its own insurance risk and so should not be subject to a statutory obligation to take out insurance policies.

SCHEDULE 1

MANAGEMENT SCHEME A

RULE 1

SCOPE AND INTERPRETATION

1.1. This scheme provides for the management and maintenance of the scheme property of a tenement.

Scope of scheme.

1.2. For the purposes of this scheme, "scheme property" means-

Meaning of "scheme property".

(a) any part of a tenement that is the common property of some or all of the owners,

(b) with the exceptions mentioned in rule 1.3, the following other parts of a tenement building-

(i) the ground on which it is built,

(ii) its foundations,

(iii) its external walls,

(iv) its roof (including any rafter or other structure supporting the roof),

(v) if it is separated from another building by a gable wall, the part of the gable wall that is part of the tenement building, and

(vi) any other wall that is load-bearing.

1.3. The following parts of a tenement building are the exceptions referred to in rule 1.2(b)-

Parts not included in rule 1.2(b).

(a) any extension which forms part of only one flat,

(b) any door, window, skylight, vent or other opening,

(c) any chimney stack or chimney flue.

1.4. In this scheme-

Other definitions.

"maintenance" includes repairs and replacement, cleaning, painting and other routine works, gardening, the day-to-day running of a tenement and the reinstatement of a part (but not most) of the tenement building; but does not include demolition, alteration or improvement unless reasonably incidental to the maintenance,

"scheme costs" has the meaning given by rule 5.1,

"scheme decision" has the meaning given by rule 2.1.

1.5. If a flat is owned by two or more persons, then one of them may do anything that the owner is by virtue of this scheme entitled to do.

Rights of co-owners.

Printed below is a guide to Management Scheme A. This is written in non-technical language so as to be more easily understood by the owners of flats who will have to operate the scheme. It is suggested that owners be given a copy of this guide. In cases where Scheme A is amended, under clause 5 of the Bill, the guide will need to be amended accordingly. The guide concentrates on those issues which are of practical importance to owners and so is not comprehensive. However, it is followed by a table which links up the rules of Scheme A to the relevant parts of the report. This table need not be reproduced for owners.

The guide is written as if Scheme A had been brought into force for the tenement.

GUIDE TO MANAGEMENT SCHEME A

Management Scheme A is a set of rules for running a tenement. "Tenement" means any flatted building.

Scheme A supplements the rules set out in the title deeds and needs to be read along with those rules. Many flats are now registered in the new Land Register of Scotland, in which case there is only a single (and simple) title deed known as a land certificate.

The scheme consists of 8 main rules which are explained more fully below.

Rule 1

This explains the meaning of some of the words used in the scheme.

Not every part of the tenement is to be managed under the scheme. The scheme applies only to "scheme property", the meaning of which is given in rule 1.2. Scheme property essentially means those parts of the tenement which are common property (that is, where ownership is shared by the owners of different flats). Section 3 of the Tenements (Scotland) Act 1997 gives the following list of the common property in a tenement:

(i) the close (ie the connected entrance passage, stairs, landings and corridors within a tenement building)

(ii) any lift, and

(iii) any other part of a tenement which serves two or more flats.

Examples of (iii) might include a path, an outside stair, rhones, pipes, flues, cables, tanks or chimney stacks. This list of common property can be altered or added to in the title deeds. In the case of flats registered in the Land Register, owners should look at the A. (property) section of the land certificate.

Certain other key parts of a tenement, listed in rule 1.2(b), are also scheme property, whether they are common property or not.

RULE 2

Making decisions

2.1. Any decision made in accordance with-

Meaning of "scheme decision".

(a) the title to the tenement, where rule 3.1 applies, or

(b) rules 3.2 to 3.13,

is referred to in this scheme as a "scheme decision".

2.2. The owners may make a scheme decision on any of the following matters-

Basic scheme decisions.

(a) to carry out maintenance to scheme property,

(b) to appoint on such terms as they may determine a person (who may be an owner or a firm) to manage the tenement,

(c) to delegate to a person appointed as mentioned in paragraph (b) power to decide that maintenance (costing no more than an amount specified by the owners) needs to be carried out to scheme property and to instruct it,

(d) to arrange for the tenement a common policy of insurance complying with section 19 of this Act and against such other risks (if any) as the owners may determine and, except where provision is made in the title to the tenement, to determine on an equitable basis the liability of each owner to contribute to the premium,

(e) to determine that an owner shall not require to pay a share (or some part of a share) of such scheme costs as may be specified by them,

(f) to authorise any maintenance of scheme property already carried out by an owner,

(g) subject to rule 2.4, to determine that a deed of conditions varying this scheme or disapplying it and applying such other scheme as may be specified should be duly recorded or registered,

(h) to modify or revoke any scheme decision.

2.3. If the owners decide under rule 2.2(a) to carry out maintenance to scheme property, they may make a scheme decision on any of the following matters-

Scheme decisions relating to maintenance.

(a) to appoint on such terms as they may determine a person (who may be an owner or a firm) to manage the carrying out of the maintenance,

(b) to instruct or arrange for the carrying out of the maintenance,

(c) to require each owner to deposit (by such time as the owners may decide and with such person as may be nominated by them) an amount of money not exceeding a reasonable estimate of that owner's share of the cost of the maintenance,

(d) to take such other steps as are necessary to ensure that the maintenance is carried out to a satisfactory standard and completed in good time.

2.4. If a scheme decision under rule 2.2(g)-

Case where decision to disapply or vary scheme not valid.

(a) would increase the liability of an owner for any scheme costs, and

(b) that owner did not vote in favour of the decision,

then the decision is not valid.

Rule 2

Rules 2 and 3 explain how decisions are to be made about the tenement. These are known as "scheme decisions". Rule 2 gives a list of the subjects on which scheme decisions can be made, while rule 3 explains the procedure for making a scheme decision.

Most scheme decisions are about maintenance and repairs. Under rule 2.2(a) owners can decide to carry out maintenance to any scheme property. The meaning of "maintenance" is given in rule 1.4. Rule 5 explains how the cost of the maintenance is to be divided among the owners. To allow for the fact that tradesmen may not be willing to start work unless money has already been collected, rule 2.3(c) permits money to be collected in advance.

A scheme decision can be made to appoint a manager (or factor), whether for a particular repair (rule 2.3(a)) or for the overall management of the tenement (rule 2.2(b)). Power can be delegated to the manager to carry out maintenance up to an agreed amount (rule 2.2(c)).

Rule 2.2 also sets out other matters on which owners can make scheme decisions.

Since a scheme decision can usually be reached by a bare majority (see rule 3.6), scheme decisions are restricted to the subjects listed in rule 2. Owners are of course free to make decisions on other matters but agreement must then be unanimous.

RULE 3

PROCEDURE FOR MAKING SCHEME DECISIONS

3.1. If- Title to prevail.

(a) the title to the tenement provides procedures for the making of decisions by the owners, and

(b) the same procedures apply as respects each flat,

then those procedures shall be followed and the following provisions of this rule shall not apply.

Case where no provision in title.

3.2. If the title to the tenement does not provide procedures as mentioned in rule 3.1(a) and (b) then decisions shall be made by the owners in accordance with the following provisions of this rule.

Allocation and exercise of votes.

3.3. Except as mentioned in rule 3.4, for the purpose of voting on any proposed scheme decision one vote is allocated as respects each flat; and any right to vote is exercisable by the owner of that flat or by someone nominated by the owner to vote as respects the flat.

Qualification on allocation of votes.

3.4. No vote is allocated as respects a flat if-

(a) the scheme decision relates to the maintenance of scheme property, and

(b) the owner of that flat is not liable in accordance with this scheme for maintenance of the property concerned.

Exercise of vote where two or more persons own flat.

3.5. If a flat is owned by two or more persons the vote allocated as respects that flat may be exercised in relation to any proposal by either (or any) of them; but if those persons disagree as to how the vote should be cast then no vote shall be counted as respects that flat.

Decision by majority.

3.6. Except as mentioned in rule 3.7, a scheme decision is made by majority vote of all the votes allocated.

Case where unanimity required.

3.7. If the number of votes allocated does not exceed three, a scheme decision is made by unanimous vote of all the votes allocated.

Notice of meeting.

3.8. If any owner wishes to call a meeting of the owners with a view to making a scheme decision at that meeting he shall give the other owners at least 48 hours' notice of the date and time of the meeting, its purpose and the place where it is to be held.

Consultation of owners if scheme decision not made at meeting.

3.9. If an owner wishes to propose that a scheme decision be made but does not wish to call a meeting for the purpose he shall instead-

(a) unless it is impracticable to do so (whether because of absence of any owner or for other good reason) consult on the proposal each of the other owners of flats as respects which votes are allocated, and

(b) count the votes cast by them.

Consultation where two or more persons own flat.

3.10. For the purposes of rule 3.9, the requirement to consult each owner is satisfied as respects any flat which is owned by more than one person if one of those persons is consulted.

Notification of scheme decisions.

3.11. A scheme decision shall, as soon as practicable, be notified-

(a) if it was made at a meeting, to all the owners who were not present when the decision was made, by such person as may be nominated for the purpose by the persons who made the decision, or

(b) in any other case, to each of the other owners, by the owner who proposed that the decision be made.

Case where decision may be annulled by notice.

3.12. Any owner (or owners) who did not vote in favour of a scheme decision to carry out, or authorise, maintenance to scheme property and who would be liable for not less than 75 per cent. of the scheme costs arising from that decision may, within the time mentioned in rule 3.13, annul that decision by sending a notice stating that the decision is annulled to each of the other owners.

Time limits for rule 3.12.

3.13. The time within which a notice under rule 3.12 must be sent is-

(a) if the scheme decision was made at a meeting attended by the owner (or any of the owners) sending the notice, not later than 21 days after the date of that meeting, or

(b) in any other case, not later than 21 days after the date on which notification of the making of the decision was sent to the owner or owners (that date being, where notification was sent to owners on different dates, the date on which it was sent to the last of them).

TABLE OF RULES SCHEME A

Rules of the Scheme	Paragraphs of report
Rule 1	
1.2	5.4 to 5.11
1.3	5.4 to 5.11
1.4	5.40 to 5.51
1.5	5.12 to 5.18
Rule 2	
2.1	5.17 and 5.18
2.2(a)	5.40 to 5.51
2.2(b)	5.71 to 5.73 and 5.78
2.2(c)	5.71 to 5.73 and 5.78
2.2(d)	5.74 and 5.78
2.2(e)	5.75 and 5.78
2.2(f)	5.54 to 5.57
2.2(g)	3.16 to 3.21 and 5.76 and 5.78
2.2(h)	5.77 and 5.78
2.3	5.52 and 5.53
2.4	5.76 and 5.78
Rule 3	
3.1	5.17 and 5.18
3.2	5.12 to 5.18
3.3	5.13, 5.15 and 5.18
3.4	5.14 and 5.18
3.5	5.15 and 5.18
3.6	5.12 to 5.18
3.7	5.27 and 5.30 to 5.32
3.8	5.33 to 5.39
3.9	5.33 to 5.39
3.10	5.33 to 5.39
3.11	5.33 to 5.39
3.12	5.28 to 5.29 and 5.32
3.13	5.29 and 5.32

Rule 3

Sometimes the title deeds set out rules for making decisions. If so, those rules are to be followed. But if there are no rules in the title deeds, scheme decisions must be made in accordance with rule 3.

Decisions are reached under rule 3 by counting votes. There is one vote per flat, and the vote is exercised by the owner of the flat or (if a flat is owned by more than one person) by any of the owners. The owner can appoint someone to vote for him. See rules 3.3 and 3.5.

Occasionally the owner of a particular flat is not liable for the cost of a particular repair. In that case the flat does not have a vote in relation to that repair (rule 3.4).

Decisions are reached by a simple majority (rule 3.6). So if there are 8 flats in a tenement, 5 must vote in favour for a decision to be made. But if the tenement has no more than 3 flats (or if, for a particular decision, no more than 3 flats have a vote), decisions must be unanimous (rule 3.7).

Voting can take place at a meeting of owners, in which case 48 hours' notice must be given (rule 3.8). Alternatively an owner can approach his neighbours one by one to collect their votes. All owners must be consulted except where this is impracticable (rule 3.9).

Once the voting is completed, any scheme decision reached must be notified to the other owners as soon as possible. Rule 3.11 sets out how this is to be done. It is safer to notify in writing, and rule 8.6 explains ways in which written notification can be sent.

Once a scheme decision is made it is binding on all the owners and (where a flat changes hands) on any incoming owner as well (rule 8.2). But rule 4 freezes the decision for a short period. During this period an owner who did not vote in favour of the decision has the right to apply to the sheriff court under section 8 of the Tenements (Scotland) Act 1997 to have the decision annulled. Similarly, rules 3.12 and 3.13 give a special right of annulment to those owners who would be liable for not less than 75% of the cost.

RULE 4

DELAY IN IMPLEMENTING SCHEME DECISIONS

4.1. Except as mentioned in rule 4.2, no costs shall be incurred in relation to the implementation of a scheme decision until- Scheme decision not to be implemented immediately.

(a) the 21 days allowed for making an application to the sheriff in relation to that decision have passed and no such application has been made and notified to the owners, or

(b) if such an application has been so made and notified-

(i) the application has been disposed of and either the 14 days allowed for appealing against the decision of the sheriff have passed and no appeal against it has been made to the Court of Session or such an appeal has been made and disposed of, or

(ii) the application has been abandoned.

4.2. Rule 4.1 does not apply if a scheme decision- Exceptions to rule 4.1.

(a) is made by unanimous vote of all the votes allocated, or

(b) relates to work which requires to be carried out urgently.

Rule 4

A scheme decision is frozen for a period of 21 days. The 21 days is counted from the day on which notification was sent to the owners under rule 3.11 (or, if no notification was required, from the day of the meeting). During this period no costs relating to the decision should be incurred. Rule 4.2 sets out some exceptions.

RULE 5

Scheme costs: liability and apportionment

5.1. Except in so far as rule 6 applies, this rule provides for the apportionment of liability among the owners for any of the following costs-

Meaning of "scheme costs".

- (a) any costs arising from any maintenance of scheme property where the maintenance is in pursuance of, or authorised by, a scheme decision,
- (b) any remuneration payable to a person appointed to manage the carrying out of maintenance by virtue of rule 2.3(a),
- (c) running costs relating to any scheme property (other than costs incurred solely for the benefit of one flat),
- (d) any costs recoverable by a local authority in respect of work relating to any scheme property carried out by them under or by virtue of any enactment,
- (e) any remuneration payable to a person by virtue of rule 2.2(b),
- (f) the cost of any common insurance to cover the tenement arranged by virtue of rule 2.2(d),
- (g) any other costs relating to the management of scheme property;

and a reference in this scheme to "scheme costs" is a reference to any of the costs mentioned in paragraphs (a) to (g).

Title prevails if full amount of costs covered.

5.2. If the title to the tenement provides that the full amount of any scheme costs (in so far as any of that amount is not to be met by a third party) is to be met by one or more of the owners, then those title provisions shall be followed as regards the costs; and the owner, or as the case may be owners, shall be liable accordingly.

Common property: title to apply to extent it makes provision.

5.3. If-

- (a) the title to the tenement provides that any scheme costs mentioned in rule 5.1(a) to (d) (in so far as any of those costs are not to be met by a third party) are to be met by one or more of the owners, but not in such a way as to account for the full amount of the costs, and
- (b) those costs relate to common property mentioned in rule 1.2(a),

then those title provisions shall be followed in so far as they apportion the costs and rule 5.5(a) shall apply in apportioning the remainder; and the owner, or as the case may be owners, shall be liable accordingly.

Determination of liability.

5.4. Unless rule 5.2 or 5.3 applies, rules 5.5 to 5.8 shall apply as respects the apportionment of liability for scheme costs.

Maintenance and running costs.

5.5. If any scheme costs mentioned in rule 5.1(a) to (d) relate to-

- (a) the scheme property mentioned in rule 1.2(a), then those costs shall be shared among the owners in the proportions in which the owners share ownership of that property,
- (b) the scheme property mentioned in rule 1.2(b), then-
  - (i) in any case where the floor area of the largest (or larger) flat is more than one and a half times that of the smallest (or smaller) flat, each owner is liable to contribute towards those costs in the proportion which the floor area of his flat bears to the total floor area of all (or both) the flats,
  - (ii) in any other case, those costs shall be shared equally among the flats;

and each owner shall be liable accordingly.

Remuneration of manager.

5.6. Any scheme costs mentioned in rule 5.1(e) shall be shared equally among the flats; and each owner shall be liable accordingly.

Insurance premium.

5.7. Any scheme costs mentioned in rule 5.1(f) shall be shared among the flats in such proportions as may be determined by the owners by virtue of rule 2.2(d); and each owner shall be liable accordingly.

Management costs.

5.8. Any scheme costs mentioned in rule 5.1(g) shall be shared equally among the flats; and each owner shall be liable accordingly.

When liability arises.

5.9. With the exceptions mentioned in rule 5.10, each owner is liable for any scheme costs from the date when the scheme decision to incur those costs is made; and for the purposes of this rule that date is-

- (a) where the decision is made at a meeting attended by the owner, the date of the meeting, or
- (b) in any other case, the date on which notification of the making of the decision is sent to the owner.

Exceptions to rule 5.9

5.10. The exceptions are that each owner is liable for-

- (a) the cost of any emergency work from the date on which the work is instructed,
- (b) any scheme costs mentioned in rule 5.1(d) from the date of any statutory notice requiring the carrying out of the work to which the costs relate,
- (c) any accumulating scheme costs (such as the cost of an insurance premium) on a daily basis.

Rule 5

Scheme decisions reached under rules 2 and 3 will often result in costs being incurred. Rule 5 explains who is to pay for those costs. The types of cost which might possibly be incurred are listed in rule 5.1 and are referred to as "scheme costs".

Look first at title deeds

Owners should look first at their title deeds. In the case of flats registered in the Land Register owners should look at the D. (burdens) section of the land certificate. Quite often the title deeds will say who is to pay. If so, then the title provisions are to be followed and rule 5 can be ignored (rule 5.2).

If title deeds silent, look at rules 5.3 to 5.8

Usually not all scheme costs are dealt with in the title deeds. If the title deeds say nothing about a particular cost, rules 5.3 to 5.8 apply instead. Rules 5.3 to 5.8 also apply if the title deeds fail to provide for 100% of a particular cost. This is unusual but does happen occasionally. (For example, in a tenement of 8 flats each flat might be made responsible for a 12% share of the cost of repairing the roof - which would leave 4% of the cost unaccounted for.)

Under rules 5.3 to 5.8, the amount due by any owner depends on what the money was spent on. The most common types of expenditure are described below.

Maintenance costs (rule 5.1(a), (b) & (d))

Liability depends on who owns the scheme property which is being maintained.

- If the property is common property, each owner must pay in proportion to the size of his share in the property (rule 5.5(a)). Usually the owner of each flat will hold an equal share, so that the cost is divided equally among the flats.
- If the property is not common property, the cost is also divided equally among the flats, except in one case (rule 5.5(b)). The one case is where the sizes of the flats are so different that the floor area of the largest is more than one and a half times that of the smallest. In that case the cost is apportioned by reference to floor area.

Rule 5.3 makes special provision for a very unusual situation which occasionally arises in relation to maintenance costs.

Running costs of scheme property (rule 5.1(c))

The rule is the same as the rule for maintenance costs. Examples of running costs might be the cost of electricity to light the passage and stair or to run a common central heating system.

Other scheme costs (rules 5.1(e)-(g))

These are provided for in rules 5.6 - 5.8.

Rules 5.9 and 5.10 explain the date on which an owner becomes liable for a particular scheme cost. This is important mainly for where a flat is sold at a time when a repair is being carried out. The outgoing owner has to pay if he becomes liable for the cost before the sale is completed. Further details are given in section 15 of the Tenements (Scotland) Act 1997.

RULE 6

SCHEME COSTS: SPECIAL CASES

6.1. Where two or more persons own a flat-

Liability where two or more persons own flat.

(a) they are jointly and severally liable for the share of any scheme costs for which the owner of that flat is liable in accordance with rule 5, and

(b) as between themselves they are liable for that share in the proportions in which they own the flat.

6.2. Where an owner is liable for a share of any scheme costs but-

Redistribution of share of costs.

(a) a scheme decision has been made under rule 2.2(e) determining that the share (or a portion of it) should not be paid by that owner, or

(b) the share cannot be recovered for some other reason such as that-

(i) the estate of that owner has been sequestrated, or

(ii) he cannot be contacted,

then that share shall be paid by the other owners in accordance with rule 5 as if it were a scheme cost for which they were liable; but where paragraph (b) applies that owner shall be liable to each of those other owners for the amount paid by each of them.

6.3. If any owner is directly affected by a procedural irregularity in the making of a scheme decision and that owner-

Liability for scheme costs where procedural

(a) was not aware that any scheme costs relating to that decision were being incurred, or

(b) on becoming aware as mentioned in paragraph (a) above, immediately objected to the incurring of those costs,

he shall not be liable for any such costs (whether incurred before or after the date of his objection); and, for the purposes of determining in accordance with rule 5 the share of those scheme costs due by each of the other owners, that owner shall be left out of account.

Rule 6

Rule 6 sets out three special rules about payment of scheme costs.

Rule 6.1 explains that, where two or more people own a flat (such as a husband and wife), any one of the owners can be made to pay the full amount due for that flat, but can then recover a share from the other owner or owners.

Rule 6.2 deals with the situation where an owner is unable to pay or where a scheme decision is taken that an owner should be exempted from payment. The other owners have then to pay the unpaid balance.

Rule 6.3 exempts an owner who, as a result of a procedural irregularity, did not know that expenditure was being incurred. For example, he may not have been notified of the original scheme decision under rule 3.11. However, it is open to the other owners to avoid this provision by making a fresh scheme decision under rule 2.2(f).

RULE 7

EMERGENCY WORK

7.1. Any owner may instruct or carry out emergency work. Power to instruct or carry out.

7.2. The owners are liable for the cost of any emergency work instructed or carried out under rule 7.1 as if the cost of that work were scheme costs mentioned in rule 5.1(a). Liability for cost.

7.3. For the purposes of this rule, "emergency work" means work which, before a scheme decision can be obtained, requires to be carried out to scheme property- Meaning of "emergency work".

(a) to prevent damage to any part of the tenement, or

(b) in the interests of health or safety.

RULE 8

ENFORCEMENT AND GENERAL

8.1. This scheme binds the owners. Scheme binding on owners.

8.2. A scheme decision is binding on the owners and their successors as owners. Scheme decision to be binding.

8.3 Any obligation imposed by this scheme or arising from a scheme decision may be enforced by any owner. Enforceability of scheme decisions.

8.4. Any person authorised in writing for the purpose by the owner or owners concerned may enforce an obligation such as is mentioned in rule 8.3 on behalf of one or more owners; and in doing so he may bring any claim or action in his own name. Enforcement by third party.

8.5. Any procedural irregularity in the making of a scheme decision shall not affect the validity of that decision. Validity of scheme decisions.

8.6. Any notice which requires to be given to an owner under or in connection with this scheme may be given in writing by- Service of notices.

(a) delivering the notice to his flat,

(b) posting it to that address or such other address as he is known to have, or

(c) transmitting it to him by electronic means.

Rule 7

This rule allows an owner to carry out work without a scheme decision where it is an emergency and, as a consequence, there is no time to consult the other owners. The work is to be paid for as if a scheme decision had in fact been taken. Few repairs will be as urgent as this.

Rule 8

Rules 8.1 to 8.4 make provision for enforcement.

Rule 8.5 explains that a procedural mistake does not make a scheme decision invalid. This is restricted to minor mistakes, such as a failure to notify an owner about a meeting or about a scheme decision. It does not excuse a failure to achieve a majority as required by rule 3.6. Rule 8.5 should be read together with rule 6.3.

Rule 8.6 sets out ways in which notice might be given. These are suggestions only and other methods can also be used.

Rule 4

4.1	5.19 to 5.25
4.2	5.19 to 5.25

Rule 5

5.1	5.59 to 5.67 and 5.79 to 5.83
5.2	5.59 to 5.67 and 5.79 to 5.83
5.3	5.59 to 5.67
5.4	5.59 to 5.67 and 5.79 to 5.83
5.5	5.59 to 5.67
5.6	5.79 to 5.83
5.7	5.79 to 5.83
5.8	5.79 to 5.83
5.9	8.1 to 8.8
5.10	8.1 to 8.8

Rule 6

6.1	5.79 to 5.83
6.2	5.79 to 5.83
6.3	5.33 to 5.39

Rule 7

7.1	5.54 to 5.57
7.2	5.54 to 5.57
7.3	5.54 to 5.57

Rule 8

8.1	5.84 to 5.86
8.2	5.84 to 5.86
8.3	5.84 to 5.86
8.4	5.84 to 5.86
8.5	5.33 to 5.39
8.6	5.33 to 5.39

SCHEDULE 2

MANAGEMENT SCHEME B

PART I

THE OWNERS' ASSOCIATION

RULE 1

ESTABLISHMENT, STATUS ETC.

1.1. The association is established on the day on which this scheme takes effect. Establishment.

1.2. The association shall be a body corporate to be known as "The Owners' Association of" with the addition of the address of the tenement. Status.

1.3. The members are the persons who, for the time being, are the owners of the flats; and where two or more persons own a flat both (or all) of them shall be members. Members of the association.

1.4. The address of the association shall be that of- Address of association.

(a) the tenement, and

(b) the manager,

or either of them.

Printed below is a guide to Management Scheme B. This is written in non-technical language so as to be more easily understood by the owners of flats who will have to operate the scheme. It is suggested that owners be given a copy of this guide. In cases where Scheme B is amended, under clause 5 of the Bill, the guide will need to be amended accordingly. The guide concentrates on those issues which are of practical importance to owners and so is not comprehensive. However, it is followed by a table which links up the rules of Scheme B to the relevant parts of the report. This table need not be reproduced for owners.

The guide is written as if Scheme B had been brought into force for the tenement.

GUIDE TO MANAGEMENT SCHEME B

Management Scheme B is a set of rules for running a tenement. "Tenement" means any flatted building.

The scheme is divided into three parts and consists of 16 rules which are explained more fully below.

PART I

Under the scheme the tenement is managed by an association of all the owners. Part I describes how the owners' association works. Part I is not very important for the day-to-day running of the tenement, and some of the rules are technical in nature.

RULE 1

The owners' association comes into being automatically at the same time as the scheme itself (rule 1.1). All owners of flats are members, for as long as they remain owners. If a flat belongs to two people (such as a husband and a wife) both are members (rule 1.3).

RULE 2

FUNCTION, POWERS AND ENFORCEMENT

Function of association.

2.1. The function of the association is to manage the scheme property for the benefit of the members.

Powers of association.

2.2. The association shall have power to do anything necessary for or in connection with the carrying out of the function mentioned in rule 2.1 and in particular may-

(a) carry out maintenance, improvements or alterations to the scheme property,

(b) enter into a contract of insurance in respect of the tenement or any part of it (and for that purpose the association shall be deemed to have an insurable interest),

(c) purchase, or otherwise acquire or obtain the use of, moveable property,

(d) require owners to contribute by way of service charge to association funds,

(e) open and maintain in the name of the association an account with any bank or building society,

(f) invest in the name of the association any money held on behalf of the association,

(g) borrow money,

(h) engage employees or appoint agents, or

(i) act in accordance with any other powers conferred under or by virtue of this scheme.

Scheme to be binding.

2.3. This scheme shall be binding on the association, the manager and the members.

Enforcement of scheme.

2.4. The association may enforce-

(a) the provisions of this scheme,

(b) any obligation owed by any person to the association.

Rule 2

Rule 2 sets out the functions and powers of the association. The association's main function is to manage the scheme property for the benefit of the members (rule 2.1). The meaning of "scheme property" is given in rule 16.1. The parts of the tenement which are not scheme property (notably the individual flats) are not managed by the association or affected by the scheme.

The association is restricted to the functions and powers listed in rule 2. Any other activities would be invalid.

RULE 3

THE MANAGER

3.1. The association shall have a manager who, subject to rule 3.2, shall be a person (who may be a member or a firm) appointed by the association at a general meeting.

Association to have manager.

3.2. Where a person nominated as the first manager in the deed of conditions applying this scheme as respects the tenement has confirmed that he is willing to act as manager he shall-

Appointment by relevant deed of conditions.

(a) act as such until the first annual general meeting is held,

(b) be entitled to reasonable remuneration, and

(c) be eligible for reappointment.

3.3. The association may at a general meeting remove from office the manager before the expiry of his term of office.

Power to remove manager.

3.4. Any actings of the manager shall be valid notwithstanding any defect in his appointment.

Validity of actings of manager.

3.5. The manager shall be an agent of the association.

Manager to be agent.

3.6. Subject to this scheme, any power conferred on the association under or by virtue of this scheme shall be exercisable by-

Exercise of powers.

(a) the manager, or

(b) the association at a general meeting.

3.7. Any duty imposed on the manager under or by virtue of this scheme shall be owed to the association and to the members.

Duties owed to association and members.

3.8. The manager shall comply with any direction given by the association at a general meeting as respects the exercise by him of the powers conferred under or by virtue of this scheme.

Manager to comply with directions.

3.9. The manager shall provide and sign any certificate required for the purposes of section 15 of this Act.

Certificates under section 15.

RULE 4

EXECUTION OF DOCUMENTS

4. A document is signed by the association if signed on behalf of the association by-

Execution of documents by association.

(a) the manager, or

(b) a person nominated for the purpose by the association at a general meeting.

Rule 3

The members can meet together in a general meeting. A general meeting of members is the governing body of the association and can make decisions on any matter on which the association has power to act (rule 3.6(b)). (Those matters are listed in rule 2). Rules 8 and 9 give further information about general meetings.

The day-to-day running of the association, and the tenement, is in the hands of a manager. The manager can be an ordinary person or a firm or a company. A member can be the manager (rule 3.1). Usually the manager is appointed by the members at a general meeting (rule 3.1). Rule 6 gives further details. However, the deed of conditions which brought the scheme into operation will probably name a person to act as manager until the first general meeting can be held (rule 3.2). The duties of a manager are set out in rule 7.

The general meeting of members has ultimate authority over the manager. The manager must do what he is told by the general meeting (rule 3.8). The general meeting can also dismiss the manager (rule 3.3). However, in some cases dismissal may be a breach of the contract made with the manager, and may lead to a claim for damages against the association.

Rule 4

This rule explains how the association signs documents (such as contracts).

RULE 5

WINDING UP

5.1. The manager shall commence the winding up of the association on the date on which this scheme ceases to apply as respects the tenement. Commencement of winding up.

5.2. The manager shall, as soon as practicable after the commencement of the winding up, use any association funds to pay any debts of the association; and thereafter he shall distribute in accordance with Part II of this scheme any remaining funds among those who were, on the date when the winding up commenced, owners of flats in the tenement. Distribution of funds.

5.3. The manager shall- Final accounts.

(a) prepare the final accounts of the association showing how the winding up was conducted and the funds were disposed of, and

(b) not later than 6 months after the commencement of the winding up, send a copy of those accounts to each owner.

5.4. Subject to rule 5.5, the association shall be dissolved at the end of the period of 6 months beginning with the commencement of the winding up. Automatic dissolution of association.

5.5. At any time before the end of the period of 6 months mentioned in rule 5.4, the members may determine that- Delayed dissolution.

(a) the association shall continue for such period as they may specify, and

(b) that it shall be dissolved at the end of the period so specified.

5.6. Notwithstanding the disapplication of this scheme, rule 5 and any other rule relating to the winding up of the association shall continue to have effect. Saving for certain rules.

Rule 5

A general meeting of members can decide that the scheme should no longer apply (rule 12.1(a)). In practice this is very unlikely to happen unless the tenement is destroyed and is not re-built. Where the scheme no longer applies the association requires to be wound up. This involves a number of technical steps which are set out in rule 5 and in rule 15.4.

PART II

GENERAL RULES

RULE 6

APPOINTMENT OF MANAGER

6.1. The association shall- Appointment of manager.

(a) at the first annual general meeting, and

(b) where the manager's period of office expires or a vacancy occurs, at any subsequent general meeting,

appoint on such terms and conditions as the association may decide the person who is to be the manager.

6.2. Not later than one month after the date of a general meeting at which a person is appointed to be manager- Certificate of appointment.

(a) that person, and

(b) on behalf of the association, a member,

shall sign a certificate recording the making, and the period, of the appointment.

PART II

Part II of the scheme describes the day-to-day running of the tenement. Rules 8 to 11 (which regulate the general meetings and the payment of service charge) are particularly important.

Rule 6

The manager is appointed at a general meeting of the members. All owners of flats are members (rule 1.3). It is up to the members to decide how long the manager should be appointed for and how much he should be paid. It is unwise to appoint a person as manager unless he has agreed to act. Rule 3 has some further provisions about the appointment.

RULE 7

DUTIES OF MANAGER

Duties of manager.

7. The manager shall manage the scheme property for the benefit of the members and in particular shall-

(a) carry out regular inspections of the scheme property,

(b) arrange for the carrying out of maintenance to scheme property,

(c) ensure that a common policy of insurance complying with section 19 of this Act and against such other risks (if any) as the members may determine is in force in the name of the association in respect of the tenement building,

(d) fix the financial year of the association,

(e) keep, as respects the association, proper financial records and prepare the accounts of the association for each financial year,

(f) implement any decision made by the association at a general meeting,

(g) enforce-

(i) the provisions of this scheme, and

(ii) any obligation owed by any person to the association, and

(h) keep a record of the name and address of each member.

Rule 7

This rule sets out the main duties of the manager. Some other duties can be found in other parts of the scheme. In practice the manager's most important task is to arrange a proper programme of maintenance. The manager can be told what to do by a general meeting of members (rules 3.8 and 7(f)), but otherwise he is free to decide himself what maintenance needs to be done. However, he is restricted in what he can spend by the budgeting arrangements described in rule 10.

Rule 8

General meetings: procedure

8.1. The first annual general meeting shall be called by the manager and shall be held not later than 12 months after the day on which, in accordance with rule 1.1, the association is established. First annual general meeting.

8.2. The manager shall call an annual general meeting each year; and a meeting so called shall be held no more than 15 months after the date on which the previous annual general meeting was held. Annual general meetings.

8.3. The manager may call a general meeting at any time and shall call a general meeting if- Other general meetings.

(a) a revised draft budget requires to be considered,

(b) he is required to do so by members holding not less than 25 per cent. of the total number of votes allocated, or

(c) he is required to do so by a member of the advisory committee.

8.4. Any member may call a general meeting if- Member's right to call meeting in certain circumstances.

(a) the manager fails to call a general meeting-

(i) in a case where paragraph (b) or (c) of rule 8.3 applies, not later than 14 days after being required to do so as mentioned in those paragraphs, or

(ii) in any other case, in accordance with this scheme, or

(b) the association does not have a manager.

8.5. Where under rule 8.4 a general meeting is called by a member- Procedure where member calls meeting.

(a) any rule imposing a procedural or other duty on the manager in relation to general meetings (other than the duty imposed by rule 8.6(b)) shall apply as if it imposed the duty on the member, and

(b) if there is a manager, the member shall send him a notice stating the date and time fixed for the meeting and the place where it is to be held.

8.6. Not later than 14 days before the date fixed for a general meeting the manager shall call the meeting by sending to each member- Calling of meeting.

(a) a notice stating-

(i) the date and time fixed for the meeting and the place where it is to be held, and

(ii) the business to be transacted at the meeting, and

(b) if the meeting is an annual general meeting, copies of the draft budget and (except in the case of the first annual general meeting) the accounts of the association for the last financial year.

8.7. Any inadvertent failure to comply with rule 8.6 as respects any member shall not affect the validity of proceedings at a general meeting. Validity of proceedings.

8.8. A general meeting shall not begin unless there is a quorum; and if there is still no quorum twenty minutes after the time fixed for a general meeting then- Quorum necessary for meeting to begin.

(a) the meeting shall be postponed until such date, being not less than 14 nor more than 28 days later, as may be specified by the manager, and

(b) the manager shall send to each member a notice stating the date and time fixed for the postponed meeting and the place where it is to be held.

8.9. A meeting may be postponed only once; and if at a postponed meeting the provisions in rule 8.8 as respects a quorum are not satisfied, then the members who are present or represented shall be deemed to be a quorum. No quorum at postponed meeting.

8.10. If a general meeting has begun, it may continue even if the number of members present or represented ceases to be a quorum. Quorum need not be maintained.

8.11. For the purposes of rule 8 a quorum is- Number required for quorum.

(a) where there are no more than 30 flats in the tenement, members present or represented holding 50 per cent. of the total number of votes allocated,

(b) where there are more than 30 such flats, members present or represented holding 35 per cent. of the total number of votes allocated.

8.12. The members present or represented at a general meeting shall elect one of their number or the manager to be chairman of the meeting; and on being so elected the chairman shall take charge of the organisation of the business of the meeting. Election of chairman.

8.13. Any member present or represented at a general meeting may nominate additional business to be transacted at that meeting. Additional business.

8.14. Except where he is unable to do so because of illness or for some other good reason, the manager shall attend each general meeting and shall- Manager to attend and keep record of business transacted.

(a) keep a record of all the business transacted at a general meeting, and

(b) not later than 21 days after the date of a general meeting, send a copy of the record of business to each member.

Rule 8

Members must meet once a year for an annual general meeting (rule 8.2). Normally they will not meet more often than this. But if the need arises an extra meeting can be requested either by the manager or (subject to some restrictions) by members (rule 8.3). It is up to the manager to organise the meetings although, if he fails to do so, any member can step in and call the meeting (rule 8.4).

Rule 8.6 lists certain documents that the manager must send to all members at least 14 days before a general meeting. These include a draft agenda, although members may add further items to the agenda at the meeting itself (rule 8.13).

All members are allowed to attend general meetings. If a member prefers he can ask someone else to attend for him, and that person is able to vote on behalf of the member if he is given written authority (rule 9.1). The manager has a duty to attend the meeting (rule 8.14). At the meeting a chairman is elected (rule 8.12).

A meeting cannot begin unless a certain number of members or their representatives are present (a "quorum"). The quorum is based on the number of votes held by those members or their representatives. There is one vote per flat (rule 9.1), and normally a quorum is 50% of the votes. So if there are 20 flats in a tenement, a quorum is reached when members for 10 of the flats are either present at the meeting or are represented there by someone else. However, if the tenement has more that 30 flats, a quorum is only 35% of the votes (rule 8.11). A quorum is required only for the start of the meeting, and the meeting can continue even if some members leave before the end (rule 8.10).

Rules 8.8 and 8.9 make special provision for cases where there is no quorum at the start of a meeting.

It is up to the manager to keep a record of all decisions reached and other business transacted at the meeting. He must then send out a copy to all members within 21 days (rule 8.14).

Rule 9

General meetings: voting

Allocation and exercise of votes at general meeting.

9.1. For the purpose of voting on any proposal at a general meeting one vote is allocated as respects each flat; and any right to vote is exercisable by the owner of that flat or by someone (not being the manager) nominated in writing by the owner to vote as respects the flat.

Exercise of vote where two or more persons own flat.

9.2. If a flat is owned by two or more persons the vote allocated as respects that flat may be exercised by either (or any) of them; but if those persons disagree as to how the vote should be cast then no vote shall be counted as respects that flat.

Decision by majority.

9.3. Except as mentioned in rule 12.1, a decision is made by the association at a general meeting by majority vote of all the votes cast.

Method of voting.

9.4. Voting on any proposal shall be by show of hands; but the chairman may determine that voting on a particular proposal shall be by ballot.

Rule 9

The main business at an annual general meeting will often be the approval of the draft budget for the following year (see rule 10). Other decisions may also need to be made. Even after a decision has been made, it can be challenged, within 21 days. For any member has a right to apply to the sheriff court, to have a particular decision annulled. Further details are given in section 8 of the Tenements (Scotland) Act 1997.

Except in the special cases listed in rule 12.1, decisions are reached by a simple majority of the votes actually cast at the meeting (rule 9.3). There is one vote per flat (rule 9.1), and the vote is exercised by the owner of the flat or (if a flat is owned by more than one person) by any of the owners (rule 9.2). An owner can give written authority to someone else (but not the manager) to vote for him (rule 9.1).

RULE 10

FINANCIAL MATTERS

10.1. Before each annual general meeting the manager shall prepare, and submit for consideration at that meeting, a draft budget for the new financial year.

Duty of manager to prepare annual budget.

10.2. A draft budget shall set out-

Content of draft budget.

(a) the total service charge and the date (or dates) on which the service charge (or instalments) will be due for payment,

(b) an estimate of any other income that the association is likely to have and the source of that income,

(c) an estimate of the expenditure of the association, and

(d) the amount (if any) to be deposited in a reserve fund.

10.3. The association may at a general meeting-

Consideration of draft budget by association.

(a) approve the draft budget subject to such variations as may be specified, or

(b) reject the budget and direct the manager to prepare a revised draft budget for consideration by the association at a general meeting to be called by the manager and to take place not later than two months after the date of the meeting at which the budget was rejected.

10.4. At a general meeting at which a revised draft budget is to be considered, the association may approve or reject the budget as mentioned in rule 10.3(a) and (b).

Revised draft budget.

10.5. Subject to rule 10.6, the manager may from time to time determine that an additional service charge shall be payable by the members to enable the association to meet any expenses that are due (or soon to become due) and which could not otherwise be met (or met in full).

Additional service charge.

10.6. In any financial year the total amount of any additional service charge determined under rule 10.5 shall not exceed 25 per cent. of the total service charge for that year as set out in the budget approved by the association; but in calculating that percentage no account shall be taken of any additional service charge payable in respect of the cost of emergency work (as defined in rule 13.3).

Limit on amount of additional service charge.

10.7. If in any financial year the manager considers that any additional service charge exceeding the percentage mentioned in rule 10.6 should be payable, he shall prepare and submit to the association at a general meeting a draft supplementary budget setting out the amount of the additional service charge and the date (or dates) on which the charge (or instalments) will be due for payment; and rules 10.3, 10.4 and 11.4(a) shall apply as respects that draft supplementary budget as they apply as respects a draft budget and revised draft budget.

Supplementary budget.

10.8. Any association funds shall be-

Association funds.

(a) held in the name of the association and,

(b) subject to rule 10.9, deposited by the manager in a bank or building society account.

10.9. The manager shall ensure that any association funds-

Special treatment of certain funds.

(a) which are likely to be held for some time are-

(i) deposited in an account which is interest-bearing, or

(ii) invested in such other way as the association may at a general meeting decide,

(b) forming a reserve fund are kept separately from other association funds.

Rule 10

The association has a financial year, which is fixed by the manager (rule 7(d)). Each financial year the manager must prepare a draft budget which is then sent to members not later than 14 days before the annual general meeting (rules 8.6(b) and 10.1). The budget sets out the projected expenditure of the association for the year, and explains how that expenditure is to be met (rule 10.2). Usually expenditure is met by levying a service charge on the members. The draft budget must state the amount of service charge and when it is to be collected. At the annual general meeting, members vote on the draft budget. If they are not willing to approve it they can either amend it, or reject it altogether and require the manager to produce a new budget (rule 10.3).

Once a draft budget is approved, the manager will ask the members to pay the agreed service charge on the agreed dates (rule 11.4). The manager has a discretion to ask for up to 25% more than was originally agreed (rules 10.5 and 10.6). This gives a certain amount of flexibility and recognises the fact that it is difficult to predict future expenditure. However, the manager cannot go beyond the 25% figure without preparing a supplementary budget and submitting that budget for approval at a new general meeting (rule 10.7).

Rules 10.8 and 10.9 control the way in which the manager is to invest association money.

RULE 11

SERVICE CHARGE

11.1. Subject to rules 11.2 and 11.3, the amount of any service charge imposed under this scheme shall be the same as respects each flat. Amount of service charge.

11.2. The association may at a general meeting decide as respects a particular owner and in relation to a particular payment that no service charge (or a service charge of a reduced amount) shall be payable. Service charge exemption.

11.3. Any additional premium on a common policy of insurance in respect of the tenement shall, in so far as it is attributable to any special characteristics of a particular flat (including the purposes for which the flat is used), be payable by the owner of that flat. Liability for additional insurance premium.

11.4. When the draft budget has been approved in accordance with this scheme, the manager- Manager to collect service charge.

(a) shall send to each owner a notice requiring payment, on the date (or dates) specified in the budget, of the service charge (or instalments) so specified, and

(b) may send to each owner at any time a notice-

(i) requiring payment, on the date (or dates) stated in the notice, of an additional amount of service charge determined under rule 10.5, and

(ii) explaining why the additional amount is payable;

and on receipt of such a notice each owner is liable on such date (or dates) for the amount to which the notice relates.

11.5. Where two or more persons own a flat- Liability where two or more persons own flat.

(a) they are jointly and severally liable for the service charge for which the owner of that flat is liable, and

(b) as between themselves they are liable for the service charge in the proportions in which they own the flat.

11.6. Where an owner is liable for a service charge but the service charge cannot be recovered for some reason such as that- Redistribution of share of costs.

(a) the estate of that owner has been sequestrated, or

(b) he cannot be contacted,

then that service charge shall be shared equally among the other owners or, if they so decide, that service charge shall be met out of any reserve fund; but that owner shall be liable to each of the other owners for any share paid.

11.7. Where any service charge (or part of it) remains outstanding not less than 28 days after it became due for payment, the manager may send a notice to the owner concerned requiring him to pay interest on the sum outstanding at such rate (being a reasonable rate) and from such date as the manager may specify in the notice. Interest payable on overdue service charge.

Rule 11

Each flat pays the same amount of service charge (rule 11.1). However, a general meeting of members has discretion to alter this rule in particular cases (rule 11.2). This is unlikely to happen very often. Rule 11.3 makes special provision for insurance premiums.

Where two or more people own a flat (such as a husband and wife), both are members of the association (rule 1.3) and either can be made to pay the full amount due for that flat (rule 11.5).

No one need pay anything until a notice is received from the manager. The notice sets out the amount due and the dates on which it is to be paid (rule 11.4). If a member pays late the manager has a discretion to charge interest (rule 11.7).

Rule 11.6 deals with the case where a member is unable to pay.

RULE 12

SPECIAL MAJORITY DECISIONS

12.1. The association may determine- Special majority required.

(a) to make a deed of conditions under section 5 of this Act,

(b) to use any reserve fund to pay for such expenditure of the association as may be specified, or

(c) subject to consent being obtained as mentioned in rule 12.2, to use any money held on behalf of the association to carry out improvements or alterations to scheme property (not being improvements or alterations which are reasonably incidental to maintenance);

but only if they so determine at a general meeting by majority vote of all the votes allocated.

12.2. Where any scheme property is not common property as mentioned in rule 16.1(a), a determination mentioned in rule 12.1(c) may be implemented only if at the time when it is proposed to carry out the work the owner of the property in question consents in writing to the improvements or alterations being made. Consent of owner to be given where not common property.

RULE 13

EMERGENCY WORK

13.1. Any member may instruct or carry out emergency work. Power to instruct etc.

13.2. The association shall reimburse any member who pays for emergency work. Reimbursement of member.

13.3. For the purposes of this rule, "emergency work" means work which requires to be carried out to scheme property- Meaning of "emergency work".

(a) to prevent damage to any part of the tenement, or

(b) in the interests of health or safety,

in circumstances in which it is not practicable to consult the manager, or call a general meeting, before carrying out the work.

Rule 12

Usually decisions at general meetings are taken by a majority of the votes *cast* (rule 9.3). But in the three cases listed in rule 12.1 a decision requires a majority of the votes *allocated.* Each flat is allocated one vote (rule 9.1). So in a tenement of 20 flats, a majority of the votes allocated would be 11 votes.

The three cases are:

(a) *A decision to alter the scheme, or to replace it with another scheme, or to disapply the scheme.* Changes of this kind are made by a deed of conditions signed by the manager under sections 5 and 6 of the Tenements (Scotland) Act 1997.

(b) *A decision to use money from any reserve fund.* A reserve (or "sinking") fund is money put away for long-term expenditure of various kinds such as the replacement of the roof (rule 16.2). Sometimes a part of the service charge is ear-marked as a contribution to the reserve fund (rule 10.2(d)). Not all tenements have reserve funds, but members can decide at a general meeting to set one up.

(c) *A decision to carry out improvements or alterations.* However, *ordinary maintenance* can be carried out by the manager without the need for a decision by members (see rule 7(b)).

Rule 13

This rule allows a member to carry out work to scheme property in an emergency, where there is no time to consult the manager. The association reimburses the cost of the work.

RULE 14

ADVISORY COMMITTEE

14.1. The association may at a general meeting elect such number of the members as they may specify to form an advisory committee whose function shall be to provide the manager with advice relating to the exercise of his powers under or by virtue of this scheme. Power to elect advisory committee.

14.2. Where an advisory committee is formed, the manager shall from time to time seek advice from the committee. Manager to consult advisory committee.

RULE 15

MISCELLANEOUS

15.1. Any member may require the manager to allow him to inspect a copy of any document, other than any correspondence with another member, which relates to the management of the tenement; and the manager shall, if the document is in his possession or it is reasonably practicable for him to obtain a copy of it, comply with the requirement. Information about management of tenement.

15.2. Any member who sells or otherwise disposes of his flat shall, before the date on which the person to whom the flat is to be sold (or otherwise transferred) will be entitled to take entry, send a notice to the manager stating- Notice to manager on sale of flat etc.

(a) the entry date and the name and address of that person,

(b) the name and address of the solicitor or other agent acting for that person in the acquisition of the flat, and

(c) an address at which the member may be contacted after that date.

15.3. Any document which requires to be sent to a member under or in connection with this scheme may be sent by- Service of documents.

(a) delivering the document to his flat,

(b) posting it to that address or such other address as he is known to have, or

(c) transmitting it to him by electronic means.

15.4. Any funds distributed under rule 5.2 shall be shared equally among the owners. Distribution of funds on winding up.

Rule 14

This rule allows a general meeting of members to set up a committee to give advice to the manager. Such a committee is consultative only. The manager must listen but he need not take the advice. Only a general meeting of members can tell the manager what to do (rule 3.8).

Rule 15

Rule 15.1 gives members access to documents concerning the management of the tenement.

Rule 15.2 requires a person who is selling or disposing of his flat to give certain information to the manager.

Rule 15.3 sets out ways in which documents can be sent to members. Other methods can also be used.

Rule 15.4 explains how surplus assets are to be distributed in the event of the association being wound up under rule 5.

PART III

INTERPRETATION

RULE 16

INTERPRETATION

16.1. For the purposes of this scheme, "scheme property" means-

Meaning of "scheme property".

(a) any part of a tenement that is the common property of some or all of the owners,

(b) with the exceptions mentioned in rule 16.2, the following other parts of a tenement building-

(i) the ground on which it is built,

(ii) its foundations,

(iii) its external walls,

(iv) its roof (including any rafter or other structure supporting the roof),

(v) if it is separated from another building by a gable wall, the part of the gable wall that is part of the tenement building,

(vi) any other wall that is load-bearing.

16.2. The following parts of a tenement building are the exceptions referred to in rule 16.1(b)-

Parts that are not included in rule 16.1(b).

(a) any extension which forms part of only one flat,

(b) any door, window, skylight, vent or other opening,

(c) any chimney stack or chimney flue.

16.3. In this scheme, unless the context otherwise requires-

Other definitions.

"advisory committee" means any such committee formed in pursuance of rule 14.1,

"association" means the owners' association of the tenement established under rule 1.1,

"general meeting" means an annual or other general meeting of the association,

"maintenance" includes repairs or replacement, cleaning, painting and other routine works, gardening, the day-to-day running of the tenement and the reinstatement of a part (but not most) of the tenement building; but does not include demolition, alteration or improvement unless reasonably incidental to the maintenance,

"manager" means the person appointed to be manager of the association,

"member" means a member of the association, and

"reserve fund" means money held on behalf of the association to meet the cost of long-term maintenance, improvement or alteration of scheme property or to meet such other expenses of the association as the association may determine.

PART III

Part III consists of a single rule (rule 16) which explains the meaning of some of the words used in the scheme.

Rule 16

Not every part of the tenement is to be managed under the scheme. The scheme applies only to "scheme property", the meaning of which is given in rule 16.1. Scheme property essentially means those parts of the tenement which are common property (that is, where ownership is shared by the owners of different flats). Section 3 of the Tenements (Scotland) Act 1997 gives the following list of the common property in a tenement:

(i) the close (ie the connected entrance passage, stairs, landings and corridors within a tenement building)

(ii) any lift, and

(iii) any other part of a tenement which serves two or more flats.

Examples of (iii) might include a path, an outside stair, rhones, pipes, flues, cables, tanks or chimney stacks. This list of common property can be altered or added to in the title deeds. In the case of flats registered in the Land Register, owners should look at the A. (property) section of the land certificate.

Certain other key parts of a tenement, listed in rule 16.1(b), are also scheme property, whether they are common property or not.

TABLE OF RULES: SCHEME B

Rules of the Scheme	Paragraph of report
Rule 1	6.7 to 6.10
Rule 2	
2.1	6.7 to 6.10
2.2	6.7 to 6.10 and 9.9 to 9.14
2.3	6.19 to 6.24
2.4	6.19 to 6.24
Rule 3	
3.1 to 3.5	6.11 to 6.15
3.6 to 3.8	6.19 to 6.24
3.9	8.18 to 8.24
Rule 4	6.62
Rule 5	6.63 to 6.67
Rule 6	6.11 6.15
Rule 7	
(a)	6.42 to 6.46
(b)	6.42 to 6.46
(c)	9.9 to 9.14
(d)	6.33 to 6.41
(e)	6.33 to 6.41
(f)	6.25 to 6.32
(g)	6.19 to 6.24
(h)	6.59 to 6.61
Rule 8	
8.1 and 8.2	6.25 to 6.32
8.3	6.16 to 6.18 and 6.25 to 6.32
8.4	6.25 to 6.32
8.5 to 8.14	6.25 to 6.32

Rules of the Scheme	Paragraph of report
Rule 9	
9.1 to 9.4	6.25 to 6.32
Rule 10	
10.1 to 10.9	6.33 to 6.41
Rule 11	
11.1 to 11.7	6.33 to 6.41
	8.1 to 8.8
Rule 12	3.16 to 3.21
	6.30 to 6.32
Rule 13	5.54 to 5.58[1]
Rule 14	6.16 to 6.18
Rule 15	6.59 to 6.61
15.1, 15.2 and 15.4	6.63 to 6.67
15.3	5.35 to 5.5.39[2]
Rule 16	5.4 to 5.11[3]

1 These paragraphs cover the equivalent rules in Scheme A.
2 These paragraphs cover the equivalent in Scheme A.
3 These paragraphs cover the equivalent rule in Scheme A.

Appendix 2

List of those who submitted written comments on Discussion Paper No 91

The British Branch of the International Commission of Jurists
British Insurance & Investment Brokers' Association
British Gas plc (Scotland)
S Brymer and C T Graham, Thorntons, WS, Solicitors
J Butters
The City of Edinburgh District Council-Department of Housing[1]
The City of Edinburgh District Council-Department of Technical Services[2]
The City of Glasgow Council
G F Collie, Solicitor
Committee of Scottish Clearing Bankers
Convention of Scottish Local Authorities
Council of Mortgage Lenders
D J Cowperthwaite
S J Cumming, Solicitor
Professor D J Cusine, University of Aberdeen
K W Donnelly, Solicitor
Dunfermline Building Society
East Kilbride Development Corporation
Edinburgh New Town Conservation Committee
The Faculty of Advocates
J S Fair, Thorntons WS
Falkirk District Council
G P Fletcher, Solicitor
J A Fox, Architect
Professor W M Gordon, University of Glasgow
Professor G Gretton, University of Edinburgh
Hillhead Community Council
The Institute of Housing in Scotland
D A Johnstone, Solicitor
The Keeper of the Registers of Scotland
The Lands Tribunal for Scotland
The Law Society of Scotland
A Lawson
W Leslie, WS
V T Linacre, Consultant Valuer & Development Surveyor
R J Livingstone, Solicitor
The Lord President
Marchmont and Sciennes Community Council
L D Most, Solicitor
W Muirhead
Property Managers Association Scotland Limited
Professor K G C Reid, University of Edinburgh
The Royal Incorporation of Architects in Scotland
The Royal Institution of Chartered Surveyors in Scotland
Scottish Chambers of Commerce
Scottish Chief Housing Officers' Group

1 Now the City of Edinburgh Council Housing Department.
2 Now the City of Edinburgh Council Property Services Department.

Scottish Consumer Council
Scottish Homes
Scottish Homes Legal Services
The Scottish Law Agents Society
The Sheriffs' Association
Society of Writers to H M Signet[3]
J A A Speirs, CA, FRICS
R J W Stiven, Solicitor
K P D Strachan, Solicitor
J S Wilson
R W Wishart, Solicitor
W Wylie

3 The response was written by R W McIntyre WS and while it was approved by the Council of the Society, according to their normal practice, it has not been formally adopted by them.

Appendix 3

On 7 September 1995 the Department of Private Law of the University of Edinburgh and the Scottish Law Commission held a seminar on the reform of the law of the tenement. Seminar participants were invited to comment on a revised approach to reform outlined in the Commission's paper *Further Thoughts on the Law of the Tenement*. They were also invited to comment on a questionnaire prepared by the Commission. The following is a list of those who submitted written comments.

J Clarkson, Solicitor

S J Cumming, Solicitor

Professor D J Cusine, University of Aberdeen

G P Fletcher, Solicitor

D A Johnstone, Solicitor

R McCluskey, Assistant Secretary, Convention of Scottish Local Authorities

Professor A J McDonald, Thorntons, WS Solicitors

L D Most, Solicitor

A A Noble, Solicitor

Scottish Consumer Council

Professor J H Sinclair, University of Strathclyde

A J M Steven, Research Student, University of Edinburgh

Appendix 4

On 25 September 1996 the University of Glasgow and the Scottish Law Commission held a seminar on the reform of the law of the tenement. Seminar participants were invited to comment on the Commision's Position Paper *The Reform of the Law of the Tenement* and a draft Tenements (Scotland) Bill. They were also invited to comment on a questionnaire prepared by the Commission. The following is a list of those who submitted written comments.

A D Anderson, Solicitor

I S Bruce, FRICS

S Brymer, Thorntons WS, Solicitors

Convention of Scottish Local Authorities (incorporating comments from the Legal Services Division of the City of Edinburgh Council and the Director of Housing, Glasgow City Council)

Council of Mortgage Lenders (including the Building Societies Association)

S J Cumming, Solicitor

Dunfermline Building Society

G P Fletcher, Solicitor

A Flint, Ann Flint and Associates, Housing & Planning

The Keeper of the Registers of Scotland

Professor A J McDonald, Thorntons WS, Solicitors

L D Most, Solicitor

Property Managers Association Scotland Limited

D Reid, Solicitor

The Royal Incorporation of Architects in Scotland

The Royal Institution of Chartered Surveyors in Scotland

Professor J H Sinclair, University of Strathclyde

A R M Stewart, FRICS

Sun Alliance Insurance UK Ltd

Printed in the UK for The Stationery Office Limited
on behalf of the Controller of Her Majesty's Stationery Office
Dd 293533 C10 3/98 J40993, CCN003808